AF599055

THE LORD HOLDS US BY THE HAND

POPE BENEDICT XVI

The Lord Holds Us by the Hand

Private Homilies for Seasons and Feasts

Edited by
Riccardo Bollati, Luca Caruso, and Federico Lombardi, S.J.

Translated by Michael J. Miller

IGNATIUS PRESS SAN FRANCISCO

Original Italian edition:
Il Signore ci tiene per mano

To preserve the phrasing and personality of these homilies, Scripture quotes have been translated directly from the text of Benedict XVI.

ISBN 978-1-62164-918-2 (HB)
ISBN 978-1-64229-411-8 (eBook)
Library of Congress Control Number 2026932833
Printed in the United States of America ♾

CONTENTS

HOLY WEEK

EASTER SEASON

FOREWORD

"Christ triumphs over no one who does not want it. He conquers only by persuasion: He is the Word of God." In these words of Origen, which Cardinal Joseph Ratzinger quoted in his speech on the occasion of his admission to the Académie Française, we find the key to the singular importance of the preacher's activity. Proclaiming the Word of God means, for Joseph Ratzinger, testifying to the splendor of truth that was made flesh in the only-begotten Son of God. Thus, proclaiming the truth became for him a mission and a passion.

During his life, he gave innumerable homilies, which for the most part are available in his *Complete Works* in the original German edition, at the Vatican website, and in other published books. A peculiar circumstance makes this edition of the unpublished homilies of Benedict XVI unique. Not one of these homilies was presented publicly to a large congregation; rather, all of them were given "privately" with only a few persons attending, either during his pontificate or after his resignation.

It should be emphasized that neither the *Memores Domini* nor the undersigned asked Benedict XVI to preach at those celebrations of the Eucharist. It was his own initiative, and for us, the few members of his household, it became an unexpected and invaluable gift. We were often asked, especially after his resignation, how the Pope Emeritus ever managed to give homilies for "four cats", given that his strength was fading little by little. Among us we found a reason, which is to say that we came to the conviction that Benedict XVI wanted to give a discreet sign of gratitude to the little papal family for the company they offered during his "final stage of earthly life", as he himself said on the balcony of the Pontifical Villa at Castel Gandolfo on the evening of February 28, 2013.

Joseph Ratzinger—Benedict XVI sees the proclamation of the Gospel as the irrevocable duty of a priest, bishop, cardinal, pope, and even of the Pope Emeritus. He gave unequivocal proof of this in the final years of his earthly journey. As was the case throughout his life, each one of the homilies published here is based on Sacred Scripture, in its unity of the Old and New Testaments, takes into account the tradition of the Fathers and the teaching of the Church, and concludes with a simple prayer addressed to the Lord that His grace may transform our life and grant salvation.

His attentive, in-depth reading of the biblical texts, not with the eyes of a detached exegete, but rather marked by a lively participation, involves the listener. It is evident that meditating on Scripture, allowing himself to be questioned by it and questioning it in turn, was a practice that accompanied him throughout his long life; in a certain sense it is his very life, not only as a theologian, but also as a believer and a priest in the community of the Church. It is what he always did, but with the passage of time it became in a way even more dominant with the diminution of his other obligations and activities. It is noticeable that he lives in God's presence, in communion with the divine mystery, seeking to know more and more the face of Jesus, feeling the weight and sometimes the difficulty of the Word of the Lord.

I adopt as my own the following words of Father Federico Lombardi in his extensive and important introduction to the homilies collected here:

> The coherent and harmonious synthesis between in-depth listening to Scripture, reflection on the faith and its "content" as transmitted by the Church, and the application of it to Christian life is an impressive and fascinating characteristic of the preaching of Joseph Ratzinger—Benedict XVI. Exegesis, theology, catechesis, and spirituality intertwine and join together, leading the listener to enter in depth into the heart of the mystery of Christ. This goes well beyond an intellectual and conceptual exercise so as to become involved in a personal relationship with God in all its richness and intensity.

The final years of Benedict XVI were an example of a long human diminishment, experienced in the presence of God in communion with the Church and in ever more perfect truth in the Lord. This can be deduced from the fact that his homilies always end with a brief prayer, which reveals a lot about the authenticity and humility of his life as a believer in Jesus Christ. Prayer and faith are never something taken for granted, not even for someone who was pope. Reading these homilies, we are left struck by the continuity of spirit and method that characterize the entire preaching of Joseph Ratzinger—Benedict XVI from the beginning. Now that these homilies are finally published, they are a precious testimony of the spiritual magisterium, not only of an exceptional theologian, but also and equally of a great preacher.

Archbishop Georg Gänswein

INTRODUCTION

The daily celebration of Holy Mass, but particularly on Sundays and feast days, was a fundamental event in the priestly life of Joseph Ratzinger. He could not think of his ministerial service on the Lord's day without giving due place to the Word of God, listening to it, and proclaiming it, even though sometimes, given the circumstances, the celebration took place in an assembly of much reduced size, not in a church or a public place, but in a "private" chapel. For him it was always that way.

Therefore, even during his pontificate, when Benedict XVI did not preside at the celebration of Holy Mass in public, in Rome (at Saint Peter's or in the parishes), or in other places during his apostolic journeys, it was his custom on Sundays to celebrate in his private chapel, preaching a carefully prepared homily on the readings prescribed by the liturgy, even if a very small number of people were present.

Normally this restricted congregation was made up of his secretaries, His Excellency Archbishop Georg Gänswein and then-Monsignor Alfred Xuereb (between 2007 and 2013), his very faithful secretary Sister Birgit Wansing, the four *Memores Domini*—Carmela, Cristina, Loredana, Manuela and (after the death of the last-mentioned), Rossella—and sometimes concelebrants or guests who were traveling.

This custom was continued even after the resignation from the papacy. Thus it became more frequent and regular, since all the public liturgies had ceased, and it lasted as long as the strength and above all the voice of the Pope

Emeritus allowed him to give the Sunday homily. After that he concelebrated, but asked one of the priests present to say a few words to those in attendance.

There never was a handwritten text by Benedict XVI for these homilies. As his Secretary, Abp. Georg Gänswein, explained several times, or sometimes even the preacher himself did, Benedict XVI prepared the Sunday homily throughout the preceding week, reading and studying the liturgical texts attentively, making them the object of reflection and prayer, and also taking notes in a suitable notebook. But whereas for the occasions of public liturgies that he celebrated during his papacy he used to prepare a complete written text—which was published each time—he did not do so for these "private" Masses, because he had an extraordinary memory and great clarity when speaking without notes. However the method of preparation and the care put into it were essentially the same.

The *Memores Domini* were faithful and attentive witnesses of this invaluable spiritual service by Benedict XVI; realizing its great value and wishing to preserve the wealth for themselves and eventually for others, they took the initiative to record these homilies discreetly and to make an initial summary transcription of most of them.

After the death of Benedict XVI, the executor of his last will and testament, Abp. Gänswein, mentioned several times these homilies and the existence of the related recorded material; finally he made it available to the Fondazione Vaticana Joseph Ratzinger—Benedetto XVI and to Libreria Editrice Vaticana [the Vatican publishing house] with a view to possible publication. So this collection was born; two volumes are planned. The texts were edited by the undersigned with the invaluable collaboration of Msgr. Riccardo Bollati and Dr. Luca Caruso.

❧ ❧ ❧

After attentive work of listening, revising the already existing transcriptions, and transcribing the homilies for which there was only an audio recording, a total of around 135 homilies were prepared for publication, dating from the time between 2005, the year when the pontificate began, and 2017.

They were given by Benedict XVI in Italian. Benedict XVI had a perfect command of this language, even though naturally one sometimes noticed a Teutonism, since it was not his mother tongue.

In almost all cases, the Masses were celebrated in one of three places: until the end of the pontificate, chiefly the private chapel of the papal apartment in the Apostolic Palace; then, in the initial months after the resignation, the private chapel of the Palace in Castel Gandolfo; finally, the chapel of Mater Ecclesiae Monastery in the Vatican Gardens, the last residence of Benedict XVI.

In preparing the publication, we adhered as faithfully as possible to the text that was actually spoken, keeping the discursive, oral character and the vocabulary habitually used by the preacher. The work of revision was mainly to correct the punctuation so as to facilitate comprehension and to make the reading fluent, to eliminate some repetition, and to reorder the sentence structure according to Italian usage where it was affected too much by the preacher's German origin.

With regard to the original text, for each homily a title was added, which therefore must be attributed, not to Benedict XVI, but rather to the editors of this publication. Also added were references to the biblical texts quoted by Benedict XVI in the course of the homilies, which sometimes were not included in the readings from the Lectionary on which he was commenting. There are many references of this kind. It must be noted that Benedict XVI had an extremely profound knowledge of the Scriptures and familiarity with them, so that often he quoted "the meaning" without consulting a specific Italian translation of the Bible. Rather, as far as the New Testament is concerned, he prepared for the most part using the Greek text, which he knew perfectly, and on the basis of it he sometimes also made a critical observation about the Italian translation used in the Lectionary. Therefore in no case have the editors sought to insert into the homilies the citations according to the official Italian [or English] translations; instead, we have respected the personal and original way in which the preacher presented the biblical texts. As is well known, Benedict XVI was also an expert on the Fathers of the Church—particularly but not exclusively on the works of Saint Augustine—so that likewise there are frequent citations from them in the homilies, quoted not verbatim but "by the meaning". To the extent possible, textual references were added for these, too.

As was mentioned, there are around 135 of these unpublished "private" homilies in all, and they are being published in two volumes. According to the criterion already used in Volume XIV of the German version of the *Complete Works*, in the publication the editors preferred to follow, not chronological order, but rather the order of the liturgical calendar. Therefore, the first volume is a collection of homilies for the major "seasons" of the liturgical year (Advent, Christmas, Lent, Easter) and for other particular feast days, while the second volume will be a collection of homilies for Ordinary Time. Of course the collection is by no means a complete commentary on the three-year lectionary; nonetheless, it is quite rich.

Besides the index arranged according to the liturgical calendar, which the structure of both volumes faithfully respects, a chronological index of the homilies is also offered, as well as a biblical index. The last-mentioned is not compiled with the criterion of analytical completeness of all the citations, but rather with the criterion of pointing out all the scriptural passages about which Pope Benedict actually offers a commentary or at least a brief examination in his preaching.

❦ ❦ ❦

Of course, in presenting a new collection of homilies by Benedict XVI, we cannot fail to recall that this is a relatively small part of an immense activity of preaching, developed regularly and passionately over decades, in response to his priestly vocation of service proclaiming the Gospel to the people of God. As a priest, as a bishop, as pope, Joseph Ratzinger—Benedict XVI gave several thousand homilies in all, most of which have been published in several languages and are available in various anthologies that he himself reviewed and explicitly approved. We are thinking about the three thick tomes of Volume XIV of the *Complete Works* in the German edition, with hundreds and hundreds of homilies preceding the pontificate. We are thinking about the website vatican.va, which makes accessible all the homilies given in public during the pontificate, even on all the major solemnities, for which we do not find corresponding homilies in our collection. The whole liturgical year, the feasts of Our Lady and of the saints, sacramental celebrations, countless occasions of the Christian life, both communal and personal, were accompanied and illuminated theologically and spiritually by the homilies of that great pastor.

Benedict XVI is generally considered, with good reason, one of the greatest contemporary Catholic theologians, but we must not forget that he can just as well be considered one of the greatest preachers of our time, particularly in the liturgical and sacramental sphere. And the two things go together: teaching and preaching the faith was the mission of his entire life.

In reading and meditating on these homilies from the last stage of his long life, we cannot help being struck by the continuity of spirit and method that characterizes the entire preaching of Benedict XVI from the beginning.

In one of his first sermons after his priestly ordination, in 1954, the young Ratzinger said:

> If I may relate something from my remembrances, I will say that even as a student I was very often cheered by the thought that one day I would be able to preach, to proclaim the Word of God to people who, although often forgetful of God in the muddle of their everyday routine, nevertheless must have looked forward to this Word. And I was gladdened especially when a passage from Scripture, or a connection between our faith and our life, appeared to me in a new light and filled me with joy.[1]

In 1973 Professor Ratzinger wrote: "The inner tension of preaching depends on the objective arch spanning and upheld by the pillars: Dogma-Scripture-Church-Today; not one of them can be taken away without the whole thing eventually collapsing."[2]

As he did throughout his life, so too in each of the homilies published here, Benedict XVI starts from Scripture, in its unity of Old and New Testaments, reviews and runs through the patristic tradition and the teaching of the Church of which we are members, and arrives at today's questions and difficulties with the faith and the Christian

[1] Quoted in Joseph Ratzinger, *Gesammelte Schriften*, vol. 14 (Freiburg im Breisgau: Herder, 2019), p. 34.

[2] Foreword to *Dogma and Preaching*, trans. Michael J. Miller and Matthew J. O'Connell, 2nd ed. (San Francisco: Ignatius Press, 2011), p. 7.

life, which are clearly and sincerely outlined. Finally, he concludes with a prayer, a humble, direct, and affectionate conversation with the Lord, that His grace might transform our life and grant us salvation. It is always this way: from attentive listening to the Word of God, to the faith in Christ that forms and transforms our life, to the communion in charity with His Body which is the Church, to the final humble request, full of hope and love, addressed directly to the Father, the giver of every good thing.

The coherent and harmonious synthesis between in-depth listening to Scripture, reflection on the faith and its "content" as transmitted by the Church, and the application of it to Christian life is an impressive and fascinating characteristic of the preaching of Joseph Ratzinger—Benedict XVI. Exegesis, theology, catechesis, and spirituality intertwine and join together, leading the listener to enter in depth into the heart of the mystery of Christ. This goes well beyond an intellectual and conceptual exercise so as to become involved in a personal relationship with God in all its richness and intensity. Even when the biblical images reach their culmination in depth and beauty, when the Cross of Jesus is likened to the fiery chariot on which the prophet Elijah is carried off to heaven, we realize that the preacher is not guided by aesthetic considerations but is bringing us to perceive intuitively the splendor of truth.

❧ ❧ ❧

Yet given the essential structural and spiritual continuity of the Ratzingerian homilies over the course of time, it is fair to ask whether the homilies being published now present specific characteristics relative to the general ones already noted. It is a question that will deserve further examination. Probably an adequate answer would have to be situated within the framework of a comprehensive rereading of the immense homiletic production that we mentioned earlier, reflecting on its development in the light of the various stages of the long life of Ratzinger the preacher. However, several aspects can be delineated even now.

First of all, the common feature of these homilies, which were given either during the pontificate or after the resignation, is the fact that they were presented to a small, or rather an extremely small, assembly, without particular circumstances due to the situation of the celebration. In various public circumstances, on the contrary, the preacher of course had to take into account adequately the congregation that was present or the important or specifically urgent themes that he could not help addressing. Certainly even in these homilies there is no lack of references to events or circumstances, but the essential thing is always a clear itinerary from listening to the biblical texts to the light of the mystery of Christ, and then to the fundamental aspects of personal and communal Christian life. The digressions from this simple central theme are rare and restrained. Therefore, it seems to us that reading these texts transmits to us almost naturally the characteristic timbre of Ratzinger's personality, as a believer and a formator in the faith, with his intelligence and his honest and profound reflection, his love for Jesus Christ and His Church, his balance and his rare sense of spiritual harmony.

Anyone who is well acquainted with the great trilogy by Pope Benedict on Jesus of Nazareth, and also with many other writings or homilies of his, will often find again thoughts and even formulations that are already familiar to him, but he will never have the sense of reading something that is merely repeated. Besides, Ratzinger the preacher never even remotely wished to say things that were "his own", "new", or "original", but always sought only to interpolate the service of his voice into what he himself calls the "roar of many waters", that is, into the streams of Scripture that speak about Christ and are His voice (see Rev 1:15). Indeed, even in listening to those roaring waters, Ratzinger feels distinctly that same joy that the young, newly ordained Ratzinger said that he experienced in discovering a new glint of daylight in every word of Scripture. Every time he listens to it, he experiences again the taste of the water drawn at the source. And the source is inexhaustible. This is verified also in several homilies of this collection. Given that the Sunday Lectionary follows a three-year cycle, the preacher finds himself commenting on the very same biblical texts every three years. But even though he sometimes cannot help returning to the same themes, Benedict completes once again each time the process of preparing for the homily in prayer, and each time he has new things to tell us, new references to cite, new lights to let shine.

Even though in this publication the homilies are arranged according to the liturgical calendar, we must not think of them as being delivered all at the same moment and in the same situation. This is the great importance of the chronological index. It tells us that the homilies are distributed over the course of about twelve years. Most of them are from the years 2013 and 2014, the first ones after the resignation; then they become less numerous in the following years, when the preacher's voice begins to weaken, until the last one, on April 2, 2017, a little before he completed his ninetieth year, on April 16.... Almost all of them were preached, then, between the ages of eighty and ninety, and from March 2013 on, the preacher "withdrew to the mountain" to spend the last stage of his life in prayer and reflection. We almost get the impression that, as time goes by, the exegetical analysis of the texts becomes abbreviated and simplified, and our attention is gradually drawn more and more to our spiritual participation in the heart of the mystery of Jesus, who leads us to the Father. Perhaps it is no accident that the last homily, on the Gospel of the Raising of Lazarus, is precisely a meditation on the dialogue between Jesus and Martha on eternal life and concludes with a beautiful prayer that the Lord may hold us forever by the hand and in His hand without letting us fall.

In the gathering of the little "family" that surrounds and accompanies him in his prayer, we therefore notice also his progress on his journey and the weakening of his voice. These homilies thus become a precious and, in a certain sense, unique testimony to the experience and the spiritual magisterium of a great pontiff, theologian, and preacher, but first of all a believer in Jesus Christ: "My Lord and my God!"

Federico Lombardi, S.J.

ADVENT SEASON

Advent: The "Coming" of Christ into Human and World History

December 1, 2013
Private Chapel, Mater Ecclesiae Monastery

First Sunday of Advent (Year A)
Readings: Is 2:1–5; Ps 122; Rom 13:11–14;
Mt 23:37–44

The word "Advent" is taken from the Latin spoken at the time of Jesus, from the political and religious language of the era. It meant the first visit of a great personage to a certain place. For example, we have coins from first-century Corinth that speak about the "advent of Augustus"—that was Nero—or news of the fourth-century calendar that speak about the advent, the *adventus ibi* of Constantine. But the visit of a figure of a deity to a temple can also be called an "advent", that is, the coming of that deity, for a certain time, into that temple.

Christians knew that the true emperor of the world, the true deity, the Son of God, made a visit to this world. This is Advent, the visit of the emperor of the world, our brother, our Lord Jesus Christ. Theology speaks about two advents of the Lord: the first advent in the flesh, in His earthly life in Palestine, from the beginning of this first millennium to the year 33; and the second advent, that is, His coming as judge at the end of time.

But a problem arises here: if that is the case, Christianity belongs to the past, because the first advent happened in a distant past; the second advent, then, is equally distant, because no one expects it anytime soon; it is almost something utopian and unreal. Thus Christianity would have no present, but only a past and an uncertain future. That is not so.

Saint Bernard of Clairvaux, in the early twelfth century, spoke, not of two, but of three advents of Jesus Christ: the first, a middle one, and the third.[1] This middle one happens continually in the Church. In reality, the Church Fathers, too, had already understood the matter, so that Advent is not merely a fact from the past. Saint Augustine, for example, interprets Scripture in this sense, saying that the clouds described by the prophet Daniel on which the judge comes (see Dan 7:13–14) are the Word of God, and he says that the proclamation of the Word happens in this cloud, which is at the same time a mystery and a presence.[2] The cloud would therefore have a double meaning: the cloud indicates, on the one hand, God's presence in the temple and in worship (see 1 Kings 8:10–12) and, on the other hand, this continual movement of God in speaking with us.

In reality, it seems to me that one can speak about at least three modes of Christ's ongoing Advent: the first is in the Word, the second in the sacraments, the third in history. We should note immediately that this coming of the Lord is not a unilateral movement, because it implies that we, too, must go to meet the Lord. Today's liturgy gives us the key words for this: the first is "I lift up my soul": "I lift up", *sursum corda* ["let us lift up our hearts"], "I go to meet the Lord"; the Letter of Saint Paul speaks

[1] See Bernard of Clairvaux, *Sermon 5 on Advent*, nos. 1–3.

[2] See Augustine of Hippo, *Letters*, 119.11.41; *Exposition on Psalms*, 96.13.

to us then about being clothed in Christ, and, finally, the Gospel speaks to us about being "worthy", which is to say, being ready for His coming. But let us look a little more closely at these advents, still in this perspective of God's movements and our movements.

First of all, God, Christ, comes in His Word, which is not a word from the past. He speaks with us, and this word is proclaimed in the Church, which thus shows where the presence of the Lord is. Every generation receives anew this Word of the Lord, who speaks with us. Since the beginning, the Lord is not a lifeless book, but lives in the proclamation of the Church, in which we see how even today the Lord speaks, speaks with me, speaks with us.

We must add that this Word is not a theory that concerns only our reason, our thought, but rather is a reality; it is a journey. Thus, the first reading today tells us: "Let us walk in the light, in the Word of the Lord!" and, in this context, it shows a world penetrated by the Word of God, which really walks in this light. This would be a world that lives in peace, a world where swords are turned into plowshares and spears into pruning hooks.

Chapter 11 of the prophet Isaiah takes up this vision and makes it even more radical (see Is 11:1–9): it speaks about a situation in which the lamb lives together with the wolf and the calf with the lion. It seems rather unreal, but it is not unreal insofar as the Word of God really enters into this world. This same chapter 11 of Isaiah gives us the key when, at the conclusion of this vision of the reconciled world, it says that "the knowledge of God will fill the earth as the waters cover the bottom of the sea."

Where there is knowledge of God, where the knowledge of God really is fully real in the life of man, God is present and the reconciled world grows. The great problem of our time is just religious illiteracy, the lack of knowledge of God, the absence of God. For a true renewal of the world, before all the other reforms that may be necessary, this reform is fundamental: the new presence of the knowledge of God, a listening that becomes activity and action. The knowledge of God is not like the knowledge of a phone number, for example, but it is knowledge in the way that I know a person whom I love, and whom I really know only in love. This knowledge of God transforms the world; where this knowledge exists, the reconciled world appears. We can see it in these little paradises that grow where there are religious communities that truly live in the light of the Lord.

Let us pray that the Lord may enlighten us and help us really to listen, to let ourselves be permeated by the Word of God, to be formed interiorly, to begin really to know God and to live with God; and in that way to receive the light, which becomes light for others, also, and thus becomes a force of peace and renewal.

The second mode of the coming of Jesus, of God, into this time, into the present of every generation, is in the sacraments. Just think of the Eucharist. Here Jesus really enters into our midst; the bread is no longer bread, it is the Lord; the Risen Lord comes, visits us, is with us, and even remains in our hearts. And the Eucharist does not end with the celebration of Holy Mass; the Lord remains present, dwells with us, visits us, and we can visit Jesus, speak with Him, and He enters into this friendship with the world. Another example: in absolution, in confession, the Lord really speaks to me and says: "I start over with you, your past no longer counts, now there is a new present based on my forgiveness, my grace." And so on in all the sacraments.

The Church's liturgy as such is another way by which God enters into our time and makes Himself heard. On this day, we want to allow ourselves to be penetrated deeply by the fact that God, Christ, really visits us and has conquered now, precisely in the Holy Mass: He is with us; He gives Himself into our hands. Let us pray that our life may really be guided by Him.

In the second reading, there is talk about "putting on Christ". In the Second Letter to the Corinthians, Paul describes the body as man's clothing and the resurrection as a process of being clothed again (see 2 Cor 5:1–5). The Risen Lord enters into our mortal life and thus begins this "re-clothing" of our life; the resurrection begins with the Risen Lord; in the moment when the Risen Lord touches us, everlasting life begins: life with God. Let us really be clothed again with Christ, with His risen body, with His eternal life, with the joy of His love, with the strength of His presence. Let us truly celebrate in the Eucharist the advent of the Son of God, who has become our brother, who clothes us again with Himself, so that already in this world we are the body of Christ, of the risen Christ.

Finally, Christ Jesus comes in history, too, in large-scale history and in small-scale history. Think of the example of the work of Saint Benedict, who created a new way of living that joins work and worship, created new communities, and thus created a new continent: Europe. The arrival of this way of life was a "coming" of Christ: with this Rule, with this man, with this activity of his, God Himself once again entered into history and gave history a new form.

Think of the twelfth century, with Saint Dominic and Saint Francis. With them, too, the Lord returns; it is a "coming" of the Lord, a true advent. Saint Francis was rightly considered by his contemporaries as an icon of Christ with his stigmata: Christ Himself appears to be identified with him, and he with Christ. With him the Word of God arrived on the scene with a new, experiential freshness; his word was living out the Word of the Gospel always, without annotations, without additional commentary, a word that transforms our situations; living out the Word so that it is present among us in all its power. With this Franciscan movement, with this Dominican movement, a new dynamism thus enters into the wealthy and somewhat stodgy Church of that era: a new joy, proclamation to the poor, and proclamation also outside of the European Christian world. Christ arrives in this way in history: this is a true "coming" of Him into history.

Think of the sixteenth century. On the one hand, there is Saint Ignatius, with his new joy in fighting for Christ, in bringing the Lord's power to bear against what is opposed to it. On the other hand, there are Saint Teresa of Avila and Saint John of the Cross, and this intimacy with Jesus, which really enters into man, into being, transforms him and makes him see the presence of Jesus.

And in the nineteenth century, too. Think of the great religious communities that were born in that era: they are a "coming" of Christ. It was a very large-scale social movement: men and women came together to serve Christ in the poor, in the sick, in order to offer education to the poor, in order to make present the Word of Christ, the Life of Christ. We all live now on the fruits of this great apostolate, of a new "coming" of the Lord in that "enlightened" century that was against Christ, the century that said that Christ is antiquated, that His time has passed. Precisely in that time there was a new birth of the Church, a new birth of her message, of her life.

And if we are attentive, we can see that in our generation, too, even today Christ arrives and is Advent. What great figures: Mother Teresa, John Paul II, and others are the entrance of Christ into this time, which gives us the strength to live once again in the presence of the Lord, as in the past, so also today and in eternity.

In large-scale history, then, there are Advents, the Advents of Christ. But also in our small-scale personal history. If we are attentive, we can feel that in various situations the Lord touches me, knocks at the door of my life, makes me feel His tenderness, His goodness. We must have more sensitivity, more ability to perceive this mysterious and real presence.

Let us pray to the Lord to help us, so that our heart, our sensibility may be open to understand that now the Lord is touching me: this gesture is for me, now He calls me, informs me, speaks to me, guides me. The Lord is present with many gestures in my life, too. Into the life of each one of us the true Advent comes, the Advent of Christ, today. Christ is not only a past time; He is a today, He is a future! Lifting up your hearts, going to meet Christ, putting on Christ, being true and sensitive to His presence: this is the interior rhythm of Advent.

Let us pray to the Lord that in these weeks we may really celebrate his Advent. Amen!

Enter into Our History, Lord!

November 30, 2014
Private Chapel, Mater Ecclesiae Monastery

First Sunday of Advent (Year B)
Readings: Is 63:16b–17, 19b; 64:2–7; Ps 80;
1 Cor 1:3–9; Mk 13:33–37

"O that you would tear the heavens and come down, return, O Lord!" These words from the first reading are Israel's prayer, an Advent prayer, after their return from the Babylonian exile.

Recall: for seventy years, Israel was as if nonexistent; it was dispersed, in exile. God seemed to have forgotten them; He seemed no longer to exist. And then the unexpected happens: the King of Persia, Cyrus, destroys the Babylonian Empire and gives Israel permission to return. It is a gift from God. The Israelites see that this great king of the Persians, in reality, is a servant of God, who opens the doors for Him. And we know these beautiful words: "Prepare the way ..." (see Is 40:3): this is the idea of a highway of God in the desert by which to return to their homeland.

And so there is a second exodus; once again they return from the house of slavery to the Promised Land; it is a great moment, in which God's coming is visible. But then, when they have returned to their homeland, Israel finds tremendous poverty: they are abandoned by everyone, the land is neglected, they have to start from zero, no one helps them, the earth gives no fruit, there is no temple; God is once again totally absent and silent. In this situation, after the great joy of God's intervention, in the great mystery of His silence, this prayer is born: "Return, tear the heavens and come down!"

We can see a certain analogy with our situation, with the situation of the Church. God has come! He has come to us, He was born in the stable in Bethlehem, He is a child, God let Himself be touched, He lived with us, we know His voice, we know His face, we know His goodness, His humility, His power. He has come! This is the joy of the Christian.

And yet it is also true for us that we must cry: "O that you would tear the heavens and come down!" Because we see, even in countries that are already Christian, so many problems, such great violence, such great disbelief, such great destruction of the faith, of man himself; and in the world we see so many refugees, so many wars, and so we must cry out: "God, do you not see? Come! Descend!" This is our Advent. What does Advent mean? God has come, and we know Him, we are never after Christ, we are with Christ, not before Christ, because God has come. But we are far from Him.

Usually we speak about two advents or comings of Christ: the first in Bethlehem, the second at the end of the world. But this way of speaking is absolutely insufficient. If that were the case, we would have, on the one hand, an increasingly distant past: Bethlehem, the life of Jesus; on the other hand, an undesired future, because none of us desires the end of the world, with all the tremendous things that the Gospel speaks about. And so the time of Christianity would be this: a distant past, an undesired future, and the present would be empty.... But it is not like that!

Saint Bernard of Clairvaux said that we must speak instead about three advents of God: the first in Bethlehem, the intermediate one, and the final one.[1] And the intermediate coming is the one that concerns us. God did not come so as to return to heaven, after a brief visit, and to leave us alone again. He always comes! He remained with us, He is with us in the Holy Eucharist, He dwells with us, He is our fellow citizen, gives Himself into our hands, comes continually in His Word, in all His graces, comes with the saints, in whom we again know His presence, His face, his humility, and His power. God always comes! This intermediate Advent is the continuation of the first and the anticipated presence of the second. The two are not purely past or future, but meet in a humble and nevertheless true present.

Advent therefore means *attesa*, an Italian word with the twofold sense of attention and expectation. *Attesa*, attention to the real presence of the Lord. He is with us! It is only that we do not perceive Him, because we are deaf and blind with regard to Him. And then Advent tells us: open your heart, open your mind, open your senses, open your ears, and see the humble and real presence of the Lord every day, in so many realities and above all in the liturgy, in His Word, in the sacrament. But it also means expectation, a cry so that God might show Himself more and more, as in the great moments of history.

So we pray to the Lord today also to enter again into our history: "Show Your presence, as You did in the fall of the Berlin Wall, in many historical events that came ultimately from You; enter into our history and open our hearts." To be expectant, attentive to the presence of the Lord, awaiting, praying that He might show Himself more and more to me in my life. This is Advent!

[1] See Bernard of Clairvaux, *Sermon 5 on Advent.*

The liturgy presents Advent not only in thoughts, in ideas, but also in a person. For the Church, Mary is Advent in person. In Mary we see all this, this sensitivity to God, this ability to perceive His presence, this moderation, this courage to say: "But what do you want me to do?" And this willingness to obey and, above all, this silent joy also, despite all the problems and difficulties that she had, such as the difficult birth of the Baby Jesus in a stable; this marvelous joy; the Child is born, God is with us! This is precisely what should be reborn in our hearts: this joy in His presence, this joy that He is with us, is humble and good to us and—in precisely this way—powerful!

So we pray to the Lord to help us to be attentive and open and to give us the humble and beautiful joy of this season, in which we perceive that He is with us: I am with you, God says. And we respond: "Thank you, Lord, increase in us this joy in Your presence." Amen!

How We Should Spend Advent

December 3, 2006
Private Chapel, Apostolic Palace

First Sunday of Advent (Year C)
Readings: Jer 33:14–16; Ps 25; 1 Thess 3:12–4:2;
Lk 21:25–28, 34–36

The Advent liturgy offers us different images, different visions of what Advent is essentially, what movement of our life is expressed and will be accomplished in the season of Advent. Among the themes that the Church proposes, there is also the Invitatory Psalm for the Advent liturgy, Psalm 25: "To you, O Lord, I lift up my soul, to you, O Lord, I raise my soul."

The first words are already important: "to You". Christianity has discovered the "You" who makes Himself visible to us. For a Christian, it is not a form of introspection, as most Asian mysticisms are, but rather a departure from self; it is an exodus toward the You of God. Here the profound essence of Christianity is expressed, the relational character of our existence, which is not self-enclosed but rather awaited, willed, loved, and called by the You.

Therefore the first community, along these lines, said "to You": it is this opening of self, perceiving the reality of the You who created me, who loves me, who calls me. "To You I lift up my soul." The movement "to You" is the movement of elevating, and, here, Psalm 24 coincides with the introductory words of the Eucharistic Prayer, which are common to all the major liturgies, which say, from the very beginnings of the Church's liturgy: "Lift up your hearts." Hearts uplifted, lifting up the heart is a movement toward the You of God.

In reality the heart can be "down", can be rather consumed by the little routine things, the ones that wear us out every day. The heart can be down, discouraged by the preoccupations of this world. It can be down, consumed by amusements, by all the material things, as the Lord says in today's Gospel: "Take heed to yourselves lest your hearts be weighed down with dissipation and drunkenness, by the cares of this world." This is a description of the media world, which, although it tells us to amuse ourselves, to be well, in reality burdens the heart and pulls it down.

"Lift up your heart": the heart moves upward, ascending toward this You. An old comparison comes to mind: Peter, who gets out of the boat and walks on the water toward Christ, and as long as he sees Christ he can walk on the waters of the world (see Mt 14:24–33). But the moment he sees the things beneath him, he starts to sink; the force of gravity drags his weight down. And he must reach toward a new force of attraction, the one in Jesus' eyes that lifts him up. Walking on the waters of the ages, with our eyes fixed on the You, on Jesus, creates a new gravitational force and lifts up the heart. In the heights there is also this joy of being loved and not being in an empty world, but being in a movement, in an attraction toward the heights, where there is true beauty, true happiness.

A second image corresponds to what is said in the Church's prayer, which mentions the key word of the Advent liturgy: *Excita*, "Wake up", "Awaken us", Lord. This presupposes that man usually runs the risk of not being awake, that is, of being closed off in dreams, of not perceiving reality in its entirety. "Sleep" means that man is self-enclosed because of the dream and does not perceive reality as such, but only the reflections that arise in his subconscious and appear like reality, but are only reflections—albeit curious reflections intermingled with reality—and not reality itself.

"To awake" means to break through the veil of sleep and thus to see reality as such, not only the reflection of reality that remained in me. The Fathers of the Church tell us: even those worldly persons who think that they are very attentive are in reality fixated on material things, on anxieties, on afflictions, on all this, but they are asleep and dreaming, because they do not see reality in its entirety; they see only a sector that appears as the whole but is not all, it is only a sector, which derives its true significance only from the light of all, from the divine light. And thus the Lord says to us, to the world: "Wake up! With this life that you are living, with this life presented in the media, you are dreaming, you do not perceive reality. All this is wrapping yourself up in a veil that hides the true reality. Wake up and perceive the light, God Himself, the You of the Lord who comes!"

This is our prayer in this Advent season: May the Lord help us to see reality itself. And we see it only if we perceive the presence of God, in the Word of God, in the sacraments, in the life of the Church, in personal conversation with God, with the Lord.

Finally, the prayer offers us an image to meditate on: "Stir up in us the desire to go to meet the Lord who comes, with good works, praying with our lamps lit." This is the idea, the image of the journey, of walking. All that appears in the heart, in waking, points to a journey, a setting out on a journey toward the Other, and it is well expressed in another Advent image: setting out on a pilgrimage, on a journey toward the You.

Naturally we wonder how we are to accomplish this journey of the heart: How is this walking of the heart done? Prayer shows us two fundamental answers. The first: by doing good or, as we say, by good works, that is, by acting according to the Word of God, according to the directions that are given to us by the lives of the saints, who put into living practice the Word of God and the commandments of God and thus show us the way, the true way to live, to ascend—many times with difficulty—toward the heights, toward reality itself.

And the second direction: prayer. Praying is a manifold concept, but as a first step it always involves listening, because how could we speak to God unless we listened to Him? This interior attention, that allows itself to be penetrated by His Word, enters into the depths of His Word, which also personalizes this Word—because I must understand that this Word concerns me, too. To listen, to meditate, to respond, to speak with the Lord, to tell Him our problems, our inabilities, our desire, our determination to love Him. And in this way really to move along the path of the heart toward this You who comes to meet us.

Because this is the other side of it: we are not alone in having to lift ourselves up toward a distant God who always remains in himself. No. God comes once again, descends, and thus takes us by the hand and makes us ascend toward Him. Descending and ascending meet in this movement of doing good, of praying, at the moment of the sacrament, in which the Lord really descends, gives Himself into our hands, and causes our hearts to be uplifted.

Let us pray: "Lord, come and help us to come toward You." Amen!

Advent: The Desert, the Highway, the Voice

December 7, 2014
Private Chapel, Mater Ecclesiae Monastery

Second Sunday of Advent (Year B)
Readings: Is 40:1–5, 9–11; Ps 85; 2 Pet 3:8–14; Mk 1:1–8

The liturgy tells us what Advent is by bringing to our attention both persons—Saint John the Baptist, Our Lady—and great images. In today's readings we find especially three great images: the desert, the highway, the voice.

First of all, the desert. Saint John the Baptist preaches, not as Jesus would do, in the temple or in the synagogues, but in the desert. Anyone who wants to hear him must go out of the town, must take some time, several days, and must bring with him only the necessities. He must take a break from his usual activities; he must be free precisely in order to hear the message.

In reality, in the history of religions the desert is of great importance: we can say that monotheism was born in the desert, and it is important especially for the history of Israel. It begins with the encounter of the burning bush. Moses knows God personally, with His name, with His voice, in the desert, not in the royal court, not in the context of the labors of the oppressed Hebrews, but precisely by going out into the desert, he finds God and God speaks with him.

Israel finds itself as a people on Sinai: here it hears the voice of God, here it receives the Law that gives form to it, that creates it as a people. Then Elijah, too, after the slaughter of the priests of Baal, must once again return to Sinai, to Mount Horeb, in order to receive again the voice of God, so as to renew the covenant that had been broken in the previous history.

Jesus, too, begins His mission in the desert. This means: in the town, in everyday life, there is almost no encounter with God; we are so full of our own affairs that God cannot enter into our heart, into our eyes, into our ears. In order to hear God, in order to come into contact with the Lord, we need an exodus, we need to go out in order to be free, to leave our affairs, to hear, to wait for His voice.

The second image: the highway. A highway is communication; it opens up a connection between two points; it is a relation. To create a highway means to create a bridge, an access road between two points that per se do not communicate. The network of highways in our country, in the world, is precisely the network of communication that allows humanity to communicate. Highway: it is the highway from God to us. Inherently, for us God is distant; it does not seem possible to find a highway that ends in God, a highway that finally arrives at Him. In reality only God can create a highway toward us, or rather He made Himself the Way. However, we too must collaborate, we must make our way in order to build this highway, this communication. The readings—both the prophet Isaiah and the Gospel about Saint John the Baptist—speak in this context about the construction of the highway, about the overture of communion, of reality's access to God; above all, they speak about the obstacles that we must remove in order for this highway to be able to exist, and they show us two: the mountain and the valley.

The mountain, in this case, obstructs the highway, blocks access to the other, and is a symbol of being closed in on ourselves, of pride, of the fact that we consider ourselves so great that access to God no longer remains. Removing the mountain means, therefore, removing this enclosure in ourselves, this mountain of things, realities, ideas that separate us from God. In this context, Saint Augustine spoke about love of self, about self-love as the true mountain that prevents us from finding the love of God.[1] The false love of self, the self-centeredness that thinks only of oneself and does not allow us to go out from ourselves, is for Saint Augustine, throughout history, the force that is opposed to our communion with God. He says: history is a battle between two loves: the love of self to the point of denying God, and the love of God to the point of freedom, martyrdom. In this sense, therefore, the mountain to overcome would be that infatuation with self that closes me off in myself.

Saint Augustine points out three elements that express this false love, which becomes a mountain and obstructs access to God. The first is "vainglory", which means seeking to be loved in an egotistical way, seeking to be admired, trying to be accepted by everyone. This is not true love; it is only love of oneself: I wish to use other people for my purposes. And so this love of myself, this search for vainglory, to be accepted, creates a mountain that does not allow me to go out of myself. The second is "power": man in search of power, man who tries to be God himself. The third is gain [*guadagno*], that is, material things that dominate us.

[1] See Augustine of Hippo, *Commentary on the Gospel of John*, 123.5.

These three elements of self-love—vainglory, power, "gain"—build the mountain that obstructs our way; Augustine contrasts them with the three values that open the path: obeying, helping, loving. We ourselves can meditate on how obedience (that is, opening our eyes so as to hear the voice of God and follow it willingly), how helping (not helping ourselves in the first place, but helping others), and finally, loving, saying our "Yes" [to God], are the way to remove the mountain, by replacing this desire for vainglory, power, and gain with obedience, aid to others, and true love.

The other obstacle, the valley, signifies a way of living at a low level, which does not raise itself up to God's height but is completely lost in the futility of daily routine and material things, in banal, everyday things, and one's perspective is directed to something other than God; this is not the way to build. We know that man today, with all his apparently great occupations—the pursuit of money and so forth—in reality lives a "low" life, because he does not go beyond material things and is not open to the greater perspective of life. The Church counteracts this valley with the prayer *sursum corda*, "lift up your hearts": being open to the greatness of our vocation, seeing that there is something more, and opening our hearts so that God can come to us.

The third image: the voice. A voice in the desert. The "voice" means also that behind the voice stands a person, a person who speaks to my reason, to my heart. In the story of Elijah, on Mount Horeb, it is interesting that God is not in the storm, not in the earthquake, but in the voice (see 1 Kings 19:9–13). The true translation says, in other words, that God is not a force of nature, not a power; God is a person, reason, and heart, and He speaks to me, to my reason, and to my heart, with His word. Today we heard how the prophet, after threatening the judges of God, says at the end: "Speak to the heart of Israel: be comforted...." Advent is this voice, the voice of God who speaks to our heart and says with great tenderness: "In all the terrible things of this world, do not forget my heart; remember that I am with you."

Let us pray to the Lord that we might truly listen to His voice: by listening to His word in Scripture, both when it speaks about Him directly and also in the Psalms, which are the voice with which God speaks to our heart.

Let us pray to the Lord that He may truly be for us the highway that opens up our path toward Him, that in the desert we may find His voice and that His voice might enter into our heart and give us the joy of His presence. Amen!

A Voice: "Rejoice! The Lord Is Near!"

December 15, 2013
Private Chapel, Mater Ecclesiae Monastery

Third Sunday of Advent (Year A)
Readings: Is 35:1–6, 8–10; Ps 146; Jas 5:7–10; Mt 11:2–11

The Church shows what "Advent" means, especially with two persons, who are almost Advent in person: Mary, the Mother of the Lord, and John the Baptist.

Mary, who is not self-enclosed, but totally open to the Lord, is [mankind's] "yes" to the Lord. Thus she becomes the sacred tent where the Lord resides, the dwelling place, the new Zion, where the Lord is present. Mary, who offers her own flesh so as to give flesh to the Son of God, so as to give Him our humanity, is that very openness of the world to the presence of the Lord and to His coming.

The figure of Saint John the Baptist appears different, almost contrary. Mary is penetrated with the joy of Advent, of the Lord's arrival; the angel's first word to Mary is at the same time the first word of the New Testament, it opens the New Testament: "Rejoice! Because the Lord is coming, this distance no longer exists. God is no longer unknown ... rejoice!" (see Lk 1:26–28).

In contrast, Saint John the Baptist appears severe. In Saint John, man's moral duty appears, the threat of judgment appears, the severe judgment that can also say: "No, you are not mine!" However, even Saint John is not only a threat, he is not only a moralist; even Saint John deep down is a messenger of joy. We see him thinking about his presentation, in all four Gospels, in terms of a verse from the prophet Isaiah: "A voice in the desert: prepare the way of the Lord" (see Is 40:3).

"A voice in the desert", Isaiah says five hundred years before Christ. Israel had been in exile for seventy years; there was no longer a land of Israel. Israel no longer existed as a people; it was nonexistent. God no longer spoke; there was no temple, no possibility of adoring God in a common liturgy: God was silent, He had been absent for seventy years, and the great fear was that God had withdrawn from history, that He had forgotten Israel, that salvation history had ended and Israel had disappeared among the nations in a sad situation of exile and poverty.

And behold, a voice in the desert, a voice that announces the new presence of God: here is God's love, which still exists, which returns to Israel and brings it home. The voice in the desert, the voice after seventy years of silence, is a sign of hope; it is a sign of joy; a voice that announces the new presence of God, that announces the return. This was the joy that awakened Israel and made it capable of returning.

And now, five hundred years later, John is once again this voice, with his whole person he is "voice", voice of God, which speaks once more with us. The situation was very similar to the one after the exile. Israel was at home, but under the domination of others: Herod was an Idumean, Rome ruled; Israel was no longer autonomous but was a conquered people, and for two hundred years no prophet had spoken. The common opinion was that the time of the prophets, of God's speaking, had ended and that God would no longer speak. In this hopeless, joyless situation, behold:

a voice in the desert; God speaks with me, God has not forgotten me. The "voice" is the certainty that God knows us and loves us.

The whole ethical, moral plan, the whole moral challenge of Saint John is ordered to this voice, serves this voice. Morality is not a self-contained thing, a sort of spiritual gymnastics. The labor [of morality], moral duty serves this love, is ordered to this love; the purpose of the labor is to go out and meet, to open the highways, to go and meet God, therefore it is totally penetrated by the reality that God is near; it is a response to love, it is an expression of love, thus morality is renewed, because it becomes part of a love story, it responds to the joy of the voice that proclaims: God has not forgotten us.

This task, the labor of love, is a common task. Yes, the world must be changed; it is a desert, and desert means death, the desert is not a highway; the world must be changed, and the desert must become a highway. And changing the world begins in individual persons: in order for the world to be changed, everyone must change himself, must open his life, make sure that his life is not closed, but is an opening to the Lord, is a highway for the Lord. But at the same time, this voice of the Lord, which encourages us to change the world by changing ourselves, is prolonged in a common labor. The people of God together change the world, working together so that the desert might be a highway. And this work, with all its burdens, is a labor of love; because the fundamental melody remains: "Rejoice!" Joy remains.

The "voice": many think that now, too, revelation is over and that we live in a world in which God does not speak. But that is not true; even today the voice of God is there; the Church gives God a voice and at God's request speaks to us and makes herself this same voice. And in order to be God's voice, she takes the words of Saint Paul, which are the recurring theme of this whole Mass: "Rejoice, I say to you again, rejoice. The Lord is near!" (see Phil 4:4–5).

Saint Paul wrote these words in prison and had his death sentence to look forward to; he was near death and at precisely that moment he writes: "Rejoice!" And he wants this to be his last word to the Christians, to us, like his testament before his death: "Rejoice, because the Lord is near!" Even death, illuminated by the light of the Lord's presence, is no longer death; it is a change that unites us to Christ. "Rejoice, the Lord is near": this is true even today. And Saint Paul continues: "Let your goodness be seen by all." The joy of the single Christian is communicated and becomes goodness for the others. In reality, someone who carries joy within him must give a bit of light to others, too, illuminate the others; joy communicates itself and, thus, becomes common joy. Rejoice and show your joy and in that way manifest God, the voice of God, to the world.

In our big cities today, it is difficult to hear His voice; there is so much noise, and it is almost impossible. Interior noise, exterior noise, and it appears difficult to hear this decisive voice that gives us joy and hope. Therefore John the Baptist spoke in the desert, where there is no noise but a great silence, and therefore there is the possibility of hearing the voice. Saint John invites us, even today, to go out a bit from the noise of the big cities, to seek a bit of desert so as to hear the voice of God. And to make this voice heard by others, so that they, too, might know: there is a reason for joy, because they are loved with an indestructible love.

Let us pray to the Lord: that this voice might touch our hearts, too! Let us pray that He may create in us the joy of being loved and give us a light so as to give light to others, too, so as to make the people of our time hear the voice of God, so as to make them feel the love of God and thus to receive true joy, the joy that makes us able to change ourselves, to change the world. "Lord, help us, give us Your joy." Amen!

Joy, Because We Know That We Are Loved

December 14, 2014
Private Chapel, Mater Ecclesiae Monastery

Third Sunday of Advent (Year B)
Readings: Is 61:1–2, 10–11; Lk 1, Canticle of Mary; 1 Thess 5:16–24; Jn 1:6–8, 19–28

This third Sunday of Advent, according to the Church's liturgical tradition, is the Sunday of joy. We see this in the colors of the vestments;[1] we see it also in the Church's entrance antiphon, which prays, according to the new liturgy, with the words of the Letter of Saint Paul to the Philippians: "Rejoice! Again I say: Rejoice!" (see Phil 4:4–5).

What can we say? Joy cannot be commanded: either it is there, or it is not. This is true: joy cannot be commanded ... but joy can be brought. News can be brought that becomes a transformation of reality. For example: a friend of mine was in a Russian prison, in a very dismal situation, with hunger, cold, and cruelty, for month after month. One day a letter arrived from his wife that told him: "I love you, I am faithful to you, and we are waiting for you." Everything was changed! Life as such is to be welcomed, because this light is there: "I love you, we are

[1] The vestments are rose colored and not violet, as during the rest of Advent.

waiting for you." He knows why he exists, knows why he should face all this: joy has arrived! The little flame of joy in the midst of the sorrow of that situation. Another example: someone takes part in a competition with many participants and few chances to win.... The news arrives: "You won!" and life is changed. Or someone is looking for work, and they tell him: "You are hired!"

These situations of Christians contain the reality of the Gospel; in other words, God Himself tells us: "You are loved, you are awaited, you have won, you are hired!" This is our joy; it is news that involves the transformation of our life. In all the problems of the world there is this flame: "You are loved, you are awaited, you won!"

I would like to say the same thing with another example: there is an anecdote about the great Spanish mystic and theologian Ramon Llull, born in 1232. The story goes that one day he met a very thin hermit, with a long beard and a very sad face. And he asked him: "What happened to make you so sad?" He replied: "I decided to seek perfection, and I decided to start with me, to overcome my sins, to change myself so as to reach God. But in this task, with all the penance that I do, everything makes me sadder and sadder...." And Ramon said to him: "You have been tricked by Satan! The contrary is true: if you start with yourself, you still remain with yourself, and your sadness keeps increasing, because you do not see the light. No! You must not start with yourself; you must start with God, and thus you walk toward the light; that way you see the beauty of creation, of creatures, and that way you see love as the source of everything! That way, although your brothers and sisters may be disagreeable, you see them also in another light; you see in them, too, the little light of the Creator shining through. And so you walk toward this light of God, purified, perfected, and, at last, holy!" This is the decisive message: start not with yourself, but with God. The important thing is that the first glance be at God: only by starting with God is our view enkindled, and we, too, can be enlightened and purified and, thus, find the true life, find in Him also our brothers and sisters.

Saint Augustine once said: "Knowledge saddens",[2] linking sadness and knowledge. It is nice to know many things, but if finally I know all these things and sadness remains, then they are so many sad things, and there is no meaning in all that. Only when the light of God's love appears do things go well; only in that way can sadness be transformed into joy. Therefore, this is the joy of this day: that we, without our knowledge, not only can know and teach, but also in a world full of injustice and sadness we can see the light that shines through in all things and gives us joy.

In the Sixties it was fashionable to say: after Auschwitz joy is no longer permitted. In a world where those terrible things happened, we can no longer write poetry, we can no longer achieve beauty, because that would be to despise the sadness: because we cannot rejoice. This, too, was a trick of the devil, just the opposite of what is necessary. The world needs people who bear within them the light of God's love, who bear within them the joy of presenting a little light in the night of this world.

"Rejoice!" Saint Paul says. This is above all a gift. He brings us this gladness, this joy, telling us: "You are loved!" And this aspect should be combined closely with the other; that is, we must really keep alive this God-given flame, the flame of the Gospel. As Saint Paul says to Timothy: "Rekindle the flame in yourself!" (see 2 Tim 1:6). This is the meaning of Christian feast days and of this Third Sunday: "Rekindle this flame!" Let us pray that the Lord may

[2] See Augustine of Hippo, *Letter 167*, 11; *On Christian Doctrine*, 2.7.10.

make us feel this truth profoundly: "You are loved, you are awaited, you have won!"

We pray that the flame of God's joy may not be extinguished in us and that we may be able to bring this light, this joy to others: we are loved! Amen!

Saint Joseph: The Just Man Who Listens and Acts

December 22, 2013
Private Chapel, Mater Ecclesiae Monastery

Fourth Sunday of Advent (Year A)
Readings: Is 7:10–14; Ps 24; Rom 1:1–7; Mt 1:18–24

Besides Mary, Mother of the Lord, and Saint John the Baptist, today the liturgy presents to us a third figure, in which Advent is almost a person, a figure who embodies Advent: Saint Joseph. In meditating on this text, it seems to me, we can see three constituent elements of this vision.

The first and decisive one is that Saint Joseph is called "just—*sadich*". This is for the Old Testament the greatest description of someone who really lives according to God's Word, who lives by the covenant with God. In order to understand this, we must think of the difference between the Old and the New Testament.

The fundamental act of a Christian is the encounter with Jesus and, in Jesus, with the Word of God who is a Person. By encountering Jesus, we encounter the truth, the love of God, and thus the relation of friendship becomes love, our communion with God grows, we really are believers, and we become saints.

The fundamental act in the Old Testament is different, because Christ was still in the future and, therefore, at most a believer went out to meet Christ, but there was not yet a true encounter as such. The Word of God in the Old Testament essentially has the form of the Law—Torah. God guides (this is the meaning of it), God shows us the way, and it is a journey of education in which he forms man to be like God and makes him capable of encountering Christ. In this sense, this justice, this life according to the Law, is a journey toward Christ, an act of reaching out toward Him, but the fundamental act is the observance of the Torah, the Law, and thus being "just". Saint Joseph is a just man, an exemplary man, but still of the Old Testament.

But there is a danger here, together with a promise, an open door. The danger appears in Jesus' discussions with the Pharisees and especially in the letters of Saint Paul. The danger is that if the Word of God is essentially a Law, it is to be considered as a set quantity of precepts and prohibitions, a packet of norms, and the attitude should therefore be to observe the norms and thus to be correct. But if religion is like that, if it is only that, then the personal relationship with God is not born and man remains in himself; he seeks only to perfect himself, to be perfect. And so, on the one hand, this gives rise to bitterness—as we see in the second son from the parable of the prodigal son who, having observed everything, is bitter at the end and also a bit envious of his brother, who, as he thinks, had life in abundance (see Lk 15:25–32). This is the danger: the mere observance of the Law becomes impersonal, a mere doing; man becomes hard and even bitter and ultimately cannot love this God, who appears only with norms and possibly also with threats.

This is the danger; on the other hand, the promise is: one can see these precepts not only as a legal code, a packet of norms, but also as an expression of God's will, in which God speaks with me and I speak with Him. By entering into this Law, then, I enter into a dialogue with God, I learn the face of God, I begin to see God, and thus I am journeying toward the Word of God in Person, toward Christ. And so it is for a true just man like Saint Joseph: for him the Law is not a mere observance of norms, but appears as a word of love, an invitation to dialogue; and life according to the Word of God is entering into this dialogue and finding within it the norms and, in those norms, the love of God; and understanding that all these norms are not valuable for their own sake, but are rules of love and serve to increase love in me.

Thus we understand that ultimately the whole Law is only love of God and of neighbor. If that is discovered, then the whole Law is observed (see Mk 12:28–34; Mt 22:34–40). If someone lives in this dialogue with God—a dialogue of love in which he seeks the face of God, in which he seeks love and it is understood that everything is dictated by love—then he is journeying toward Christ, he is a true "just man". Saint Joseph is a true just man: thus in him the Old Testament becomes New, because in the words he seeks God, His Person, he seeks His love, and the whole observance of the Law becomes life in love.

We see this in the example that this Gospel reading offers us. Saint Joseph, betrothed to Mary, discovers that she is expecting a child. We can imagine his disappointment: he was well acquainted with this girl and the depth of her relationship with God, her interior beauty, the extraordinary purity of her heart; he had seen that this girl was entirely transparent to the love of God and love of His Word, of His truth, and now he finds himself seriously disappointed; what should he do?

Look, the Law offers two possibilities, in which the two ways appear: the dangerous, fatal way and the way of the promise. He can bring a suit in court and thus expose Mary to shame, destroy her as a person. He can do it privately, with a letter of separation. And Saint Joseph, a true just man, although greatly suffering, arrives at the decision to take the latter path—which is a path of love in justice and of justice in love—and Saint Matthew tells us that he struggled with himself, in himself, with the Word of God. In this struggle, in this journey to understand the true will of God, he found unity between love and the norm, between justice and love, and thus, while journeying toward Christ, he is ready and open for the apparition of the angel, open to the fact that God gives him the knowledge that this is a work of the Holy Spirit.

Saint Hilary of Poitiers, in the fourth century, once said, while discussing the fear of the Lord: "All our fear is situated in love."[1] This is only one aspect, one nuance of love. Thus we can say here, for us: the whole Law is situated in love; it is the expression of love and is to be fulfilled by entering into the logic of love.

We must keep in mind that, for us Christians, too, the same temptation exists, the same danger that existed in the Old Testament: even a Christian can arrive at an attitude in which the Christian religion is considered as a packet of norms, of prohibitions and positive norms, of precepts. It is possible to arrive at the idea that it is solely a matter of carrying out impersonal precepts and thus perfecting oneself: but in doing this, the personal basis of the Word of God is emptied out and one is left with a certain bitterness and hardness of heart.

In Church history, we see this in Jansenism. All of us, too, are acquainted with this danger: personally we know that we must always overcome this danger anew and find the Person of God and, in the love of the Person, the path of life and the joy of our faith. To be "just" means to find this path. And thus we, too, in reality, are always once again journeying from the Old to the New Testament, in our

[1] Hilary of Poitiers, *Tractates on the Psalms*, 127.

search for the Person, the face of God in Christ. Advent is precisely this: emerging from the pure norm toward the encounter of love, emerging from the Old Testament, which becomes the New. This, therefore, is the first and fundamental element of the figure of Saint Joseph, as he appears in today's Gospel.

Now, two very short remarks on the second element and the third.

The second: in a dream he sees the angel and hears his message. This presupposes an interior sensitivity to God, an ability to perceive the voice of God, a gift of discernment, which can discern between dreams that are dreams and those that are a true encounter with God. Saint Joseph could discern only because he was already journeying toward the Person of the Word, that is, toward the Lord, toward the Savior; God could speak with him, and he understood: this is not a dream, it is the truth, it is the apparition of His angel. And so he could discern and decide.

For us, too, this sensitivity to God is important, this ability to perceive that God is speaking with me, and this capacity for discernment. Of course, God normally does not speak with us as He spoke through the angel with Joseph, but has His particular ways of speaking with us, too. They are gestures of God's tenderness, which we must perceive in order to find joy and consolation; they are words of invitation, of love; also of request, perhaps with regard to persons who are suffering, who need a word from me or some concrete gesture of mine, a good deed: and here it is necessary to be sensitive, to know God's voice, and to understand that, right now, God is speaking with me and it is necessary to respond.

And so we have arrived at the third point: Saint Joseph's response to the word of the angel is, first, faith and, then, obedience, a deed. Faith: he understood, this really is God's voice; it was not a dream. Faith becomes a foundation on which to act, on which to live: it is recognizing that this is God's voice, it is an imperative of love, which guides me along the path of life; and then [secondly] it is doing God's will.

Saint Joseph was not a dreamer, even though his dream was the door through which God had entered into his life, but rather a practical, sober man, a decisive man with organizational abilities. It was not easy, I think, to find in Bethlehem—because there was no room in the houses—a stable as a discreet, protected place that, despite the poverty, was worthy of the Savior's birth. Organizing the flight into Egypt, finding a place to sleep each day, and then one in which to live for a long time, required a practical man who could take action and was capable of responding to challenges and finding the means of survival. And then, on their return, his decision to return to Nazareth, to establish there the homeland of the Son of God: this, too, shows that he was a practical man, who earned a living as a carpenter, which made their everyday life possible.

Thus Saint Joseph invites us, on the one hand, to this interior journey into the Word of God so as to be ever closer to the Person, to the Lord; but, at the same time, he invites us to a sober life, to work and practical, everyday service so as to do our duty in the great mosaic of history.

Let us thank God for the beautiful figure of Saint Joseph. Let us pray: "Lord, help us to be open to You, to find Your face more and more, to love You, to discover love in the norm, to be rooted and fulfilled in love. Make us open to the gift of discernment, to the ability to listen to You and to the moderation needed to live according to Your will in our vocation." Amen!

Mary's "Yes" and the Fulfillment of the Promise

December 21, 2014
Private Chapel, Mater Ecclesiae Monastery

Fourth Sunday of Advent (Year B)
Readings: 2 Sam 7:1–5, 8–12, 14, 16; Ps 89;
Rom 16:25–27; Lk 1:26–38

This Gospel that we just heard is certainly one of the most beautiful passages in all of Sacred Scripture. The angel says to Mary: "Rejoice! Rejoice, because God is entering into history and is becoming one of us." In Mary's "yes", the Incarnation is accomplished; God is made man.

But in order to understand correctly the profundity of this event, of this passage, we must first of all listen to the message of the first reading, taken from the Book of Samuel. We are one thousand years before Christ. The story starts here. David, having arrived at the height of his power, after dramatic deeds, was finally able to unite all twelve tribes of Israel under his reign. He is the undisputed king of all Israel; he managed to win all the wars with the various kings who surrounded Israel and, at last, against all expectations, succeeded also in taking the city that was considered impregnable, Jerusalem, and thus created for himself a capital really worthy of a king.

In this moment, David thinks about God. He now lives in the palace—as he says—while God is still in the tent: God is still an itinerant God, in the tents of the Exodus. Therefore David wants to build a house worthy of God. God will be the guest of his city, will live in his city; the temple will be the glory of God, and God will also be the glory of his city and of his kingdom.

We can consider this plan of David as being motivated by a true love of God, a desire for the true glory of God and zeal for the primacy of God, but also a bit of human vanity: to have a glorious temple, to have God in one's own city and, with his temple, to have also more prestige outside of Israel. In any case, through his prophet, Nathan, God gives him different orders. He tells him: "You wish to build a house for me, but I will build a house for you."

Man cannot build a house for God; he is incapable of it. God does not live in houses made by human hands; God does not live in the middle of stones, in the middle of rocks. Only God can build a house for Himself; God is not our guest, but rather we are God's guests; God does not live with us, but rather we live with and in God. This is the great promise that occurs in this moment: God Himself will build a house for Himself through David and his son. This is already an announcement of what Jesus will mention before His Passion: "In three days I will build the new, true temple, my body, which is really the temple of God" (see Jn 2:19; Mt 26:61). Hence we all become God's temple, by being drawn into His body. And so we enter both into the mystery of the Incarnation and into the mystery of the Eucharist, in which He gives us His body and we become His body.

God promises three things. He promises a son of David, who will say to God: "Father". God will say to this king: "My son", and therefore promises him his dignity.

Finally, God says: "Even if your sons must be punished, I will punish, but I will not renounce my faithfulness." And so this house does not depend on man's morality, but only on God's fidelity: because it is an eternal kingdom. All this appeared rather fantastic and, after the exile, no longer realistic, either; it seemed to be a sign that God had forgotten His promise. But this promise appears in its profound reality only at the moment of the annunciation in Nazareth. Now, God knocks at the door so as to become man definitively and thus to give us the king, the kingdom, and to show us His fidelity.

We see again briefly: "Rejoice!" This is a Greek greeting. In Israel the greeting was: *Shalom*—"Peace!", while in Greek it is: *Chaĩre*—"Rejoice!" And so today, in Israel, the universality of this promise unfolds: God will be not only king of Israel, but king of the entire world. Therefore "Rejoice!" is the greeting spoken to all of us. And, at the same time, this word of total fidelity to the promises made to David, to Israel, is also a word taken from the prophet Zephaniah, who says, "Rejoice, Zion, because the Lord will be in you; the Lord is with you!" (see Zeph 3:16–17). Literally the text says: "The Lord is in your womb." This is the expression used for the Ark of the Covenant: it is in Israel's womb, and through the Ark of the Covenant the Lord is to be in the womb of His people. All this takes on in the Gospel a totally unexpected significance: Mary, the living woman, is the living Ark of God; the Lord God really will be in her womb.

But we must also think of the dramatic character of this moment, which was explained well by Saint Bernard in one of his homilies.[1] God knocks at the world's door, at humanity's door. He makes Himself dependent on the free

[1] See Bernard of Clairvaux, *Homilies on Our Lady*, 4, 8–9.

"yes" of a human person. Many are awaiting him, and Saint Bernard says to the Blessed Virgin: "I truly and profoundly await the answer that you will give me." If Mary, perhaps moved by humility, frightened by the greatness of God's will, were to say: "I am not worthy", what would happen? God could not enter into the world; He would not find a house. But, while everyone is waiting, Mary says: "Yes, I am the servant of the Lord." This is the moment of the true turning point in history: from this moment on, God is man, and with us, and He never abandons us again, not even in all the sorrows, in all the catastrophes, in all the situations of history. "Yes, I am your handmaid": this single event makes us truly rejoice.

We want to keep in mind also the fact that, in a certain way, this situation is repeated: God also knocks at the door of my life, of my heart, and wants to be conceived, wants to be born also in me and from me. And He still says: "I want to be born from you", and He waits for our "yes". Let us pray that the Lord will help us to say: "Yes, I am the servant of the Lord." In this way, we accomplish the impossible. It would occur to us instead to say: "I am too little; no, no, I cannot; I would like to live in my own way", but nothing is impossible for God. The Gospel gives us this great confidence: if we say "yes" to Him, God will carry us and guide us. Let us give thanks to God for the great gift of His Incarnation, and let us pray that we, too, may be able to say: "Yes, every day I am Your servant, may Your will be done in me!" Amen!

CHRISTMAS SEASON

The Baptism of Jesus, the Servant of God, and Our Baptism

January 12, 2014
Private Chapel, Mater Ecclesiae Monastery

Baptism of the Lord (Year A)
Readings: Is 42:1–4, 6–7; Ps 29; Acts 10:34–38; Mt 3:13–17

In the first reading of this liturgical feast of the Baptism of Jesus, we heard the first of the four Servant songs, which are distributed from chapter 42 to chapter 53 of the Book of the Prophet Isaiah. The fourth song is central to the liturgy of Good Friday and speaks about the Servant of God, who suffers much for us and thus brings us true life.

These four songs of the Servant of God are important, because they show us a dimension of Israel's hope, and therefore of the hope of our faith, which normally we almost do not see, since we are too focused on the line of the Messiah, as the central expectation of Israel, the Messiah king, the new David who was to reign again over Israel. But this other vision, of the Servant of God, is important, precisely because it shows the whole depth of the hope that faith opens up for us.

A first point. This hope does not speak about a king; it speaks about the Servant of God and thus already clarifies one fundamental aspect: God's way of reigning is different from the way in which the kings of this world reign. God reigns by serving, and He tells us that all true dominion is service; that only by serving can one really reign, that is, build up the world in such a way as to be open to God.

This divine humility is of great importance, because it shows us the way. Then, a few words describe it even better; through the prophet, God says that "my servant does not raise his voice and does not quench the wick", the little flame, and He does not break man. He does not raise His voice: in other words, this Lord, God, does not come with the great power of propaganda, with an amplified outcry that obliges us to listen; He does not come with this mechanism that shapes public opinion, which oppresses us and easily and necessarily gets us involved; He comes, not with a loud voice, but with a silent voice, and only by entering into this silence of God can we hear the truth. We must therefore learn to listen to the One who does not raise His voice, who speaks to the depths of our heart in truth, and who does not quench, in other words, is not a violent man, who governs, not with violence, with external power, but with interior goodness.

Here we see precisely what Jesus replied to John when he asked: "But are you the Lord, the Messiah?" (see Mt 11:2–6; Lk 7:18–23). He does not make a great cry, does not make big headlines in the worldwide press, but interiorly, humbly, He heals and cures. And this is precisely God's way of governing, in the service of the Lord Jesus.

A second point. God is not only king of Israel, but light of the nations, light for all, because all need to be enlightened. Israel is only the point of departure so as to reach the entire world. The light of the nations: the Gospel of John repeats this expression when it says: "He, Christ, is the light that enlightens every man who comes into this world" (see Jn 1:9–10). The liturgy thinks also about the star that guided the Magi. This means: Christ Himself is the true star, which guides us in the night of the world and shows us the way. The night of the world is ignorance of God. If man does not know God, he really is in deep darkness and does not know where to go and how to walk: he discovers it only when the truth about God appears, because that truth is the light that guides us. We all need this central truth in order to see correctly what we are. Someone who does not know God does not know man, either; someone who knows God also understands man and his own existence. The light that guides us, the Light of the world, Christ, really is light; He is the appearance of the face of God, of truth, and thus He shows us the way.

And finally a third point: the reading says with great intensity, a good three times, that the Servant of God establishes justice, brings forth justice to the nations. What does that mean? Here Jesus, the Servant of God, is shown as the true Moses; He is not only the true David, the true Solomon, but also the true Moses; because Israel awaited also the new Moses, who would renew the liberation of the people and lead them toward the Promised Land. We usually think that the essential thing about Moses' work was the liberation from Egypt, but that is not so; the essential aspect is that he led the people to the mountain of God, created the contact, the covenant with God, and brought the Law from God to Israel.

Only with justice is a people liberated. True slavery is the absence of justice; anarchy is the opposite of liberty, and today we see in all parts of the world how anarchy, the absence of justice, and corruption destroy peoples and create slavery. Only justice liberates us; justice is not the opposite of liberty but rather the condition and cause of it. Only when there is justice—that is, a sharing of liberty in the light of the truth—is there liberty, too. Thus, Moses is a liberator precisely because he brought forth justice. And Jesus completes this work, extending it to all peoples: He gives us justice, and thus liberty, showing us God, leading us to the mountain of God. In the Most Holy Eucharist, He brings us into contact with God through Himself; we recognize in His word the face of God.

Thus we know also the fundamental lines of the Law, which is centered on the twofold commandment of love and on a reinterpretation of the Decalogue in the light of Christ. Moses brought a complete legal code for the people of Israel, which could not be extended to the world; Jesus gave us Himself, the light of God, the light of His face, of His words; He gave us the twofold commandment of love and thus gave us the liberty and the ability to create law, which according to Roman legislation is truly the cause of liberty, but also depends on our knowledge of the light of God.

At this point, an approach opens up for us to the mystery of the Baptism of Jesus, which is celebrated in today's liturgy. In His Baptism, as we saw, Jesus presents Himself as one among the sinners and enters into the service of the Servant of God. According to the information in the Gospel of Saint John, the true locality of the Baptism of Jesus is the lowest point on earth.[1] This fact has an important symbolism: Jesus, who descended to the lowest point on earth, symbolically descended to the lowest depths of human existence, to the lowest depths of our misery; He identified with us.

This Baptism is His entrance into the mystery of the Servant of God, who identifies with us, bears our sins, and

[1] This is a reference to the fact that the Baptism of Jesus occurred near the place where the Jordan empties into the Dead Sea, which is in fact the deepest depression on earth, more than four hundred meters below sea level.

thus gives us the opportunity to live once again. Jesus, in His Baptism, identified with us in our Baptism. He unites us with His Baptism, and, precisely thereby, we come to be identified with Jesus. This is the essential point of the Baptism: we go out from our own identity, enter into this identification with Jesus; it identifies us with Him, and insofar as we enter into this identification with Jesus, He also enters into an identification with us.

To this extent, we, too, are children of God, children of his "good pleasure". At this point, there is also an echo of the mystery of the Nativity, because the angels had said to the shepherds: "Peace among men with whom [God] is pleased" (Lk 2:14).[2] Who, then, is the man with whom God is well pleased? It is Jesus, and we are, too, insofar as we are identified with Jesus, insofar as we truly enter into the mystery of Jesus' Baptism and of our Baptism.

Let us pray that the Lord will help us, too, become servants of God and serve with our life the mystery of Truth, Light, and Goodness. Let us pray that He may grant to us to be identified with the Lord Himself, to live more and more by our Baptism, and thus to be truly redeemed in the light of God. Amen!

[2] Benedict XVI, in translating the verse "peace among men with whom God is pleased", highlights the fact that Luke uses the same Greek word as the voice from heaven at the Baptism of Jesus: *eudokia*.

LENT

What Must the World's Redeemer Do?

March 9, 2014
Private Chapel, Mater Ecclesiae Monastery

First Sunday of Lent (Year A)
Readings: Gen 2:7–9, 3:1–7; Ps 51; Rom 5:12–19;
Mt 4:1–11

With His Baptism and the solemn proclamation that He is the Son of God, Jesus formally, officially embarked on His mission as Messiah. The first task imposed on Him by the Holy Spirit was to go into the desert to be tempted, or, as today's prayer says, to enter into the Lenten sacrament, into the sacrament of the forty days.

In the language of the early Church, the word "sacrament" not only refers to our seven sacraments but is also a translation of the word "mystery", that is, it indicates the essential structures of salvation history, and one of the elements of these structures is the mystery of the forty days or years. Israel journeys for forty years in the desert, in a time of special closeness to God, who speaks with His people and acts with His people; but it is also a time of great temptations, in which Israel rebels against God and no longer wants to walk with God: it is the time of the initial love and the time of the great temptations.

Then, Moses remains for forty days on Sinai, high up and alone, far from everyday matters, on the interior height of God's mountain, in the silence of the world: in his great fast, he can thus perceive the Word of God for all times. Finally, Elijah walks for forty days with the strength from the bread given to him by the angel and, after Israel's apostasy, must return once again to God's mountain and renew the encounter with God.

Jesus Himself enters into this tradition of the Forty Days, and with Him the Church introduces us into it each year, once again, along this road. It must be said that, for Jesus, the content of this season is precisely temptation, that is, entering into the drama of human existence. Only in the desert, in solitude, with all its specters, in need, in the poverty of absolute hunger, in exposure to the elements and to solitude with God, He experiences the human drama, being tempted, that is, finding Himself tempted to choose, not God, but apparently better solutions, which in reality are destructive. As it says in the Letter to the Hebrews, it is part of Jesus' mission to enter into our temptations, to be tempted as we are, only Jesus does not fall into sin and, precisely thereby, helps us to overcome temptations (see Heb 4:15–16).

But what are these temptations of Jesus? I would say that they are the temptations of the Messiah, of the man who is the Redeemer. The question that arises is: If someone wants to be the redeemer of the world, what must he do? The answers that appear humanly obvious are in a way the proposals that the devil makes to Jesus: these are the great temptations.

In the first place, someone who wants to redeem mankind must above all respond to the sorrow of hunger, to the misery of poverty; someone who does not overcome this misery, who does not give everyone something to eat, who does not give everyone the means to live in a dignified way, does not redeem the world. One could say: as long as there is hunger, together with all these sad things that we see every day on television, as long as this tangible misery prevails on earth, mankind is not redeemed.

Satan's second proposal is this: the Messiah must give certainty. As if to say: "Dear God, if You want us to believe in You, You must be clear; this cloud in which You show Yourself is not enough; we need clarity, certainty."

And, with his third proposal to Jesus, the devil declares: you must give power to what is good; the good must not always be overcome and destroyed by human arrogance.

Well, then, let us return to the first point: in order to be able to see humanity redeemed, you must overcome the misery of hunger, all this sorrow of poverty. The devil offers this to the Lord. But the Lord says: This is not the way of redemption! And He makes us understand that, even if all human beings had enough to eat and well-being was extended to everyone, mankind would not be redeemed.

Indeed, we see how, precisely in the well-to-do countries, in social circles that have wealth, riches, and abundance, man is destroying himself, is self-destructing. Although a man may have enough to eat and to wear, he is not yet a good man; on the contrary, he tends to self-destruct, because he forgets God and thinks only about his riches. Hence it is not possible to start this way; there has to be a different order of priorities.

Jesus was confronted three times with this problem: here in the temptations of the desert, then in the multiplication of loaves, and finally in the true multiplication of loaves, in the Last Supper, in the institution of the Eucharist. In these three contexts, especially in the multiplication of loaves, Jesus tells us, or says to his disciples: "You give them something to eat!"

This implies that God first offers sufficient food for all human beings: the earth gives food for all; God already offers everything, but you human beings must enter into God's care, you must participate in God's love; you must become part of the network of goodness, you must give, and only this shared responsibility with the Creator fosters the true victory over evil, over poverty, and fosters redemption.

In the multiplication of loaves we should note the request to sit in groups: this implies love and the courage and willingness to share, and the miracle takes place only in this shared responsibility of man, and hunger is overcome. This is therefore an initial aspect: we must enter into this shared responsibility. And then the condition that makes this possible is the gift of the new bread from heaven, the true manna: Jesus Christ Himself. God gives Himself, through Jesus, to us in bread, and this is the bread on which we fundamentally live, and this bread is precisely what transforms, renews, and redeems the world. Hence the Lord invites us to responsibility, to share God's responsibility, and He gives us Himself, so that then we might effectively be able to give a little of ourselves to others.

We see what this means for our Lent, for our experience of the mystery of the forty days. The bread of God is Christ Himself, and an initial requirement is that we must really be open to this greatness; the second condition is, naturally, fasting, that is, self-mastery, the ability to do without things. Fasting is an expression of all religions, because they all tell us that, in order to be truly human, I must have a lively will, one capable of ruling my life; I must be capable of self-denial and self-control.

However, this self-denial and this discipline are never ends in themselves. In the Church's tradition, fasting and almsgiving, fasting and charity, fasting and responsible love always go together; fasting and self-denial are means to the end, which is shared responsibility, the sharing of goods and active love. This is a fundamental aspect of our Lent:

together with the ability to deny oneself, it is necessary to learn to love with Christ, to distribute ourselves together with Christ, who distributes Himself to mankind.

The second point: certainty. By letting Himself fall from a height, Jesus supposedly would demonstrate that God protects him absolutely and thus prove experimentally that God exists. But God finds this very thing unacceptable: God is not the subject of our experiments. In Psalm 95, in looking back on the time in the desert, God says: "You had seen my works, but you tried to put me to the test" (see v. 9). We can see God's action, but that is not enough for us, and so we want to perform an experiment; God is supposed to submit to our experiment, is supposed to go into our laboratory to let us verify whether or not He exists.

But while God really shows Himself and makes Himself visible in many things, He does not agree to be the subject of our experiments, to be subjected to our measurements and to our way of gaining certainty. This type of certainty, that claims to test God, is not possible, and certainly we all suffer from the fact that something like a final "fog" always remains. In the hour of the Last Supper, the Apostle Jude Thaddeus expressed in a really convincing way what we all would like to say; he said to the Lord: "But, Lord, how is it that you decided to manifest yourself only to us and not to the world?" (see Jn 14:22).

This means: the Risen Lord should not show Himself only to a small group of the elect, but should also go and see Pilate, should go and see the high priests, the Sanhedrin, should convince them by the very force of His presence. When Thaddeus says: "What has happened? You should not show yourself only to us, you should go also and see the others!", we too are tempted to say the same thing. But God is different; God leaves us free and waits for us to make a journey in search of Him; along this journey He offers us a place in which He makes himself visible, so that we can be sure. Let us pray that the Lord will help us to journey with Him and, thus, to see Him and to be certain.

Here we are at the second point of our Lent. We spoke about fasting and charity. The journey of prayer is part of the mystery of Lent. The prayer of today's Mass tells us that the meaning of Lent consists of grasping the secret (*arcanum*) of Christ, of entering into this secret, into this elevation that is entering into His mystery and knowing Him truly, so as to find correct certainty. We dare to do this only by the journey of prayer, by this ongoing relationship with the Lord, which seeks Him and finds Him. Saint John Chrysostom says: "Prayer is basically only the exercise of the desire for God, the desire to know his face."[1] This Lent let us allow ourselves to be seized by the desire to seek His face, to pray: "Lord, show Yourself!"

The third temptation, power: only if someone has power can he also create a good world. This seems very obvious to everyone, but here, too, Jesus says: "No!" And just as the other two temptations accompany Him throughout His life, so too this temptation appears several times over the course of His life. Think of the example at the moment in Caesarea Philippi, when Peter had understood and confessed: "You are the Messiah." Jesus praises him and tells him: "Yes, you did understand this; the Father gave you this knowledge." But then He continues: "You have not yet understood what the Messiah truly is; the Messiah must suffer, be betrayed, handed over to the pagans and crucified." Then Saint Peter takes Jesus aside and says to Him: "No! You are the Messiah, and a Messiah does not suffer!" Here Jesus feels just as He did in the situation in the desert, in front of the devil, and says: "Begone, Satan!" (see Mt 16:13–28).

[1] John Chrysostom, *Homily 6 on Prayer.*

This same temptation always remains, even in the history of the Church. Many times with the Christian empires we have tried to give power to Jesus, to rule out the weakness of God; even today we make many attempts along these lines, and Jesus tells us: "No! This is not the way for me to be your king. I can be your king only on a very different journey, on a journey that involves passion and love." In other words, Jesus did not come to liberate us from suffering, but to liberate us through suffering, so as to enter into this mystery of transformation, which is part of the essence of love.

For us it is very difficult to understand this: we all want there to be a world without the sorrow of suffering; we want God to liberate us from suffering, and not through suffering. But the Lord tells us: "Come with me in order to understand and to enter into the true mystery of redemption and the battle against evil." Thus finally, although early Christianity spoke about the "*Militia Christi*", about the war in which we must serve as soldiers, we can say: "Yes! It is the holy war of love against cold-heartedness, and only in this way is God victorious."

Let us pray that the Lord will help us to enter into the Lenten mystery, to become Christians indeed, and to learn true redemption. Amen!

To Change the World, We Need to Adore God

February 25, 2007
Private Chapel, Apostolic Palace

First Sunday of Lent (Year C)
Readings: Deut 26:4–10; Ps 91; Rom 10:8–13;
Lk 4:1–13

Today the Lord appears as the Second Adam, whose mission is to restart this human history that had started badly. Although today there is little talk about original sin, we all see that in reality human history started badly. All politicians, of all stripes, say that we want to improve the world, create a better world, presupposing that the present one is not going well. Everyone feels that something in the world ought to be changed, because, as it is, it is not on the right path.

If in the world we see hunger, violence, drugs, terrorism, there is no doubt that something in the world is not working right and that something has to be changed, that history ought to start over again. The language of the Church calls this necessity to make amends "redemption".

The temptations of the Second Adam are therefore different from those of the first; they are questions and temptations that concern the redemption of mankind and its redeemer. The common question that concerns these temptations is: If someone wants to be the redeemer of mankind, what must he do? In what does redemption consist? And in this story, the devil's view, which at first glance is very obvious, quite understandable, meets God's view, which is not so obvious, because in order to understand it we must enter into the depths of the human being, into the mystery of God.

First temptation: the devil says: "Create bread." This means: someone who wants to be redeemer of mankind must above all overcome hunger in the world. This is the essential foundation for any redemption: that there be no more hunger in the world. Someone who has not done this, who has not given everyone food, who has not overcome this calamity of hunger, has not redeemed mankind. And it seems absolutely true.

Jesus does not say that bread is unnecessary for mankind, but He says that bread is not enough. In order to understand Jesus' response, we will have to take into account the two other great stories concerning bread in His life: the multiplication of the loaves in the desert and the great and definitive multiplication of bread in the Last Supper.

I would like to highlight only one small point in the Lord's discourse after the multiplication of the loaves (see Jn 6:26–51). It is immediately interpreted in this sense: finally redemption is beginning and Jesus gives us bread so that there will no longer be hunger. The Hebrews refer to Moses, who was the true liberator, not the perfect, complete, definitive redeemer, but still the liberator of the people, the true envoy of God. The great proof that he really was the liberator, sent by God, was that he had given bread from heaven. Hence the new and definitive Moses—the Messiah would be the definitive Moses—would have to give at least what Moses gave: bread from heaven for everyone. This would be the proof that the new Moses is present.

In His discourse, Jesus seeks instead to make them understand that the manna was not the essential gift from Moses, because, even though this bread came from heaven, it was still earthly bread; it was a passing, transient thing. The true bread from heaven that Moses gave was the Torah: the Word of God, the knowledge of God. To know God, to know His will, and thus to stand in the light—in this way, by drawing near to His will, one can really and radically change the world.

Thus Jesus demonstrates that He is the true Moses, because He gives the true Word of God, or rather, He is the Word of God in person, the finally accessible God, the divine light who is with us and gives Himself into our hands and into our heart. Hence the Lord's response is as follows: material things are important, but well-being as such does not redeem mankind; it is too little. On the contrary, if it is taken as an absolute and considered as sufficient in itself, it becomes a diabolical temptation that destroys mankind and does not redeem it. This is the content of His response: bread does good, but well-being as such, material things in themselves, when taken as absolutes, are not redemption if the essential thing is missing: the knowledge of God. An in-depth change can result only from the encounter of our heart with the heart of God.

Second temptation: adoring the devil, that is, receiving power from the devil. This is the content of this offering of the devil: the fundamental good of the world is peace. But peace can be given only by someone who has power to create the peace, to conquer those who do not make peace, and to keep them within their boundaries. Thus power would be the fundamental condition for creating peace and consequently for redeeming.

In this way, someone who does not succeed in creating universal peace in the world is not the redeemer, and for that reason someone who does not have political and military power cannot give it. But the Lord—even though I do not wish to go into the details now—demonstrates that human power alone, political and military power, always remains ambiguous, and even if it appears as an instrument of peace, if it is taken as an absolute, it does not redeem; on the contrary, even if it is initiated with the best intentions, it becomes oppression. This is not what redeems mankind, and structures, in and of themselves, do not redeem mankind.

If God is missing, human structures become an oppression of liberty and do not redeem. Once again the priority of the true good appears: if the primary good is lacking—the knowledge of God and His love—the rest, even with good intentions, becomes destructive and an instrument of the devil.

The most difficult temptation is the third. Jesus on the pinnacle of the temple is supposed to throw Himself down to see whether God will protect Him. Here it seems natural to me to recall a story related in the Book of Numbers (see Num 20:1–11). In the desert there was no water, and the people said: "Now God must show that He is God", and the Lord God replied: "They put me to the test although they had seen my blessings" (see Ps 95:9). In other words, God would have to submit to our proof, to our test, to our "experiment". And if something is not demonstrable in the experiment, it does not help and is not real.

This is the view of modern science, which intends to redeem mankind with science and its power; hence God, who is not accessible in an experiment, would not be a valid reality for human life. Here, too, the Lord tells us that the relation with Him is something else, that with God one cannot treat God as we treat material things. If we want to submit God to the experiment, we have already denied Him as God. We have access to God, not by forcing Him, not by subjecting Him to our criteria of certainty, but by opening our heart. This is how God's heart opens.

In reality, Jesus does not remain on the pinnacle of the temple but, in the end, is lifted up on the high "pinnacle" of the Cross; here He gives Himself confidently into the hands of God, who even in death does not let Him fall, but raises Him to life again.

The whole meaning of this story appears in the first reading, which we heard from the Book of Deuteronomy. Ultimately we must adore God. Only by recognizing God, by knowing God and acknowledging Him as God, by adoring Him and giving ourselves into His hands, and by learning from God our way of life, do we act in truth. Because God is God, we are His creatures, and only by acting in truth, that is, by experiencing adoration, do we live well and change the world.

Let us pray that the Lord will help us to live the Truth and to know Him as the true Redeemer of the world. Amen!

The Light of the Transfiguration

March 16, 2014
Private Chapel, Mater Ecclesiae Monastery

Second Sunday of Lent (Year A)
Readings: Gen 12:1–4; Ps 33; 2 Tim 1:8–10;
Mt 7:1–9

Last Sunday's liturgy was marked by the symbol, by the place of the desert. The desert, a place of austerity, of extreme creaturely poverty, and therefore a place of temptation, but also a place of openness to God. A place in which only nothingness and God confront each other.

Today we have a different location: the mountain. The mountain, too, is a very important symbol for the geography of the soul. It starts with the mountain of the sacrifice of Abraham and Isaac, Mount Horeb, Sinai, and finally the Temple Mount, where heaven and earth touch. In the life of Jesus, too, the mountain appears again and again as a place of prayer; Jesus withdraws to the mountain to pray, He withdraws to the heights, far from everyday things, to be near God. Thus the readings this Sunday invite us to climb with the Lord and His Apostles up the mountains of the meeting with God, on the heights of Tabor. How are we to do this?

The early Church, on this Sunday, used to celebrate Mass by starting just a little after midnight, and it continued initially with twelve, later on with seven readings, until Sunday morning, and it ended with the ordination of priests. There were seven readings corresponding to the seven orders, four minor and three major, and they ended with the Transfiguration on the mountain of the Eucharist, on the mountain of closeness to Christ. This showed also what the priesthood means: being transparent to the light of God. We could say that this journey of the seven orders reflects not only the journey toward the priesthood, but also the journey of Christian life as such, with this ascent that is also precisely the meaning of Lent.

It starts with the order of porter: opening the door to Christ, having the sensitivity to listen as He knocks at our door, understanding that we must open to Him, so that He might enter into us, and, on the other hand, having discernment, that is, knowing also when to close and not to open. Opening with wisdom, learning discernment, opening the door to Christ and closing it to the world. Then the second order of exorcist: that is, accepting the battle against the evil one, against all the spirits of hypocrisy, arrogance, lying, and evil. After that, the order of lector: familiarity with the Word of God, learning to love this Word, learning to understand this Word, allowing oneself to be penetrated by this Word. Then the order of acolyte: carrying the light of Christ. The subdiaconate and the diaconate: being servants above all else; the Christian ascent is not like worldly careers that lead to a high-ranking position, but rather it leads to being a servant; this is the true height, the height of Jesus Christ, the height of love: this is where we should arrive. Finally, the priesthood: that is, letting oneself be penetrated by Christ, letting oneself be penetrated by the light of God.

On the mountain itself, the Gospel tells us, there are two things: on the one hand, the light, about which I would like to speak today, and, on the other hand, the word of the prophets; Moses and Elijah speak with Christ and thus show that He is the center, the true content of Sacred Scripture; it is not only a word but is the Word of God. And then come the word of the Father—"This is my Son"—and the cloud, which causes the disciples to fall into a tremendous fear, because this cloud that surrounds them is what happened when the sacred tent was set up in the desert, and the cloud of God came and covered everything and showed that "God is here!" Thus, after the word: "This is my Son", the cloud comes, which shows Christ Himself as the true tent of God, as the true temple in which God dwells.

But now we see what the Transfiguration is. Saint Luke is in this case the most precise Evangelist; he says: "While Jesus prayed, his face changed." The Transfiguration is an event that takes place in prayer. In prayer Christ becomes transparent, He shows Himself in His true reality, which is dialogue with God; He not only speaks with God, but is with His whole being a dialogue with the Father, He is entirely light from light. And so this light shines through, to the point where He Himself is all light; it shows who Christ really is and how Christ's prayer, this exchange of being with the Father, is His true essence.

What does this tell us? The Fathers of the Church were convinced that in the beginning, before sin, man had been clothed in light, with the light of God, and that only with sin, when man no longer wanted to be a son of God, but rather to take life by himself, did he lose that light and become merely animal matter. Man lost the light, that is, his first garment, as the Church Fathers say. And Jesus came precisely to restore to us our true garment, to clothe us once again in His light. Christ enters into us, and thus the light enters into us, and we can be clothed once again with His glory.

About this point, the Book of Revelation tells us that the angels and saints in heaven will be clothed in white, that is, in pure light, like God, because they are penetrated by the divine light. And in chapter 7 it adds a very interesting detail, saying: "Their robes are white, are light, because they washed their robes in the blood of the Lamb" (see Rev 7:9, 13–14). We would like to say: "What? Blood does not make a garment white; that cannot be!" We must instead understand that it is not material blood that purifies; the redemptive force, the death of God, is not the act of killing, but rather the interior act in which men's hatred is transformed by Jesus into an act of love, into an act of total self-giving to the Father. This gift of self, which is the true blood of Christ, the self-gift of Jesus to God, is an act of drawing man out from his sadness toward the light of God; this act of love, this transformation of human hatred into love, with which Jesus gives Himself for us to the Father, is the true "washing", it is the purifying force that makes our garments—that is, our being—shine also.

In this sense, it seems to me that this passage speaks precisely about the mystery of our redemption: the world is full of filthiness, full of sad things, but Christ came with this "cleansing", so to speak, purifying force, which with His immense love is so great as to be sufficient to cleanse all humanity from this mass of lies and hatred and all the evil that we find everywhere. In the Eucharist we enter into this reality, Jesus draws us into the interior of this love of His and washes us and thus makes us once again light, even though we still need to journey again so as to arrive finally at the true transfiguration of our being, at the state of being light with Light itself.

In the Book of Exodus, we find a detail that seems to me very beautiful in this context. The Book of Exodus says: "When Moses came down from the mountain from his meeting with God, he did not know that his skin was radiant because he had spoken with God" (see Ex 34:29). Moses had spoken with God, and this conversation with God had made his skin radiant. In the Eucharist, we speak with God and He speaks with us; we let ourselves be touched by His love, we receive into us Christ, who is pure light. Let us pray that the Lord will help us so that we, too, may be a little radiant, that some ray of His light may be visible in us, too, when we come down from this meeting with the Word of God.

At the beginning, we spoke about our "ascent"; we must add that descending is also part of the Christian vocation. We must "ascend", but we must also, again and again, have the humility, the willingness to "descend", to descend into the valley of routine and our everyday activities. Precisely in this descent, in this humility of doing our work each day, we are on Christ's road, because before opening up the way that leads on high, Christ descended from the glory of God, He descended as far as the Cross, "he became a slave for us", Saint Paul says (see Phil 2:7).

Therefore let us follow Christ, descending humbly to complete every task in the everyday routine of our life, performing it in the light of Christ, and thus, precisely while we descend, we also ascend with Him.

Let us pray to the Lord that His light may penetrate us; let us pray that He may help us to descend and to ascend and to arrive at last to be in His light. Amen!

Listening in Order to Go Out and Be a Blessing

March 12, 2017
Private Chapel, Mater Ecclesiae Monastery

Second Sunday of Lent (Year A)
Readings: Gen 12:1–4; Ps 33; 2 Tim 1:8–10;
Mt 7:1–9

The three readings of today's liturgy, and also the prayer, are dominated by two fundamental words: "listening" and "seeing". I would like to meditate a little with you especially about the word "listening".

In the first reading, we see Abraham, with whom salvation history begins. This is after the incident of the tower of Babel, and God pledges to make a new beginning; God starts over, because He wants to arrive at the salvation of mankind. And so, we see that Abraham must first of all listen. Listen to God, who tells him: "Go!", and he must go out, leave his land, so as to walk toward God's promise. The first point is therefore to listen, and then to go, to follow God's voice. This imperative is valid for us, too: "Listen!" Listen to what God says. Listen not only to the many voices of the world, which impose their message ever more forcefully and radically, but listen to God. And how can we do this?

Today's Gospel gives us the answer: "This is my Son, listen to him!" And the faith of the Apostles is transmitted;

our faith passes on through this listening. God Himself helps us all, speaks as a man with us, so that each of us can listen and understand. Therefore the first imperative of our human life is to listen to Christ. We must learn over and over again to listen to His Word, to listen with humble obedience, to listen to it with a willing mind and heart. Listen. It is a fundamental fact that God became man and speaks as a man: for this reason He does not remain an indecipherable enigma, but rather really speaks to us through Jesus. This Jesus, in turn, is not alone, but brings and accomplishes in Himself the whole dialogue of mankind with God. By listening to Jesus, we do not listen to one single person, but to the whole history of truth, and we listen to God Himself.

Then the reading speaks to us about Abraham's response: he departs, goes out from his land, and travels where the Lord had ordered him. In what sense can we, too, do something similar? I think that we must remember chapter 11 of the Letter to the Hebrews, which describes the journey of believers. It is a passage that relates what it means to journey, to listen, to carry out the will of God, and in the richness of this journey we understand what faith is and what it means to believe. Precisely this chapter recalls that Moses was like a son for Pharaoh's daughter, and could have been rich and powerful, but he preferred the poverty and sorrow of his people to the wealth of Egypt. He went out from the splendor of the royal court to live in poverty, because in that way he kept his gaze fixed on the fulfillment of God's promise (see Heb 11:24–26).

I think that here the letter speaks about something that has permanent value. Believing is always going out from a convenient situation toward the truth, giving up the things that offer a transient pleasure. This can be verified in many ways. For example, we see politicians who want to please the most constituents, instead of building up the common good, whereas they always ought to abandon that attitude and not seek their own success as much as they seek the true good. This is the fundamental decision to make. When this does not happen, we see how original sin leads politicians to put their own success ahead of the truth, so that the attempt to be well thought of by everyone prevails over the truth. But this is not the way of the Cross; it is the way of evil. To believe, in the sense of Abraham's faith, is to go out from my will, from the search for success, toward the truth. Only in this way is the world saved; only in this way do we follow the right path.

The second reading confirms this with the example of Saint Paul. Already in prison, he writes to Timothy: "Suffer with me for the Gospel!" This is willingness to suffer for the truth; suffering for the truth is contrasted to one's own convenience. In history we see that the honor of mankind always is based on a willingness to embrace martyrdom. The Church is founded on martyrs, who do not submit to the yoke of power, but rather suffer for the Gospel: thus they save the honor of the truth, they save the true life. We see this well in the life of Cardinal Ernest Simoni, who was persecuted for his refusal to create a Church without the pope.[1] For the Albanian Catholics, too, it was necessary to "go out".

Finally, we see where the path of Abraham finally leads, what the Lord promises him and what He promises us as well. He promises him descendants, but this is not the essential thing. The essential thing is: "You will be a blessing and in you all the families of the earth will bless themselves." We know persons in our own life who were, or

[1] The Albanian priest Ernest Simoni (born in 1928) had been created a cardinal by Pope Francis in November 2016, after enduring eighteen years of forced labor and other persecutions by the Communist regime.

are, like the splendor of the sun; they are like fresh water, they are a blessing. But the Lord adds: "In you all the families of the earth will bless themselves"; in other words, the blessing is not for Abraham alone, but for the others. The essential thing of the blessing is to be for the other person, for others. Thus Jesus, too, came to be a blessing for us and for all the families of the earth. Being Christians is not being privileged, fortunate individuals. Universality, "catholicity" is essential for the right perspective on the promise of salvation. Therefore let us thank the Lord that the "catholic" Church exists for the blessing of all the families of the earth.

And I conclude with the prayer for this Sunday, which, as we said at the beginning, contains the two fundamental words of this liturgy: "listening" and "seeing".

"Lord, help us to listen and purify our interior vision so that we might see Your glory." Amen!

The Transfiguration: Listening to Jesus to Learn the Way

March 4, 2007
Private Chapel, Apostolic Palace

Second Sunday of Lent (Year C)
Readings: Gen 1:5–12, 17–18; Ps 27; Phil 3:17–4:1; Lk 9:28b–36

In the ancient Roman liturgy, this Sunday had no proper Mass. In the night between Saturday and Sunday a long, solemn liturgy was celebrated, which ended on Sunday morning. During the course of this long liturgy, the seven sacred orders were conferred, starting with the order of porter, one of the four minor orders, and ending with the priesthood.

This ascent from the order of porter to the priesthood was accompanied by a series of readings, beginning with the Book of Deuteronomy, up to the First Letter to the Thessalonians: "This is the Lord's will for you, your sanctification" (see 1 Thess 4:1–8), concluding with the Gospel of the Transfiguration. This series of seven readings, each with a responsory and prayer, was the spiritual interpretation of what took place in the conferral of holy orders and made the participants understand what was happening, what reality and what obligation were connected with these orders. Thus the final reading, the Gospel of the Transfiguration, speaks essentially about the mystery of Christ, but in this night it was understood also as an interpretation of the priesthood, which is inseparable from the mystery of Christ.

Perhaps we can see this Gospel in that light, starting from the fact that Jesus takes aside the three Apostles and goes up the mountain with them. This is the first condition for the priesthood; letting oneself be taken aside with Jesus, going up the mountain with Jesus, entering in a very personal communion with Him, not merely knowing Him as the people know Him, seeing Him here and there superficially, but rather knowing Him in a true, intimate, and personal encounter.

Eight days before the Transfiguration, Peter's confession of faith had taken place, "You are the Christ, the Son of God", and Saint Luke tells us that this confession was born at the moment when they had observed how Jesus was praying (see Lk 9:18–22). They had, so to speak, entered into His interior life, having seen how the Son speaks with the Father, and thus this prayer of Jesus became transparent and allowed the mystery of the communion between Son and Father to shine through. They understood: This is the Son who speaks with the Father. And they sought to learn to pray with Jesus so as really to enter into communion with God.

Thus the Transfiguration, too, occurs while Jesus is praying: the Transfiguration makes visible what the Son's prayer is. The Son is conversation with the Father, He is the Word, as Saint John says, He is precisely this being-in-response (Word) to the Father, He is the fact of being light from light. In this interpenetration between Son and Father in the divine conversation, which is a luminous penetration, it becomes evident that the divine light penetrates the whole figure of Jesus, because He is the Light with the Light, because, being conversation with the Father, He is precisely a presence of the divine light.

Thus it appears that the priesthood should be a participation in Jesus' conversation with the Father and, thus, should enter into His light and allow us, too, to be penetrated by His light, because only if we become light can we also be witnesses to the Light. And as this is true in a specific, sacramental way for the priesthood, it is true in a profound sense also for all of us. To enter into the conversation of the Son with the Father, to learn from Jesus to speak with the Father, to let ourselves be penetrated by His word and thus by His light; to transfigure our life, which thus really takes the form of the image of God, of the appearance of the divine light.

Then Moses and Elijah appear, in other words, the essentials in salvation history, because God owns His action in history, and it appears as a history centered on Jesus, a history in conversation with Christ. The two great witnesses, Moses and the prophets, in the Greek text speak about the "exodus" of Jesus—not about His "departure", as it is translated in the Italian version that we just heard—they speak about the "exodus" of Jesus. "Exodus" was the great key word of Israel's salvation history.

The exodus was the journey in which Israel became a people and found itself because it found God. It was the journey of the knowledge of God: knowing His face, knowing His will, and thus journeying with God and finding the land, togetherness, freedom, and communion. But this exodus, this journey with God, this knowledge of God—learning to walk with God and thus to find freedom and communion—had remained incomplete.

Israel had gone out from Egypt and had arrived in its own land, but it often forgot God, and its life was often far from God; therefore the new exile follows, the new slavery, and a new return exodus, but still under the oppression of the major powers. It does not find true freedom, because it does not find true communion, and it does not find it because it does not find God. Only from God can all these things be learned.

Therefore this exodus, of which Moses was the great guide, becomes ever deeper, but it still remains only an image, a shadow; it was not yet the true exodus. Moses and Elijah speak with Jesus about Jesus' exodus, the true exodus that belongs to Jesus. Both men suffered with God and for God, they are witnesses of the Cross and thus interpret what the exodus is with their life more than with their words.

Exodus is communion with the Cross, and only in this way is it liberation from our selfishness and a landing on the shore of true freedom and a capacity for true communion. The exodus of Jesus is his exodus leading to the Cross and Resurrection, and by following this exodus we find freedom and we find communion. And we see that all salvation history—we could add all human history—is a conversation with Jesus, a conversation about how to find the way: we find it only by knowing God, by living in communion with God, and by journeying with Jesus on the way of the Cross, too.

Now, allow me to mention only briefly the words of Saint Peter about "three tents". An attentive reading by exegetes found that Peter's confession, eight days before the Transfiguration, had taken place on *Yom Kippur*, the major day of atonement. Indeed, this declaration of Peter is closely connected to the rite of *Yom Kippur*, the essence of which was pronouncing the mysterious name of God. In Peter's confession, this act of the high priest becomes Peter's act in a new way: it is pronouncing the divinity of Jesus and, thus, really making present the name of Jesus, God himself, on earth.

Then after the day of *Yom Kippur*, the day of atonement, follows "the feast of booths". The tents—the "booths"—were considered as a prefiguration of freedom, of a life in freedom, beauty, and joy. Thus the feast of booths was considered also as the moment of the return, the arrival of the Messiah, of definitive freedom, when the exodus will have really arrived at its destination.

Peter, seeing Jesus with Moses and Elijah, with all of salvation history, on the feast of booths says: "Let us build three tents here, because it seems that here the definitive feast of booths has occurred, the definitive freedom." But Jesus shows the Apostles that they are still on a journey and the tents are a sign of a provisional state; they still live in this provisional state of journeying with Jesus and also with His Passion.

One final point, the cloud from which the Father's voice comes: "This is my Son, listen to him!" To make another reference to the Old Testament, exegetes have shown that this whole narrative, from the ascent of Jesus with the three Apostles, reveals traces of the other Old Testament narrative, when Moses ascends Mount Sinai with Aaron and Hur, and Moses disappears into the cloud and there receives the Torah, the Word of God (see Ex 24:13–18).

Now this conclusion of the Transfiguration, with the word coming from the cloud, shows us that Jesus is the Torah. The Torah of Moses was only a provisional word, for a provisional period of time. Jesus is the true Torah; He is the incarnate Word of God, His living Word. Everything that is concentrated in this divine command—"This is my Son, he is my word, listen to him!"—is the command for this Sunday, and it was also the command for the newly ordained priests, as the motto for their whole life: to keep listening to Jesus and thus to learn the Way, to learn the path of freedom. And it is also a command for us, it is precisely the program for Lent: to listen to Jesus, to heed what he says, and thus to learn to travel on the path of true freedom. Amen!

Entering into the Light, Becoming Light

February 21, 2016
Private Chapel, Mater Ecclesiae Monastery

Second Sunday of Lent (Year C)
Readings: Gen 1:5–12, 17–18; Ps 27; Phil 3:17–4:1; Lk 9:28b–36

Today's Gospel is very rich in symbolism, in essential words: the light, the cloud, the voice from heaven, and so on. I would like to reflect a little with you on three of them.

First of all: the light. Jesus climbs the high mountain with these three Apostles: John, Peter, and James. This is the same company with which He will climb another mountain, the Mount of Olives. While Jesus shows Himself here in all His beauty, His glory, on the Mount of Olives the same Apostles will see in Jesus' prayer His Passion, the mystery of evil, and our redemption. Here it is important to note what Saint Luke tells us that is not said in the other Gospels, namely, how the Transfiguration happened. Saint Luke says: "While he prayed, his face changed", that is, this is a prayerful event. The Transfiguration occurs at the moment of prayer, the prayer is a transfiguration, that is, entering into the light of the Father, being penetrated by the light of the Father. Jesus is in an exchange with the Father. The *Logos*, the Word, at last speaks with the Father, He is transparent, He is living light, in His prayer He makes the Father visible. This is the important point: the Transfiguration simply makes visible the reality of Jesus' prayer, of His being-with-the-Father. Thus we can understand what is essential in Jesus.

In the current discussions about the figure of Jesus of Nazareth, there are many conjectures about what is the essential thing, about what is the characteristic thing in Jesus. Now it is clear that the essential thing is precisely this: His being in a permanent relation with the Father, His unique, specific relation with God: only in this way is He truly the One who reveals God. The Torah had said that Moses spoke with God as a friend (see Ex 33:11) and therefore was the model of the true prophet. Indeed, they used to say that the true prophet would be like Moses, who spoke with God as a friend. But Jesus speaks with God not only as a friend, but as a son, and thus, seeing him eye to eye, heart to heart, is immersed in the light of God. As Saint John says, in the first chapter of his Gospel, He alone has seen God and can tell who God is, can reveal the face of God (see Jn 1:18). Saint John also says that He is "light from light" (see Jn 1:4–5, 9; 8:12ff.; 1 Jn 1:5), and he interprets this mystery this way: Jesus, being in immediate dialogue with the Father—as light from light, heart from heart—is the One who reveals, the Son of God.

Precisely in this moment of the Transfiguration, which occurs eight days after Peter's confession, what Peter confessed becomes visible: "You are the Son of God!" Since Jesus is light from light, in prayer He is immersed in the divine light. Thus, while we learn who Jesus is, we can also learn to pray. What is prayer? It is entering into God's light; it is letting oneself be transformed by God's light. Certainly the prayer of Jesus is unique, because the Son is one with the Father, He is *Logos*, the Word, the Alpha and Omega. Nevertheless Jesus is also man and therefore draws man, our human nature, into this unity with God.

We, too, can pray in this way, entering into communion with Jesus. Learning to pray means entering into communion with Jesus, which brings us forward and causes us to be illuminated by the divine light, so that we ourselves become light.

Let us pray, therefore, that the Lord will help us to know Jesus, to love Him more and, thus, to enter into Jesus and to start to see God, to live with God, so that we ourselves are transformed into light. There is a hymn in the Breviary that says: "No one in the presence of the light can pray while remaining in conflict with the light. If we enter into the light, we ourselves become light, the light purifies us and illumines us."[1] Let us pray to the Lord that we may be able to enter into His light—to be illuminated, purified, in communion with Jesus!

The second aspect on which I decided to reflect with you is that Jesus speaks with men also: Moses, Elijah, the Law, the prophets, the entire Old Testament. At first glance, this seems a bit contradictory: Jesus speaks with the Father and not with man. But no, it is not contradictory. In speaking with the Father, Jesus speaks with us, and in speaking with us, He speaks with the Father, because He draws us into the Father. I find that it is a very beautiful thing that within God, where Son and Father speak, they speak about us. It is fascinating: precisely where God is Himself, in His interior life, He speaks about us. Thus we are sure that we are in His hands, in His light. And in this case, too, Saint Luke is the only one to mention what they spoke about. They spoke about the "exodus" of Jesus. The exodus of Moses who led Israel out of Egypt is the paschal

[1] The reference is probably to the "Hymn for the First Hour of Sunday": "Jam lucis orto sidere, Deum precemur supplices, ut in diurnis actibus, nos servet a nocentibus" (Now that daystar [the sun] has risen, let us humbly pray to God, that in our daytime activities, he may preserve us from harmful things).

supper, the exodus of the passage from slavery to freedom, but also the exodus of suffering in the desert, in poverty, in dangers. The exodus is suffering and joy together. Thus the exodus of Jesus is an exodus on the Cross, because the Cross is the exodus [i.e., departure] of Jesus; nevertheless, it is also a Resurrection, it is also glory, because on the Cross He accomplishes the exodus that leads to the Resurrection, to new life, to glory.

Thus, in a few words, Saint Luke explained to us the mystery of Jesus and also answered the question that we had asked last Sunday concerning the Old Testament.[2] Are the promises fulfilled in Jesus or not? Did the Messiah come or not? It seems now, because eternal peace has not come; paradise on earth has not come: there is hunger, there is all that suffering just as before, or rather, it is increasing. Nevertheless, Jesus is the fulfillment of the promises, because God's promises were different. God does not promise us comfort, a convenient world, but rather promises us the exodus, the transformation of our life. Moses and Elijah are witnesses to the Passion; they are also two biblical figures acquainted with suffering. We know how Moses suffered, so much that he finally said: "Destroy me, so as not to destroy all the people" (see Deut 9:27–28); we know how he entered into the desert, into the mystery of the Cross and finally remained excluded from the Holy Land. Elijah, too, is a man of suffering. They both not only speak but also give witness to the exodus; they teach us to study, to learn, to read the Old Testament in the correct way. By reading it in a new way with Christ, we see that God promises exactly this: the Cross, and with it new life. God does not come as an emperor with a large army.

[2] The Gospel of the preceding Sunday, the First Sunday of Lent, was the one about the temptations of Jesus, in the passage from Luke that is used in Year C.

God comes as a lamb among wolves, for the journey of love. He is the Paschal lamb, and this very thing is the newness of God: that a lamb among wolves renews the world. We too are in His image if we are lambs on His journey, the way of the Cross, and thus we enter into the mystery of light. This is the mystery of God that engages us throughout our life, which we will never be able to understand completely. But let us allow our hearts to be touched again by this fact: God comes as a lamb; this is the promise, and thus He renews us, He transforms the world and, little by little, in silence, in the midst of all these sufferings, the world of love grows, the true world of God.

Finally, a third note. From the cloud, a symbol of the mystery of God, of His greatness, comes the voice: "Listen to Him!" It has been observed correctly that the account of this ascent of Jesus on the mountain of the Transfiguration is modeled on the ascent of Moses on Sinai, and it renews it. On Sinai, Moses received the tablets of the Law, and we receive the word: "Listen to Him!" This means that the true Torah, the true Law of the Lord, the true gift of God is Jesus in person. We no longer have written tablets, but we have Jesus who is the Word. Thus, we see that in Him this ascent has indeed arrived at its destination: Jesus is the living Word of God. This is also the greatest consolation: we are not bound to tablets of stone, because Jesus has a heart! We must learn to love this heart of Jesus: in this way we listen to God and are in the light.

Let us pray that the Lord will help us truly to know His heart and thus to be in the fullness of the divine light. Amen!

The Samaritan Woman and the Well of Living Water

March 23, 2014
Private Chapel, Mater Ecclesiae Monastery

Third Sunday of Lent (Year A)
Readings: Ex 17:3–7; Ps 95; Rom 5:1–2, 5–8;
Jn 4:5–42

In the major discourses of Jesus that Saint John presents to us, images of the fundamental elements of human life appear: water, light, bread, wine. These fundamental elements of our biological life become, from Jesus' perspective, sacramental elements also, a way in which we can encounter God.

In every people that, like Israel, was still exposed to the desert, and therefore to the problem of a lack of water, the very gift of water was perceived in all its greatness: only water gives life, and a well that does not dry up in the hot seasons, a well that always gives water, cool water, water that is not bitter, is a gift, a gift of life: thus someone who created and built the well really is a father. Jacob, in giving the well to Israel, remains a father, because his gift of life remains forever, the gift of the water that it offers us.

A human being needs water; water is life. However, we sense that our thirst is deeper, because our life is not only biological, a human being is not only biology, but is also soul and spirit. For this reason our thirst is deeper; we want life profoundly; water is life, but we want a life that is still more radical: our heart thirsts and seeks Life itself.

Even the perversions of thirst, which we see today, prove the very fact that this thirst for Life itself, for the Infinite, for absolute Good, is rooted in the human heart. How are we to find this water that is Life itself? What does it consist of? Where do we find it? Obviously the water, the life that we desire and need, is true love, happiness, truth, light. The only persons who can be true parents of humanity are those who give us this life, who make springs of true water gush forth, the water of Life: it appears also that this thirst has something to do with God.

In the conversation between Jesus and the Samaritan woman, these problems appear little by little, and above all two questions appear. The first is the question about guilt, about the destructive acts in our life that make us incapable of drawing this water. Just as in physical life, there can be fractures of the hip or the back, etc., there can be blindness or hearing loss, so too in our deeper life, in the life of our heart, there can be infirmities that make it impossible for us to move any more or to feel and see any more; this gives rise to the question about who will help us, who will save us, so that we can have access to the life-giving water.

But together with the question of salvation, of restoring true life to us, this shows the tremendous magnitude of the problem of God: Does God exist? And if He exists, where do we find Him? Only if God exists does this water exist. In other words, Jesus makes the Samaritan woman understand that the true water that mankind needs can come only from the true God. Thus at the end it appears that He, Jesus, is the source, the spring of living water. Thus it becomes clear also that His Spirit appears in the Trinitarian mystery, that the Father in the Son gives us the Spirit and thus gives us Life, the fountain of true life, of the true water.

But the question still remains about how to arrive at this life. Where is the well? Where do we find the means of drawing this water from the depths? By ourselves we are not able to arrive at this depth and to draw Life. The essential answer is that Jesus, in His Spirit, is the Life; in Jesus the water of life has come, it has been made accessible to us.

However, over the course of all human history, too, we need builders of wells, those who help us to find this Life and give us the means of drawing it. Of course the truest, most real, and most essential well is Scripture itself; it is the Word of God, which we approach in order to drink of the water of life. But the same Sacred Scripture is a deep well, and thus we need other helps also.

Therefore, in the history of the Church the great saints, the great doctors, the great teachers of the faith are these builders of wells, who help us and become for us parents of life. Think of the Fathers and Doctors of the Church, such as Saint Augustine, Bonaventure, Thomas Aquinas; and then of Saint Francis, Saint Dominic, Saint Teresa of Avila and Saint John of the Cross, down to the present day. Saint John Bosco is a true builder of wells of living water, who helps us, and others, too, who are closer to us, are true builders of wells, who also give us the means of drawing water from the depths. Today's Gospel invites us to be in frequent conversation with them, to go with them to the fountain of water, with them to find the living water that gives us life. In this season of Lent, we want to learn once again to go to the well, to drink of the living water, of the water that is life of the Life itself, and also to guide others to this well and, despite all our weakness, to help others to take, to draw water from the depths of the Word of God and thus to find Life.

In his conversation with the Samaritan woman, Jesus takes another step forward. Not only does He show us that with Him the living water, God Himself, has entered into history and that with His friends, with His disciples, we can draw this water, but He also says something else: God will not be worshipped on this mountain or on that, but rather He will be adored "in spirit and in truth". With Jesus begins a new period of man's relationship with God. These mountains—Gerizim, Jerusalem—are representatives of religious cultures, which in an initial phase of human history are useful in finding access to the living water. Now, with Jesus, a new period has begun: we must no longer restrict our faith to one cultural and human type, but we come out from these cultural, historical forms of religion and arrive at God Himself, who is alive in Jesus Christ, in whom we go beyond religious cultures to the Truth of God whom He Himself personifies and shows.

This is the true novelty of the "hour" of Jesus: we are no longer confined to merely cultural forms, where God remains closed and limited. Jesus opened these confines; He Himself is God with His face. The true God shows Himself in this man Jesus, speaks with us, becomes living water with us. This perpetually renews the invitation to come out from all the national cultures, from all the cultural structures toward Jesus Himself and thus toward God Himself, by praying in spirit and truth. "In spirit and truth" is not an Enlightenment program, as some have said—as though we had left religions behind so as to think only rationally—but rather spirit and truth are the name of Christ and of His Spirit. Let us pray to the Lord, therefore, that we may all be able again and again to find ourselves united, coming out of the cultural traditions so as to arrive at the truth of the Spirit of God, and thus to create the unity of the Church and, at last, the unity of all mankind. Certainly, we will still have certain historical and cultural forms, and this is good, too, but it is important that they not be the last word; through these structures people must go to the reality itself, to the Spirit, to the Truth, to Christ, the true Son of God.

I would like to touch also on the final point of this Gospel. The Samaritan woman told her fellow townspeople what happened and that she understood that Jesus may really be the Messiah, the God who shows Himself and saves us from all our difficulties and sins. The townspeople come and invite Jesus to agree to stay with them, and after a few days they say: "Now we do not believe because you said this and that, but we believe because we ourselves have understood and know that He is the Savior of the world."

In other words, from a "second-hand" faith, they arrived at a "first-hand" faith; they believe not only because someone else says so, they are no longer fellow believers with someone who has her own faith, because now they know that He is the Messiah, they have arrived at a faith, at a direct, immediate personal encounter with Jesus Christ: they believe "at first hand". This movement is important for all of us: we begin by placing our trust in our teachers and in others; we believe with them and because they believed; but it is important for us to arrive at the personal encounter with Jesus, and in this encounter we really see Him, we touch Him and can understand that He is the Savior—of us and of the world. Thus we live with a "first-hand" faith, a faith that is not only based on others; rather, with this faith our very own hearts are touched by the person of Jesus Himself. Of course, we are still on a journey, we still need the great community of the Church in order to be able to see Jesus, but we must also still be on a journey toward a profound, personal conversion, toward personal knowledge of Jesus, and thus toward a staunch faith that can enlighten others, too.

Today let us thank God, who gave us the spring of living water, who gives us wells, who gives us means of drawing from His Truth, the depths of His Word. Let us thank Him because He manifested Himself and gave us the gift of living water, Life itself.

And let us pray that we may be able to know Him more and more and thus be able to imitate the One who alone saves us, who saves us all. Amen!

The Decalogue and the Fulfillment of the Law

March 8, 2015
Private Chapel, Mater Ecclesiae Monastery

Third Sunday of Lent (Year B)
Readings: Ex 20:1–17; Ps 19; 1 Cor 1:22–25;
Jn 2:13–25

In the first reading, today's liturgy presents to us a central passage, I would say *the* central passage of the Old Testament, the Decalogue [the "Ten Words"], that is, the contents of the covenantal relation between God and mankind. What is this covenant, this content? The first consideration is that here we are not talking about a pact, a bilateral agreement between equal parties, because God is the Creator; He is immense and not on the same level with us. In reality, it is a gift, an arrangement in which God reveals to us how to live as human beings; He teaches us the art of living and reveals to us the way that leads to happiness. The Decalogue, therefore, is not per se a covenant between two equal parties. The Fathers of the Church and all of Tradition, correctly, have spoken, not about a covenant, but rather about a testament. It is an arrangement by God for us: He prepares the facts and then shares them with us and makes the covenant possible.

Naturally modern man has the impression that that is not an agreement, then, it is not a true covenant; because it is an arrangement, an imposition—they think—of a law. This provokes an opposition. Man is opposed, because he wants to be, not under a law, but rather on the same level as God. But here there is already a fundamental error, because it is not a question of a law in the sense of the imposition of a will foreign to mine, a dominating will, which would then be a form of slavery for my will. On the contrary, God shows us what the innermost part of our own will really is, reveals to us precisely how we are to live. Therefore, it is not a law in the negative sense, but rather is a revelation, a self-revelation of God in which at the same time our being is clarified, because our will is a created will and finds its path only in agreement with the will of God the Creator. It is a gift, it is a revelation, but it is also a promise, because it means that living in this way is living on the right path, on the path of life. I would say, then, that we must, on the one hand, replace the word "covenant" with the word "testament", but, on the other hand, replace also the word "law" with the words "gift" and "revelation", and also "promise", because the "law" is at the same time also a "promise".

Now the concrete question arises: What is the content of this divine testament, what path does it show us? An initial point is that these "ten words" are divided into two parts: our relation with God and our relation with man. They fundamentally describe for us the twofold love of God and of man, and in this sense they are also a geography of love: they offer us a signpost in the geography of love. In reality, they are a concrete formulation of the twofold commandment of love and, therefore, of what is essential in everything; and conversely in them we truly find everything.

Let us look now at some of the details of these two tablets about the love of God and of neighbor. In reading the passage, we see a disproportion between the first tablet, about God, and the second tablet, about man. Whereas in the second tablet we have very concrete acts—do not steal, do not commit adultery, etc.—the first appears as a treatise on God. This disproportion is important, because this shows that the right relation with God is important first and foremost. If there is no God, the rest does not work, it no longer has substance, as we see today: wherever God is taken away, all the rest no longer has substance. In all senses, it is fundamental that, first, God should be present and we should know the face of the true God. Going into more concrete details, we see that there is a fundamental fact about God: there is only one God! This is the affirmation at the basis of the Decalogue and of the entire Old Testament. From this it follows that man is free, because the world is no longer full of demons and spirits, but there is a God who governs it. There is only one God, and in order to liberate human beings it is fundamental to lead them to this monotheism, to this adoration of one God. Then, concerning God, three concrete points follow.

The first is to make no images. This is surprising, but it is quite logical. If man, not knowing God, starts to make images, in reality he makes God according to his own image and adores himself; he does not go out from himself, but reduces God to himself; man is no longer in the image of God, but instead God is in the image of man. Therefore the images must disappear and be replaced by the word, which is written—as the Book says—by God's hand on these stones. The image is replaced by the word. The word in a certain way makes us more distant from God: the greatness of the mystery appears, God is always a very deep mystery. But in this way, while, on the one hand, the mystery of God grows, so much that we can no longer imagine Him, because He is immense, especially in comparison to our ideas, to our imaginings, and the distance grows; on the other hand, there is a much greater closeness, because now we see, we hear what God says, and thus God's innermost thought appears to man. The word is, on the one hand, a greater mystery, but, on the other hand, it is also greater closeness. God speaks, and thus He speaks also to our reason, to our will. The replacement of the images with the word means that our rationality, too, is challenged, because it makes God rational, in conversation with our reason. This is a very important step in history, because in this way the demons and the spirits vanish, and the *Logos* remains: the word, the eternal reason in relation to ours; hence the whole world is opened up for us. We know that Christianity specifically spread monotheism in the ancient world, and this was a liberation, because the world was full of demons, spirits against which man had to take precautions. The same is true even today: the problem of development in various parts of the earth is the problem of a world full of demons and spirits who blockade man's rationality and impede his liberation. To say: "There is one God, the *Logos*, and the others do not exist" is to liberate man and to open up the world to rationality. This is the first, very important step, which is accomplished by replacing the images with the word.

The second point is that God has a name, or rather that He gives Himself a name, that is, He sets Himself in a relation with us. If I know a man and his name, I can call him, because name means relation. Thus God puts Himself in a position of accessibility, enters into the network of our friendships; having a name, He is almost one of us. In a certain sense, this anticipates the event of the Incarnation, and of course it involves some vulnerability also. When God gives Himself a name, He is like one of us, so much so that this name can be, as it were, defiled, offended, as in fact it happened. Therefore not defiling but defending His name is a perennial commandment for us all.

The third point is the Sabbath. The Sabbath means that God is the Creator, and creation is made precisely for a covenant, for a pact between God and mankind. The Sabbath is the day of freedom for human beings, even for the slaves. This is essential, because this way man truly enters into his being-an-image-of-God. It is a day of liberty and joy, because we are creatures of God, we are friends.

These are the "words" of the first tablet. Now we cannot examine the second in depth. Nevertheless, we wonder: "Well, if this is the Old Testament, is it abolished or not? Has it been surpassed, or is it valid at present, too?" In the Gospel of Matthew, Jesus tells us: "I did not come to abolish the Law, but to fulfill it" (see Mt 5:17). What does this fulfillment consist of? Here we can recall the true relation between the Old and New Testaments: let us review this, too, in three points.

First: no image, the replacement of the images with the word. Yes, God remains a word, but the word takes flesh, and thus God makes Himself visible. In Christ's face, we see God Himself; He is no longer totally unimaginable. Since in Christ's face we see God Himself, images are now possible: images not invented by us, but images in which God really appears with us. The incarnation of Christ overcomes the prohibitions of images. In Christianity the image is essential, because Christ is the visibility of God. And, nevertheless, the way in which God manifests Himself is renewed. The new level and its continuity consist in the fact that if Christ is the image, we are in the image of Christ and are called to see and to seek the face of Christ, to be conformed to Christ, and thus we ourselves become true images of God.

Second point: the name. In the New Testament, the name itself takes concrete form in a new way. God is "I am!", but now He adds a word, another word to the name "I am", and that is: "I am and save." God is Savior.[1] Now the name is much more concrete: Jesus Himself is the name; He gives Himself into our hands and is even more vulnerable. We see Him, we love Him, and we seek to be truly friends of the Lord, giving praise to the Lord Jesus: this is the name that saves!

Third point: the Sabbath. The Sabbath that comes from creation is indeed founded on being itself, and yet it is surpassed by Sunday, by the moment of the encounter with the Risen Lord. Yes, the meaning of the Sabbath remains, "the Lord's day" essentially remains. Nevertheless, it is renewed, because now the door is opened to the new creation, that of the Resurrection. The new Sabbath, Sunday, as a day of encounter with the risen Christ, opens up time to eternity. It is a new time that breaks in; with the celebration of the Sunday Eucharist, the Risen Lord gives Himself into our hands.

Thus everything is new, but everything has remained. Continuity: not abolition, but rather fulfillment. In conclusion we can say that the Decalogue is flesh in Christ Himself. We can say that Decalogue means loving Christ, living with Christ.

Let us pray that the Lord will help us to be more and more [faithfully] on the path of His Word and to give our flesh to His Word.

Let us ask Him to help us to know Him and to love Him and to live in friendship with Him and thus in the most profound truth of the whole redemption. Amen!

[1] See Mt 1:21: "You shall call his name Jesus, for he will save his people from their sins"; cf. Jn 5:16–17.

"I Am": God Watches Us, and We Can Call on Him

February 28, 2016
Private Chapel, Mater Ecclesiae Monastery

Third Sunday of Lent (Year C)
Readings: Ex 3:1–8, 13–15; Ps 103; 1 Cor 10:1–6, 10–12; Lk 13:1–9

Today the liturgy, in the first reading, presents to us a fundamental passage of Sacred Scripture. It shows us the profound unity of all Scripture, of the history of God with us, and also the centrality of Christ from the beginning. It is the story of the calling of Moses. Let us look, rather attentively, at the situation in which it is introduced.

In Egypt, Israel lives in slavery and hardship; it seems to have been forgotten by God, and it seems that it has forgotten its God, who no longer seems to exist and no longer seems to know Israel. Moses has fled from Egypt and now finds himself working as a shepherd of his father-in-law's sheep; he, too, seems to have been forgotten by God. But while feeding the flocks on God's mountain, he sees the burning bush and from the bush hears this voice that calls him: of all people, he is to be the person who will deliver Israel. It seems absurd: a fugitive, a man with no authority, a man persecuted by the ruler of Egypt and not loved by the Israelites ... How could he accomplish this mission? Therefore his answer to God is: "If You want to send me, do something! I need some legitimization; I must say by what God I have been sent. We live in a world where there are so many deities, I cannot say that 'God' is sending me, I have to say which God and what power He has." This poses the question of the name. We are talking about a deity in the "Pantheon"; but which one and with what power, with what authority?

The response is surprising, because what God gives is not a name. He says: "I am." "I am who am." But this is not a name; one could say that it is a non-name. In saying this, God says: "I am not a god, one of the deities; I am 'the' God." "The" God is not "a" god: He stands apart, He does not have a name like the others; He stands above the others, because He has no name. The very fact that He has no name proves that He is "the" God, not "a" god. And nevertheless this non-name, with which He emerges from the multiplicity of deities, manifesting Himself, not as one of the gods, but as the God who is unique, is in a certain sense a name: "I am." This is the momentous fact: the God who does not have a name as the others do nevertheless lets us name Him in precisely this way. Therefore this mystery of the name that is not a name remains.

Throughout its history, Israel respected this mystery, observing also the second commandment: it never dared to pronounce this "Yahweh". In the manuscripts, they used a word that is read "Adonai"—the Lord—and in the Greek translation this is replaced by *Kyrios*—which means "the Lord". Thus we see that He who has a name that is not a name is the Lord, and the Lord of the New Testament reveals Himself as Christ. With this [reverential] non-pronunciation of the name and the transformation of the name into the word *Kyrios*, "Lord", starting at Sinai a path opens up that arrives at Christ as the true name of God.

But let us examine more attentively what this "I am" means. Over the course of history, there have been many interpretations. The Church Fathers viewed it as something identical to Platonic philosophy: God is Being itself. Through them a bridge is found here between Greek thought and biblical revelation, between philosophy and revelation, between revelation, faith, and reason. Essentially they viewed it correctly. Then in the last century other interpretations came: one existentialist and another Marxist. But the true interpreter of the name is Scripture itself, particularly with Isaiah, who always focuses his prophetic discourse on this name. He calls on God the One who is: "I am." All things come and go, they pass; they arrive, are past and start again, and pass by again; "I am", God, is always present. Things can be past and future; God is present: "I am." Therefore, in Isaiah, "I am" becomes truly the definition of God. In this way, too, therefore, we find ourselves once again confronting the unity of the two Testaments. When Christ says: "Before Abraham was, I am" (Jn 8:58), He introduces Himself into this same history. In the Gospel of John, the Lord says several times: "I am", thus identifying Himself with the God of Horeb, with the God of all ages, with the God who always is. While things pass away, only the Lord is a permanent presence.

There is, however, another aspect to note. We must also ask ourselves: What is a name? A name is not a definition, it is not a concept; a name does not serve to make known the meaning of things. A name serves to call the other: it creates a relation. If I know a person's name, I can say it and thus call on that person. This is the meaning of the name: creating relation. This is precisely God's purpose in speaking on Horeb. By giving Himself a non-name as His name, He enters into relation with us, enters into the network of our relations, becomes someone whom we can call on. This is the major event: God lets Himself be named, we can call on Him, He is almost one of us. I find it truly moving that in the biblical passage God Himself expresses this relation, saying that He made Himself someone who can be called on. He says: "I have observed your situation, I have heard your cry, I know your sufferings, I have come down to deliver you." These four verbs show the essence of the name, of His entering into relation with us. We must indeed reflect that the great God says: "I know your sufferings, I have heard your cry and have come down." God is touched by the sufferings of His people and comes down, truly comes down in Jesus Christ. In Jesus Christ, God truly became one among us, with us, in relation to us. He became a name. Jesus Christ is not a word, but is a person; He is the name that shows that God exists. He is the God who allows us to call on Him, who hears our cry, sees our sufferings, and cares for us. In chapter 16 of his Gospel, Saint John informs us that in Jesus Christ the revelation of the name is completed: not the word, but the person of Jesus Christ is God's name, that is, God's being-in-relation to us (see Jn 16:23–28).

The Church, today, prays as follows in the Collect Prayer: "Merciful God, look at us and comfort us." This petition seems to me to be the consolation and the prayer of this day: "Look at us." The Lord sees the sufferings of the persons in Syria and in all parts of the world.

Let us pray to the Lord: "Look truly at how these persons are suffering, look at these acts of violence, these horrors, look at the refugees, look at the children who are suffering! Look, Lord, at those who seek You and cannot find You, look at the many sufferings of people because of thirst and hunger and also because of spiritual poverty, look at the hearts of these people who want to believe and no longer can! Look at so many people today who no longer find the presence of God, because God does not seem to be present: look and comfort. Look also at us who seek You, help us, enlighten us, comfort us! Help us truly to be touched by You, so that Your light may become a reality in us and we may distribute a bit of Your light in our time." Amen!

Becoming Children of Light in Baptism

March 2, 2008
Private Chapel, Apostolic Palace

Fourth Sunday of Lent (Year A)
Readings: 1 Sam 16:1b, 4, 6–7, 10–13a; Ps 23;
Eph 5:8–14; Jn 9:1–41

In the story of the healing of the man born blind, the Evangelist Saint John makes the whole mystery of God and man shine through; he shows us that the Lord's miracles are not simply momentary deeds but are signs, manifestations of the mystery of God, an apparition of the truth.

First of all, let us note that this man, who cannot see, represents humanity marked by original sin. This humanity is incapable of seeing God, of seeing and knowing the truth, of seeing what is essential. Of course, it can never be totally ignorant of God, because God is inscribed deep in our being, in our heart. There is always some vision, some idea of God; sometimes a human being comes very close to the true vision of God but never really arrives at it, not even in the greatest attempts of noble minds or the major religions; sometimes it becomes instead a real caricature.

Nevertheless man, marked by original sin, never really manages to see correctly who God is, the face of God. In order to heal fallen man, God Himself must intervene, must become his physician, must enter into human history.

The Fathers of the Church say that the song of the angels on Christmas sprang from their joyful surprise over the fact that God, whom they knew until then in the great wisdom of the structures of the cosmos, this Creator God had entered into history, had made Himself a figure in history. This joyful surprise happens here in a very concrete way.

Saint John relates this story in three stages. The first is represented by the mud that the Lord puts on the eyes of the man born blind. It is difficult to interpret what this means, what it signifies. Saint Augustine gave an allegorical and somewhat forced interpretation, which however seems to me to guide us onto the right path. Saint Augustine calls this mud "collyrium" [eye-salve], and this collyrium, as we see in the Gospel, is made up of two ingredients: earth and saliva.[1]

In the ancient world, saliva was considered to be materialized breath, as a communication of the soul; thus Saint Augustine sees in this compound between earth and the breath of Jesus a symbol of Jesus' humanity. Therefore, to know the humanity of Jesus, to encounter the man Jesus would be the first step toward healing. Perhaps it is forced, but in any case it seems to me that it is a symbol of the catechumenate, of the approach to Jesus, of beginning to see his figure, of beginning to know at first the man Jesus so as then to arrive at the Son of man, the Son of God. A movement similar to the one that Saint John likewise narrates for us, when the first disciples follow Jesus somewhat anxiously and finally dare to say, "Where are you staying?" (Jn 1:38). This first moment of healing is always necessary once again for us, too: to know the man Jesus, to approach Him, to learn where He stays, to follow Him.

The second stage is washing in the pool of Siloam. Saint John emphasizes that Siloam means "envoy, one who is

[1] See Augustine of Hippo, *Commentary on the Gospel of John* 2.16.

sent", the one in whom God Himself enters into history, goes forth from the greatness of His glory and becomes a man in this human history. Washing in the pool of Siloam signifies immersing oneself, being immersed in the mystery of Jesus, being penetrated by the mystery of Jesus, which washes us from within and enters into our innermost being.

It is easy to recognize that this washing in the pool of Siloam, that is, in the one who is sent, is a symbol of Baptism itself, our immersion into the mystery of Jesus that takes place in this sacrament. This means that it is not enough to know Jesus, to have ideas about Jesus, to read Scripture; rather, we need one action of His, we need His Church, we need to be immersed in His mystery, in the sacraments.

Thus, on the one hand, the uniqueness of the sacrament of Baptism appears, the act in which Jesus Himself acts, in which He immerses us in His own humanity and divinity, and, on the other hand, we see that it is also a symbol of a reality that must continue in our life, that it is necessary to be washed again and again in the One who is sent, in the mystery of Jesus, that it is necessary to let our thoughts, our affections, our will be "washed" and to enter into communion with Holy Church, in the life of the sacraments, in the life of prayer, in meditation, in the encounter with Jesus in the Church. That we need to let ourselves be immersed, penetrated more and more by the mystery of God, to be more and more baptized Christians, more and more united to His being and renewed, not only "bathed", but reborn.

Finally, the third stage. The man born blind, who knew only that the man who had healed him was named Jesus, acknowledges Him as Son of God, Son of man; he believes and adores. This verb: "he prostrated himself" in the Greek text of the Gospel is *prosekínesen* (Jn 9:38), which means not only the external gesture of prostrating oneself, but the gesture of a man's whole being, adoration by the body and the heart.

Finally the man born blind believes, and to believe is to adore, and only in this way does he finally see: he sees not only with his bodily eyes but also with his heart, he sees with his mind, he is really enlightened, becomes someone who is healed, and sees what we must see in order to live really, in order to arrive at the true life.

Only the act of faith in Jesus that becomes adoration is complete and perfect illumination. Only someone who adores God in Jesus Christ, only someone who believes in Christ and adores Him, sees correctly, has really arrived at the light, is a son of the light. This twofold act—believing and adoring—is not only an intellectual or exterior act, but it penetrates life; it means acknowledging the authority of Jesus and submitting with our whole life to His authority, and thus seeing correctly, being children of light.

As the second reading says, the mystery of this healing is that we not only receive the light passively, but we ourselves become light, children of light, or, as Saint Paul says to the Philippians, we become stars in the night of the world (see Phil 2:15). We too, with Christ, become light. For this reason, we pray that Jesus will heal us completely, so that we not only can see Him, as the object of our sight, but we ourselves actively become, with Him, light in this world.

The Church proclaims all this to us on this *Laetare* Sunday, on the Sunday of joy; in this way, it means to tell us that all that we have just heard is the reason for the true joy that the Gospel brings us. Joy: God knows me, God loves me, God cares for me. The great surprise of the angels on Christmas night, because this God whom they knew in the beauty of the world had become man in history, this joyful surprise ought to be our joy also, ever new: that the great God knows me, cares for me, loves me, and I can know Him, and I can even be in contact with Him, walk with Him, experience that He is my friend.

In the postconciliar theological trends it was said that this joy—of being known by God and of knowing Him—would involve a kind of triumphalism that is incompatible with Christian humility. This is a major error. The fact that we know is not a boast; it is a gift, it is a surprising gift! As Israel acknowledged in the Psalms and was glad, saying: "To no other people did God reveal himself; to us he showed his word" (cf. Ps 147:19f.).

What a joy it is to know Your will, Lord; what a joy it is in the darkness of life to know You and to know life, to be in contact with You! This joy is all the more valid for us, because God no longer showed Himself only as a law, as a word, but showed Himself as a man, as a son of man, as one of us, as someone who loves me and, in the sacraments, gives Himself into my hands, offers Himself to my heart. This joyful surprise ought to be the motive of this *Laetare* Sunday, of really recognizing that the faith is Good News and light.

We pray that the Lord may heal us again and again, may help us to see and may give us this great joy: "He is with me, He is light, and with Him I, too, can be in the light. His grace is always greater than my weakness; the Lord is the light of my life." Amen!

Living in the Light

March 30, 2014
Private Chapel, Mater Ecclesiae Monastery

Fourth Sunday of Lent (Year A)
Readings: 1 Sam 16:1b, 4, 6–7, 10–13a; Ps 23;
Eph 5:8–14; Jn 9:1–41

Last Sunday we listened to the Gospel about the conversation of Jesus with the Samaritan woman at the well, the Gospel about the living water and about the structure of man's thirst. Water is an element of life, and we learned that thirst goes much farther than this water; it extends to a much more radical water, to Life itself. Today in the readings, both in the Letter to the Ephesians and in the Gospel, we hear the other fundamental image of life: light.

Water and light together give life; the water of the earth and the light of the sky, together, generate life. The Lord wants us to reflect on this mystery of light. If we listen attentively, we immediately hear that this Gospel is a catechesis on Baptism, on the journey toward the light, on the journey of seeing, and in precisely this way it becomes for us an examination, a reflection on how we are being Christians.

The Gospel insists on the light—Baptism was called *Photismos* in the early Church—on being delivered from blindness and on seeing. It is obvious that this man, who was born blind, represents the human situation after sin, man marked by original sin: man sees many things, but he does not see the essential, he does not see God, where we come from, where we are going, what we are, whether God exists or not, because all this is covered by a great darkness.

The question is how the man born blind can be healed, how he can arrive at healing; because without light, without seeing, we cannot find the path of life. One thing immediately appears with great clarity from these passages: man cannot heal by himself, he needs someone else, he needs a healing that comes to him as a gift. The second reading helps us also on this point by speaking about "awaking from sleep".

But now let us reflect briefly on how the man born blind himself describes or summarizes the process of his healing: he does it with three words, which indicate the healing journey itself; he says: I went, I washed, and I see. Let us follow this journey with its three stages.

I went: the first point is being restless, listening. The man is blind from birth, but God nevertheless left in him some flame of desire, because man is not content in this state of not seeing. From the beginning of humanity, we see, on the one hand, this great night, this blindness, which today becomes even more difficult, because man appears to be less and less capable of seeing, of explaining, of understanding, of seeing God; but a desire remains within him, and the search to know, which advances in the sciences, was born from this restlessness. However, all of this knowledge that we have won, which constantly increases, does not give us the light that is fundamental for our life. But there is this restlessness, this desire to see, and it is important not to let this restlessness be extinguished.

The Letter to the Ephesians refers to an ancient Baptismal hymn, perhaps an acclamation by the priest who was baptizing addressed to the candidate for Baptism: "Awake, you who sleep, and Christ will enlighten you!" "Awake!" This is the first point, to wake up, not to be content with our present situation. This is the great danger of our time, that triviality might be sufficient for us. The trivialization of life is like this: one lives a superficial life, and one sleeps ever more soundly.

This is why the Lord says to us: "Awake! So that Christ may enlighten you!" Let us allow ourselves to be awakened by the Word of God, by the many signs that God gives us; let us not allow ourselves to slumber in the triviality of a life that is content with superficial things; let us respond to the desire, to the restlessness of our heart; let us awaken so as to obey, so as to be on a journey, so as to listen and to be attentive to God's signs.

The Letter to the Ephesians adds two more elements concerning this imperative—"Awake!"—which ought to touch our heart, day by day. There are two verbs that, in my opinion, are incorrectly translated in the Italian version: in Italian we read "search" and "condemn", but this is not their true meaning; the true meaning is "discern" and "admonish".

The first verb means to learn, to discern, to distinguish, to form little by little the ability to judge, to understand what is true, what guides us toward the truth and what helps us. The other verb is not "to condemn" but rather "to admonish"; it means fraternal correction.

It is very important in the Church that we ourselves have this responsibility of fraternal correction, of watching over one another, of not letting human life be spent in triviality, but rather of entering with our words, with our life, into these critical situations; of really being brethren who live out their responsibility for one another, and doing so in both the intra-ecclesial and the extra-ecclesial sense, that is, both in the Church herself and outside of her.

We Christians always experience the temptation to fall asleep, to let things slide; instead, we must watch over one another more and more, and draw attention to God, to Jesus Christ, and also to others, in the missionary sense that Pope Francis speaks so much about; that is, we must call to mind the Gospel, the fact that God exists and that God cares for us. Hence, the first step is to go, to listen, to wake up, to test, to distinguish, to cultivate fraternal correction, admonishment, responsibility for one another.

The second step: I washed. According to the Church Fathers, the paste made up of mud and spittle that Jesus put on the eyes of the man born blind is a symbol of the Incarnation of Jesus, in which the vital element of His divinity enters into the mud of the earth and creates new life. Hence, the anointing of the eyes with this paste signifies encountering Jesus.

As we said, we cannot be saved by ourselves; we need someone who will heal us. This is the Gospel for this Sunday: the proclamation of the Christian faith says that there is someone who heals; it is Jesus! God Himself set out on a journey to heal us with His humanity, and therefore we must direct our attention to this encounter, nourish our willingness to hear Christ and to live with Him, nourish the desire to know Him.

Today many of our contemporaries, even Christians, do not even know the rudiments of the Christian faith; this is why we hear people speak about religious illiteracy; therefore, it is important to have a desire to know, to go to meet the One who comes to meet us, to learn the reality of our faith. The Church, with her word of proclamation, and the Word of God Himself give us many opportunities to know, to see that there is a God who comes and heals me.

And then: "Go, wash." This is the act of being introduced into the life of the Church: "Go, wash" is naturally a symbol of Baptism itself, in which we are immersed in the living water of faith, of God's grace, in which we are enlightened by God. But it indicates not only the moment of Baptism, but the permanent presence of God, ongoing life in communion with the Church, through the sacraments, the Word of God, mutual love, and prayer.

From the Gospel reading it emerges that the man born blind is finally healed and sees only at the moment in which he adores Christ. At first he had said abruptly: "I do not know who He was", then that He was a prophet, because he had understood that only someone who comes from God can heal. And finally he understands: it is the Son of man, it is the Son of God, and he adores Him, and now he really sees. We are still on a journey toward this perfect, complete healing, which is to understand and to see, "He is the Son of God!" and to adore. Only in adoration are we really human beings who see. Let us allow ourselves, then, to be invited on this journey so that, by adoring Jesus, we can be truly clear-sighted.

The Letter to the Ephesians adds yet another element: living in the light must ensure that our life itself becomes light, that not only does the light come to meet us, but we ourselves must be transformed into light. The passage indicates especially three elements of our personal luminosity: goodness, justice, truth.

The first fruit of the light is goodness: we must be good; this is precisely the characteristic of being Christian in imitation of God himself. God is good, and since God is good, we too must be good: in precisely this way let us be children of God, in this way let us be light. A verse from one psalm says: "Taste and see how good the Lord is" (Ps 34:8). It is a psalm of communion: while going to communion we should see the goodness of the Lord, who gives Himself into our hands, offers Himself to us so as to transform our life.

The goodness of the Lord must be reflected in the personal goodness of the Christian. In reality, if we think about it, starting from Our Lady with her maternal goodness, and on to Saint Francis, to Don Bosco, down to Mother Teresa, we see this goodness as the characteristic of the human being who has come to the light. But this goodness, which is so fundamental for a Christian, this goodness that is a reflection of the divine light, is not merely being good-natured; it is goodness united with truth and justice.

Only goodness that is truth—that does not simply do things that are rather sympathetic, probably with a certain laziness, but rather gets to the bottom of a matter so as really to do good for someone else—is imbued with the light of truth. Truth means that we ourselves are transparent human beings, without darkness, without hidden interests, without malice in our heart. Goodness and truth go together and thus create the true justice with which we respect another person's rights and, in our desire to love him, we also seek more than his rights. Then we are really healed, and we discover that the journey toward perfect healing, in which we become really light, goodness, justice, and truth, continues until the end of our life. Let us set out on this path of healing, on the path of life.

In the Church's tradition, this Sunday of light is called *Laetare* Sunday, as we see from the vestments:[1] it is the joyful Sunday in the middle of the penitential season, because penance, too, is a journey toward the light and hence brings with it the light of joy. It is the joy that God exists, that God comes to meet us, that He does not leave us in the darkness of the night, but comes to us in Christ,

[1] Instead of the characteristic violet vestments of Lent, rose-colored vestments are worn. The Introit or Entrance Antiphon begins with the word *laetare*—that is, "rejoice".

speaks with us, anoints our eyes, opens them, washes us in His Passion, guides us and advances with us on the journey of light and goodness.

Let us thank God for this great light of the Gospel; let us pray that we may increasingly become light and experience His joy. May the Lord bless you always. Amen!

Man Lives When He Sees God

March 26, 2017
Private Chapel, Mater Ecclesiae Monastery

Fourth Sunday of Lent (Year A)
Readings: 1 Sam 16:1b, 4, 6–7, 10–13a; Ps 23;
Eph 5:8–14; Jn 9:1–41

After reading the Scripture passages for today's liturgy, it occurred to me yesterday that the content of the three readings for this Sunday can be found summarized in the famous remark of Saint Irenaeus, a second-century Church Father: "The glory of God is man fully alive, and the life of man is to see God."[1] The glory of God is man fully alive: if this creature lives, it is not because of what he does, but for the glory of God. This statement guides us in our response to the question: When does man live, what makes him alive?

Does man perhaps not have to do anything, but simply live, and this living is already glory? Or is living having a lot of things at your disposal or having economic power? No! One can have this power and not truly live. Life does not consist of having, but of being. Therefore Saint Irenaeus tells us: "Man really lives when he sees God." We must understand that man's greatness is precisely in his ability

[1] Irenaeus of Lyons, *Adversus Haereses*, 4.20.5–7.

to see beyond merely useful things. Animals perceive only the things that serve them; the rest does not exist for them. In contrast, man transcends all that; he not only sees useful things but transcends them, even to the light of God, to the ultimate reality, which is light. Man is great because he sees not only the things that are useful to him, but also those that exist. This is exactly the case: God does not serve man, but we can serve Him, and thus He truly becomes the driving force of our life. We can say that man is defined by his ability to see God. In the process of evolution, we can say that man exists when the ability to see God arises, when he is capable of transcending the mere utility of things and seeing the true light. This is the definition of man: man is really man in all his fullness when he perceives God.

Anthropology tells us that in reality the knowledge of being is positive, but it is not coextensive with the knowledge of God. It has been proved that even primitive polytheistic religions knew that their deities were not God, because God was only one and different from these deities, and He stood behind their powers. They were convinced that this God was good, but that He was not interested in us; He was not dangerous, because it was neither necessary nor useful to render Him worship, while they needed to worry about the powers that are close to us, which were dangerous or which could help us. Thus God practically disappeared behind these other powers. Thus we can understand man's situation, which I would describe in a certain way as contradictory: on the one hand, man is the being that can see God; on the other hand, humanity, as we experience it, is blind, is born blind. If we observe humanity today, we see that a certain idea that there is a God never disappears, but man is born blind and must be purified, healed.

This is what we mean when we speak about redemption from original sin. Original sin is precisely a state of blindness that prevents us from really seeing God and the beauty of reality. Redemption consists of the fact that God tells us: "Awake, O sleeper, and arise from the dead, and Christ shall give you light." These last words of today's reading, taken from the Letter to the Ephesians, are probably quoted from an ancient baptismal rite, which proclaimed exactly this: "Awake! Arise from the dead. Christ shall give you light." This is the duty, the mission of the Church: to proclaim this and to give sight and to heal blindness with the sacrament of Baptism, with its faith.

What does this mean, today, for us? I would say that, on the one hand, it should inspire gratitude, because God made Himself seen. Today this sense of gratitude is not very widespread, perhaps as a result of a certain triumphalism in the past. Nevertheless, we do not give ourselves sight by ourselves, because this is a gift from the Lord, who without any merit of ours made Himself seen so that we could truly live. Our first response must therefore be gratitude. *Laetare* Sunday shows the fundamental sentiment of Christianity: gratitude, joy, because heaven is open, because God exists, God is good, and therefore being is good, and without this good God, good could not exist. Today we see how, despite all the increase in human knowledge and power, life does not become more beautiful or more true; on the contrary, it becomes increasingly dangerous. The more we lose the vision of God, the more we lose man, also, who is in great danger. Today this is obvious. And man can be healed only if he starts to see God.

Therefore, gratitude is also a responsibility. We, too, grateful for the light that the Lord gives us, must collaborate so that the light of God enters into the world: May Christ give you light! Gratitude is also a testimony; they are two aspects of Christian existence: *Laetare*, rejoicing because the world is open and God is good; and being responsible so that this may be known and humanity may not be destroyed—humanity that in this very moment is in great danger.

To conclude, it occurred to me to remind you about a short passage from the Gospel of Saint Mark, where we find a very simple and very fundamental prayer, which we should always make our own (see Mk 10:46–52). Mark relates that Jesus is journeying toward Jerusalem, toward the final Passover. He arrives in Jericho, and there along the road there is a blind beggar, who shouts: "Jesus, son of David, help me!" He makes a lot of noise, and the disciples try to make him be quiet. But Christ calls him for a personal dialogue and asks him: "What do you really want me to do for you?" He answers: "Lord, make me see!" The founder of Opus Dei, [Monsignor] Escrivá de Balaguer, made this invocation his basic prayer. Although we have the gift of sight, we are always in danger of relapsing.

Thus let us, too, make this prayer our own: "Lord, make me see! Show me the light of Your face so that I may live!" Amen!

The Older Brother: From Bitterness to Joy

March 10, 2013
Private Chapel, Castel Gandolfo

Fourth Sunday of Lent (Year C)
Readings: Josh 5:9a, 10–12; Ps 34; 2 Cor 5:17–21; Lk 15:1–3, 11–32

I would like to say just a brief word about the older brother, because this figure concerns us more, as we will see, and it is also the point of departure and of arrival of the parable of Jesus that we just heard.

The older brother, as always, so too on this day, works in the fields and returns in the evening, we can imagine, tired; tired perhaps not only in his body but also in his soul. Then he hears this music, the dancing, the singing, and asks what is going on. The Gospel says that he "became indignant": he finds this acceptance unfair, this welcome of the dissolute son by the father. This son ought to have done a little penance before entering unexpectedly into the feast.

The father goes to meet not only the younger son, but also the older son and seeks to win him over; but the older son is embittered, feels that the father is unfair, and in his words we see this bitterness on account of his long faithfulness, which seems to have been in vain. Of course he is unacquainted with the long exterior and interior journey of his brother.

His brother had left with a rather simple idea of life, that is, the idea of taking life only for himself, as an easy life in the midst of abundance; having everything for himself, having all the beauties and opportunities, and all this in the name of an absolute freedom. He no longer wanted to obey all the orders of his father, as the older brother did; he wanted to be free, without rules, to do whatever he wanted. But through this journey of a totally self-centered life, and of an absolute freedom without rules, he ends up feeding pigs and comes to the point where he actually hungers for the food that the pigs eat.

We must keep in mind that swine are for the Hebrews absolutely unclean animals, and therefore to feed swine means to be at the utmost point of human abasement; it means being absolutely unclean, it means being in total slavery, at the lowest point of slavery. He who had lived in the name of freedom, squandering his father's inheritance, arrived by this freedom at the most profound slavery, absolute slavery; with his desire to have a whole life for himself, he arrived at a hunger in which the animals' food would have been an ideal gift for him. At this lowest point of his life, of this journey into the depths in the name of freedom and life, he understands that this is not freedom, that this is not life. He understands that when he was at home with his family, who were the owners of everything, he was truly free; by obeying he was free, by living at home in love he was free and had life. This is the interior way, this is the long interior journey in which he finally understands that obedience is truth, that obedience is freedom, and that even austerity is life in abundance.

The older brother does not know about this interior journey; instead, he thinks that the other really did have freedom and life, and therefore he ought to be repentant now. The older brother, too, must learn that just being at home is freedom and life. But we see in this way that he, too, is not totally at home spiritually, that he, too, thinks that it would be better, that it would be more beautiful to be free somewhere else, to be away from home; we see that spiritually he, too, desires this other solution for his life, for human life. Because the older brother is embittered, he does not stay at home joyfully; he is almost desperate about this life of his at home, the wine of his faithfulness has become vinegar; spiritually he is sour, sad; he does not live in the joy of faithfulness and of faith. Then the father says to him to make him understand: "All that is mine is yours; you are in the fullness of life, you have everything, you really are free; there is no reason to envy someone else for all that he has done. Come into the feast of faith!"

The Lord says this not only to the scribes and Pharisees, but to all observers of all times who are observant and obedient with a bitter heart, with a sour heart. To all he says: "You must understand that you do have life and freedom, that you are at home and all that is mine is yours!" The Lord exhorts the faithful of all times to let go of interior envy, to be happy because they really are at home. He speaks to us also, and we pray today, on *Laetare* Sunday, on the Sunday of joy, in the middle of the season of Lenten austerity. Jesus speaks to us, too: "Learn a joyful faith, learn that living with the Father, living at home, living according to the Word of God really is true happiness; it is the abundance of life."

Let us pray that the Lord will open our heart and the hearts of all believers, so that we can finally live, not with a bitter heart, but with a joyful heart, which has understood: "Yes, the Father is the source of life; at home we really are alive!" Amen!

The Joy of Being at Home with the Father

March 6, 2016
Private Chapel, Mater Ecclesiae Monastery

Fourth Sunday of Lent (Year C)
Readings: Josh 5:9a, 10–12; Ps 34; 2 Cor 5:17–21; Lk 15:1–3, 11–32

Today's Gospel reading should be called: "The parable of the two brothers and the merciful father", because the figures of the two brothers are equally important. Let us look at the context. There are sinners and publicans who have come to hear Jesus: behold the first brother, the prodigal son. But there are also Pharisees and the scribes who criticize Jesus' familiarity with the first group, criticize the fact that He treats them as though they were not sinners: behold the second brother. But let us observe the two figures a little more attentively so as to understand better the message of the parable for us also.

The prodigal son wants finally to have all the property for himself, to have life for himself, freedom, to live only for himself. In this gesture of the young son, we can easily recognize the attitude of modern man, of the modern soul, of the modern epoch. He no longer wants to be under the yoke of God's Law, of the Church's Law; he wants to be free, wants only freedom, self-determination, because freedom is the first and true value. He wants to live only for himself, to take for himself life in all its fullness: you only live once, and we want to get everything out of life. And so the prodigal son goes to a distant land; distant not only exteriorly, but also interiorly, in a different world. At first, everything seems splendid: this life that is offered there, which he seems to be able to possess with unlimited means.

But then everything is lost, and famine arrives. The young man is humbled to the point of becoming a herder of swine. Swine are unclean beasts, and so he has reached the lowest possible degree of life and cannot even eat the pods that are fed to the swine. Now he understands that this freedom of his has become slavery; he understands that instead of the fullness of life that he thought he had, he has truly lost everything, that he has fallen into ruin. It is not difficult to recognize the resemblance between this incident and the path of modern man, who falls and eventually is a slave of money and of passions; he is a slave, he lives as though in a famine, he feeds himself with pods instead of the beautiful riches of the spiritual life, of the Word of God.

Finally the young man understands: "I am far not only from my father but from myself, from life itself; I am lost, I am a slave, whereas when I was at home I was free, when I was with my father I was free, at home I had everything in life." And thus he knows the way by which to return interiorly from the distant land to his father. We can imagine how this journey has different forms in different people, but it is always a journey of passion, sufferings, and transformation. At the end, one understands what freedom is, what life is: being at home, because here we are really the owners of life and not slaves; here we can practice all our own virtues. This is the journey back to the father, we could say the journey of conversion, of renewal, of purification, by which the father can again place his hand on the prodigal who has returned and once again call him son.

The other son, who remained at home, was always faithful; he worked a lot, and everything was going well. However at the moment when the other son returns, on the occasion of the feast that the father celebrates for him, it is evident that there is a certain bitterness in him; we no longer observe in him the joy of being at home. We see that, spiritually, he, too, had dreamed a bit of another life. He had not left home, but spiritually he was envious of the other son's freedom, of his life without limits and reservations. Spiritually he, too, had emigrated, and thus, having remained in bitterness, he had not understood that being at home is freedom. He, too, therefore, like each one of us, must spiritually go home, return, and only that way will he really be with the father.

Then we understand that, although in the first part of the parable the Lord speaks about the pagans, who after all their vices have returned to the Lord's feast, in the second part he speaks to those who remained at home, he speaks also to us. There is always the temptation to make this interior emigration, to give in to a certain bitterness. We think that maybe others have more life, more freedom than we do, and we no longer can understand the beauty of being at home and of not living on pods. Therefore we, too, must set out on a journey home, be renewed and purified, understand what freedom is, what life is, and thus arrive at the true joy of the Lord's feast.

We can therefore summarize the meaning of this Sunday's invitation. The Lord speaks to us and tells us: "See how all that is mine is yours, how all of life is a feast for those who stay in the Father's house: understand, and come to the feast!" Let us keep praying that the Lord will help us to leave the interior emigration and to discover again and again the joy of being with the Father, the joy of living truly on the great food at home and not on the pods of deceptive amusements. The Lord speaks with us precisely so that those who are outside may see that we are free and that we have joy. The Lord's desire is that this joy of being at home, the joy of being free might shine through us. This is the invitation of *Laetare* Sunday.

Let us pray to the Lord that this Sunday may resonate in us; let us pray that it may help us to be interiorly at home with joy, living the full life, the true freedom of children. Amen!

Eternal Life: Held in the Lord's Hand

April 2, 2017
Private Chapel, Mater Ecclesiae Monastery

Fifth Sunday of Lent (Year A)
Readings: Ex 37:12–14; Ps 130; Rom 8:8–11;
Jn 11:1–45

Last Sunday, in the Gospel about the man born blind, we saw that man is the creature who knows God. The fact that man has the ability to know God, and thus to be open to the Immense, is the essential definition of man. But we also saw what we could call the interior contradiction of man, namely, that this same creature that is defined as capable of knowing God is born blind and does not know him. Finally, we saw that a desire to know Him remains and that God can restore our sight, heal our blindness.

Today let us take a step farther. The Gospel tells us: man is the creature who desires to live eternally, who does not want to die, who finds himself contradicting death. This, too, can be seen from the beginning of human culture. Ever since man has existed, there has been the idea of his being accompanied into the next world, the idea about a life that should continue and into which one should help one's fellow man even after physical death. But in this case, too, we confront a fundamental contradiction. Man who—as we said—is the creature who wants to live eternally, who does not want to die, who is convinced that he is destined to live forever, not only is mortal but must die, because the whole structure of our world does not allow eternal life. If no one died, it would be catastrophic, for oneself and for the others. The structure of the world contradicts this definition of man. There is a contradiction that we could call cruel: man seems to be made to live forever, he wants to live forever, but at the same time he lives in a cosmic structure in which dying is essential. In a certain sense, this is also a blessing. On the occasion of the death of one of his brothers, Saint Ambrose says, indeed, in a prayer: "Death is a blessing, otherwise this life, continued eternally, would be unbearable."[1]

What can we say? Today, in his conversation with Martha, the Lord answers these questions by taking another step into the depths of human reality. Only in this way can the contradiction be overcome. He says to Martha: "Your brother will rise again"; Martha replies: "Yes, I believe in the resurrection on the last day"; but Jesus replies in turn: "No, no. I am the life, and whoever believes in me lives, and even if he dies externally, he will live forever." That is, Jesus says that this is not merely a matter of a life that begins for an immeasurable time, and we do not know when the last day will be. No! It is a life that already starts now and is indestructible. And "I am this life", Jesus says. In other words, "He who believes in me is, so to speak, held in my hand and therefore cannot fall into death."

Eternal life is structurally impossible in this world; to this we must add also a reflection on the fact that perhaps man does not want life so much for himself as to affirm another person. When two people love each other, love is a promise of eternity, and if the other person dies, it is unbearable

[1] Ambrose, *On the Death of His Brother Satyrus*, 2.132–33.

for us, because we cannot leave him! This structure of the relation with the other is decisive: I am not the most important person, because I would like the other person not to be taken away from me, because for me the other person is essential in order to be alive. In this sense, Jesus says: "He who believes in me already has eternal life now."

Two points are essential, therefore. First of all, we cannot have eternal life from ourselves, but only if we hold the Other by the hand, if we are held in the hand of the Other who does not fall. In other words, only love can give immortality, only the love of Him who is the immortality of God. And when we can hold God by the hand, He too holds us; and the memory of Him holds not only an idea, but holds the reality of our life. Moreover, this new life begins at the moment when God gives me His hand and I can take God's hand, in other words, now, already. This depends, not on biological structure, but on the structure of divine love. The relation of being held by God's hand is essential for life: we are, so to speak, fixed in His memory, and, precisely in this way, we are kept joined to life; and this new life begins at the moment in which I believe, and it will last forever, even if I die exteriorly.

Thus, we want to pray that the Lord will help us to live in His love, because His love is immortal. To live in His love not only for me, but above all with Him and, with Him, for all those whom He calls. Let us thank the Lord for this promise.

Let us pray that we may be ever more capable of holding the Lord's hand tight and thus of not falling into the sea, like Saint Peter, who would have fallen had it not been for the Lord's hand. Amen!

Conversion

March 17, 2013
Private Chapel, Castel Gandolfo

Fifth Sunday of Lent (Year C)
Readings: Is 43:16–21; Ps 126; Phil 3:8–14;
Jn 8:1–11

The three readings of today's liturgy, despite all their variety, have a common theme, the fundamental theme of Lent: conversion.

Let us start with the Letter to the Philippians, where this theme is most obvious, most evident. Here Saint Paul teaches us above all one fundamental thing: conversion is not simply an act of the autonomous subject, an act in which I can say: "From today on I will be a different person." It is not my own work that I perform simply by myself; conversion is the fruit of an encounter, and, in this sense, it is a gift.

Only an encounter that comes from outside, that opens up and gives a new reality, can also be transformed into conversion. Saint Paul says it this way: "Christ has made me His own"; he was conquered by that encounter in which the Word of the Lord touched his heart. He was transformed, conquered, and in this sense conversion is a passive deed: the other touches me and transforms me. A passive deed also in the sense that a process of transformation is also a process of passion and of suffering: it is the encounter with Christ, with the Passion of Christ; it is entering into communion with His Passion and thus being transformed, being transformed toward the Resurrection, toward the true newness of life.

Hence, conversion is a gift, which then of course also involves my activity: I am conquered so as to conquer. From the moment when I am called by Him to leave myself and to enter with Him, with Christ, a journey remains to be completed until the true Resurrection. This is important for us: the Lord calls us, invites us with His opening to come out from ourselves, to go toward the other in communion with Christ. This essence of conversion is the result of an encounter, an act of Jesus, who then opens and conquers me permanently.

Then there are the effects of conversion. The essential effect is the change of priority in your values: Jesus changes you interiorly. For Paul—as he himself tells us—the fundamental value was to be a Hebrew, the son of Hebrews, of the tribe of Benjamin, and, therefore, also one of the circumcised. This was truly the glory of the Hebrews, to be able to say: "I know God, while the pagans do not know the true God." This was true nobility: to be one of the people chosen by God, chosen to be God's sanctuary; to be circumcised, to bear in one's body the sign of the promise made by God. For Paul, all his pride, his glory was in this.

Now instead he says: "The things that were fundamental for me are now refuse, a loss." We see the upheaval, we see that everything changes fundamentally, and how the joy of the old nobility, of belonging to that noble tribe, with a great history, yields to the nobility of the Lord, which is even greater, because it is nobility, not of the flesh, but of God's election. We learn that ultimately the only thing that matters is being conquered by Christ, touched by God Himself in the person of Christ, being on a journey toward Him, going out of oneself, giving up one's own privileges, the glory of the flesh, so as to be oriented to Christ. False privileges, the boundaries and frontiers between peoples, nations, and races, fall before the glory of being conquered by Christ. This is the first value that changes, fundamentally, for Saint Paul.

But there is also another one. He had attended the great school of the rabbis, of those who were trained to interpret Scripture: Paul was a specialist in Sacred Scripture, a great exegete, who knew how to interpret. But, later, in one of his letters, he would say: "God forgave me; he could forgive me because I was ignorant" (see Rom 2:21ff; 10:3). What a major contradiction! He, the great specialist in Sacred Scripture, understands in the light of Christ that all his knowledge was ignorance, because he had not understood the essential thing, he had not comprehended what Sacred Scripture really speaks about. He understands that now, renewed, he has received the true knowledge: to have known Christ, and thus he has emerged from his real and dangerous ignorance. Finally, not only his intellect had been formed; his will had been formed also.

He had experienced the Word of God according to the norm of the Law, in the most severe manner, being a singularly perfect Pharisee, so much so that some exegetes had invented the theory that one could not speak about a conversion of Saint Paul, because he was morally perfect, already believed in God, and therefore a conversion was not possible. But in reality, notwithstanding his faith in God, he had not known Him. He was morally perfect, but with the kind of morality that is my work, for which there is almost no need of God, because I do it.... On the contrary, now he is really renewed, coming out of himself, not doing everything by himself, but setting out on a journey toward Christ: this is the true path of sanctification, of likeness with God. Let us pray together that the Lord may help us and enlighten us, so that we, too, may be conquered, and He may touch our heart and help us to be transformed in the newness of life.

Just a few words about the other two readings. As for the Gospel, one manuscript of the New Testament says that Jesus wrote on the dust the sins of all the individuals present. This is a beautiful idea, and we do not know whether or not it is true, but the meaning is that these scribes and Pharisees—who felt that they were perfect as Paul felt that he was perfect—right before the eyes of Christ, understand that He knows their heart, that He knows what there is within their heart, and thus the mask of their false moralism falls. Before that silent presence, with Jesus looking at them, that mask under which they live is no longer true, and it falls; they understand that their moralism is in reality hypocrisy.

This moralism is the desire to be judges of other people; they want to show that Jesus is not the true prophet; they want Jesus to make a misstep in any case: either He has the woman stoned and is cruel, or else He is merciful and goes against the Law. This moralism does not seek morality, because in reality it is not concerned about good, it is not enraged against evil, but it is a way of judging others, a way of being content with the evil in the world, because they can speak about it and disparage others. We know varieties of this moralism in our time also, when people hide under the moral mask of the struggle for the truth, for transparency, but deep down they only want to destroy and are proud of the evil, because they themselves live on evil. Jesus destroyed this mask. Only if this mask of hypocrisy falls can the new life conquer, and then there is conversion.

In this sense, the Lord says also to the woman: "Go and sin no more." She, too, must start out on a new path.

Finally, the first reading speaks to us about the two exoduses of Israel. The first from Egypt to the Holy Land, the forty years in which the people arrived at Mount Sinai for the covenant with God. The second exodus is proclaimed from the Babylonian exile with the return to the Promised Land: after seventy years, salvation history starts again. The exodus is a journey of several hundred kilometers, but it is not only an external journey, it is above all an interior journey, a journey on which the people are transformed and walk toward God.

The prophet speaks about this journey above all with respect to the new exodus from Babylon, in which the people, who are like dry land, become a fertile land for God and receive the water of salvation, so that they can praise God and, through this praise, can make use of the gift of language, of speech. I think that this concerns us very profoundly: the Western world today is dry with respect to God: it lacks the living water of the Word of God, it lacks fertility, fruitfulness. The Western world today is deaf, mute, and blind with respect to God. "Exodus" would therefore mean being transformed from dry, desert land into fertile land, and from deaf-mutes to becoming once again capable of praising God and of speaking correctly.

Let us pray, on this Sunday, that the Lord will help us to live with the gift of His living water, of His grace, so as to be fertile, so that we can speak with God and about God. And let us pray for our world, that it might be on an exodus from this aridity and might become a new people of God, a people blessed by His grace. Amen!

HOLY WEEK

Eating the Passover, Desire for a Loving Encounter

March 28, 2013
Immaculate Conception Monastery, Albano Laziale

Holy Thursday, Mass of the Lord's Supper
Readings: Ex 12:1–8, 11–14; Ps 116;
1 Cor 11:23–36; Jn 13:1–15

"I have greatly desired to eat this Passover with you" (see Lk 22:15). Jesus has a great desire, and in this desire of Jesus there is the desire of God, who in turn has the desire for our love, for our "yes". For this reason, the Son of God descended from heaven, became man in order to meet us and to love us, and approaches us because He wants to eat this Passover with us. Passover: we think obviously about the Last Supper with the disciples, but the Passover of Jesus does not happen only once, and every Passover of Jesus is a unique Passover.

Jesus awaits our Passover, too. He has a desire for us, for our encounter with Him, for our love. And since God has a desire for us, He inscribed on every human heart the desire for Him. Man has this desire for the infinite, for infinite love, for joy. I would say that being created in the image of God is precisely this: having the desire for God. Through this we are in the image of God, and we cannot be in the image of ourselves; in order to go beyond, we received this desire for infinite love. Even if man forgets God, he cannot extinguish this desire. All the absurdities of our age are the product of this desire, mistaken in its form because they do not know God. But in man's heart, the infinite desire always remains, the desire for the great Love of God. And therefore the two desires, God's and ours, meet.

When, on that famous Palm Sunday, Saint Clare renounced her womanly beauty, renounced her noble position in Assisi, she was moved precisely by this desire, the desire to encounter the great love of Christ. You, too, dear Sisters, are here because you were touched by this great love of Christ: you wanted to have a close encounter with Jesus and to celebrate always with Him His Passover, the feast of His Love.

Today the desire of Christ touches us and reawakens this desire in us. There is the danger that by force of habit, in the everyday routine, this desire might be extinguished, might be hidden. Today, in the encounter with this first love of Jesus, we pray that the desire, the flame of love for Him, may be awakened once again in us.

"I desired to eat with you"—with us—"this Passover." What is this Passover? Behind this word, "Passover", two key words from the parables of Jesus appear: supper and wedding.

Supper: Christ wants to make Himself our food, our bread. Man certainly lives by material bread, but man lives also by the Spirit, by the Word of God. And Jesus Christ is the true bread, our true food, not only the Eternal Word of God, but the Word who became incarnate, died, and rose to new life. Supper: hence we eat Christ, the Passover, but this is not normal eating. It is something quite different: we enter into communion with Christ, with the risen Jesus. But how do we do this? What is this eating? It is a loving encounter.

Saint Augustine heard one day a voice that said to him: "I am the bread of the strong; you will not transform me into you, but I will transform you into me."[1] In physical eating, we take a piece of this cosmos, a piece of the material of this cosmos, which is transformed in the process of digestion into a part of me: a part of reality enters into me and is transformed into a part of me. It is the opposite here; Jesus is not drawn into me and transformed into me, but I am drawn outside of myself and am transformed into Him: in this supper, the Lord draws me outside of myself and assimilates me into himself. I am transformed into Jesus Christ. Thus we see that, in this process of the supper, there is already the reality of the Cross: the renunciation of going out of oneself and of being transformed into the body and into the flesh of Christ.

In this process of the transformation of ourselves, we see also the element of the wedding, spousal unity. Because a wedding points to the same reality, the final point of this passage is neatly indicated by the words of Saint Paul that we find in the Second Eucharistic Prayer: "We want to become one spirit and one body with You" (see Eph 4:4). This transformation into one body, into one spirit with the Lord is the true process of His Passover, is the true supper, the true marriage, the true wedding.

Let us pray to the Lord with this prayer: "Draw me out of myself, help me not to remain in myself but to be transformed into You. Thus I will be united with You, transformed in my interior life, and introduced into the process of the Cross and Resurrection. Thus eating the Eucharist is the beginning of participation in the Cross and the Resurrection. Lord, thank you for having given us this gift, help us to be worthy of Your presence, transform us into You." Amen!

[1] Augustine of Hippo, *Confessions*, 7.10.16.

EASTER SEASON

Easter: A New Creation, Forgiveness, and Mission

March 30, 2008
Private Chapel, Apostolic Palace

Second Sunday of Easter—Mercy Sunday (Year A)
Readings: Acts 2:42–47; 1 Pet 1:3–9; Jn 20:19–31

Dear brothers and sisters, I would like to offer you only a few notes on several phrases from this Gospel.

The whole New Testament tradition tells us that Jesus rose on the third day after the crucifixion and that this third day was the first day of the week; the day of creation, according to the Jewish tradition; the day of the sun, according to the Greco-Latin tradition, which now becomes, in a totally new sense, really the first day, the first day of the true sun risen in the world.

It is the first day: with this day, the new creation begins, the new time begins; from this day, new life begins; it is always the day of the beginning, the first day of our life. Thus it automatically becomes the day of the Lord. In the Mediterranean language, it is no longer called "day of the sun", as it was before, but rather "day of the Lord", *dies Domini*, day of the *Dominus*, *Domenica* [in Italian], *kyriakē' ēméra* in Greek. It is the day of the Risen One and always remains that day.

And therefore it also became—to use an alternative expression—the day of the Eucharist. The disciples know that it is His day, the day on which the Lord waits for us, is among us, and comes to be with us, to give Himself to us as food. In this way, the "supper" in which the Lord instituted the Holy Eucharist became the "morning sacrifice", the encounter with Jesus that is always renewed on the morning of the first day. With Jesus we begin our weeks, our time.

In the re-paganization of the calendar, Sunday now has again become the last day of the week, the day of rest: people work for six days so as then to rest. But for us Christians, it still remains the first day, because Christ is the beginning, and with this beginning—Christ—we begin time and enter into our work, into our life. It is the day on which the Risen One waits for us, the day on which He calls us and gives us Himself as food, surrenders Himself into our hands and enters into our hearts.

Next, the Gospel told us that the Lord greets the disciples twice with the words "Peace be with you." These words of the Lord, "Peace be with you", are in the first place reconciliation, forgiveness for their infidelity, for running away. The Lord gives them His peace, He accepts them once again into His peace, reconciles them with Himself, and reconciles them with God. Because only peace with God is true peace.

A human being is a being in relation. Essentially our existence is being in relation. The fundamental relation of our being is the relation with God. And if this fundamental relation is not right, all the other relations are disturbed, as we see in the chaotic situations in the world. On the other hand, by ourselves we do not have the capability, the strength to give to ourselves the proper relationship with God, which then has a profound influence on the whole construction of our life and of society: only God can give us this fundamental peace, from which then arises the capacity for peace in all the other areas.

"Peace be with you", therefore, says not only that in this moment the Lord reestablishes communion with the unfaithful disciples, but also that He brings reconciliation to the world with Him, that He gives us this fundamental relation that is a condition for all the other relations. He brings us His peace, the peace that He alone can give us.

The Sacred Liturgy begins with precisely these words: "Peace be with you." It always renews this moment in which the Lord enters into our communities and the Risen One gives us His peace, which is the foundation of our life. In the liturgy, it is possible to alternate the two greetings: "The Lord be with you" and "Peace be with you", and this is appropriate because it signifies that the Lord Himself is the peace that is offered to us, He Himself is our being-with-God, because He is God's being-with-us. He Himself is peace!

And so the formula of the Lord's greeting has become also an indication of the Eucharistic mystery, in which He truly gives Himself and, in this way, not only grants peace with God to each of us, but grants us the peace that we share in the great Eucharistic community, which is this great communion of peace, which extends beyond all the boundaries of the world.

Then the Lord says: "As the Father sent me, so I send you." The encounter with the Lord is a mission. To see the Lord, to receive the peace of the Lord is never a purely individual thing that concerns only me; it is always a missionary dynamism.

In Scholastic philosophy there was a key expression: *bonum diffusivum sui*, in other words, an essential feature of good is that it spreads; *bonum*, the good, spreads by its very definition. Now the Lord is the Good in Himself, and this good works, spreads, and expands with an intrinsic necessity. In this sense, the mission, the command, is not a *secondary* thing that is added upon seeing the Risen Lord, but rather seeing implies being involved in this dynamic of the good that spreads and goes beyond itself in order to transform the world. We feel that we, too, are involved in this dynamism; the Lord comes among us, greets us: "Peace be with you", gives Himself, hands Himself over to us, and thus we are really implicated, involved in the dynamism of His being for all of us. Let us pray, then, for help, really to see the Lord, and that this seeing may become evangelizing, communicating.

Then Jesus "breathed", and this fact reminds us of the creation of the first man. God, Genesis says, had formed the figure of man from the clay, but it was a lifeless thing. Then "He breathed" on this man, gave His breath to this form, and in this way man became a living being (see Gen 2:7). Here the Lord repeats the Creator's gesture, that is, a new creation comes about. The breath of the Lord, His breathing creates us as new human beings, imbued by His Spirit.

The Holy Spirit is the Lord's breathing, and we are new creatures living in closeness, in contact with Jesus, in this contact with His Spirit that introduces us into a new creation. Moreover, Jesus also says that this Spirit of His that renews us is the source of renewal in the sense of forgiveness and a new re-creation that arises from forgiveness. This is the beautiful communication, the beautiful reality of Easter Sunday: that the Church has the power of forgiveness, the power to recreate our souls again and again.

Now I do not wish to meditate again on the whole story of Saint Thomas, which we all know very well; therefore, I only come to the conclusion. At the end, Thomas replied: "My Lord and my God!" This is the shortest formula of the profession of faith in the New Testament, and at the same time it is the confession, the adoration, and the fundamental prayer of Christianity: "My Lord and my God!" The whole New Testament flows into these words, all the paths of the New Testament end here, and our journey of faith, too, must arrive at this point: "My Lord and my God!" To know Jesus, our God, is thus to be in communion with our God and to live in the dynamism of His love.

Jesus also says: "Blessed are those who have not seen and have believed", and this is a beatification for all the believers of all centuries, which consoles us and gives us joy. But Saint Gregory the Great makes an observation that to me seems important. He says that Saint Thomas saw the risen man, touched the wounds of the risen man, saw the man but did not see God. But upon seeing and touching the man, his spiritual eyes were opened, and he saw interiorly with faith what he could not see with his bodily eyes. He saw by believing.[1] He, too, in seeing the man, made the "leap" of faith, or—to put it more accurately—received the gift to believe what he could not see. By contacting the man Jesus, the eyes of his heart were opened, and he saw with the eyes of his heart what he did not see corporeally, and upon seeing with the eyes of his heart, he professed: "My Lord and my God!"

We, too, can, in many senses, touch the man Jesus who makes Himself quite present in His holy ones, in all the realities of Holy Church.

Let us pray to the Lord that, by touching and seeing these human realities, the eyes of our hearts may be opened, and thus we may be able to see with our heart what cannot be seen with the eyes of the body. Thus we, too, can see and profess: "My Lord and my God!" Amen!

[1] See Gregory the Great, *Homilies on the Gospels*, 26 (PL 76:1201–2).

The Risen Lord and the New Creation

April 11, 2010
Private Chapel, Castel Gandolfo

Second Sunday of Easter—Mercy Sunday (Year C)
Readings: Acts 5:12–16; Rev 1:9–11, 12–13, 17–19; Jn 20:19–31

In the two apparitions of the Risen Lord that are recounted by today's Gospel, two aspects of the mystery of the Resurrection appear. In the first apparition, we see above all the power of God. We see the glory of God, in which He now comes: He has the power to go through the locked doors, gives the Holy Spirit, and gives the power to forgive sins. In the second apparition, we see above all His humanity, which has remained as such: a man with a true body who can be touched, who bears His wounds for all eternity, who although He is the Son of God, living in the glory of God, remains a man, with a human body of flesh and bone, as the Gospel of Saint Luke says (see Lk 24:39). But let us examine carefully the details of the Gospel.

The date is important: the first day, the first day of the week, the day after the Sabbath. For the Jews, the Sabbath was the center of their structure of time, and here we already see a revolution in how this structure is viewed. In the First Letter to the Corinthians by Saint Paul, we see already that the first Christian community, the Christians, already gather on the first day of the week, the day after the Sabbath. And already in the Book of Revelation—this is still in the first century—this first day has a new name: *kyriakē' ēméra*, the Lord's day, *Domenica* [in Italian].

This "first" day became the "new" day of the encounter with God, the day of the assembly of believers around the risen Christ. We must keep in mind that this was a profound change, which concerns the way of viewing time in the structure of the week. The precept of the Sabbath not only was part of the Decalogue, being the Third Commandment of this fundamental law of Israel and of humanity, but was also introduced into the account of creation. Creation is structured in such a way as to end on the Sabbath, and everything is created so that it might be a place where God is revered and adored. And everything is created precisely in view of this day on which the Creator and creation are together.

For Israel, the Sabbath determines the structure of time and even of the human being himself. Now, in contrast, after Jesus, we think that this revolution in our view of time already concerns the first creation: no longer the Sabbath, but rather the first day determines the structure of the week. We see that something radical has happened. Without an incredibly powerful event that changes everything, there is no explanation for this change in the structure of time, with the passage from the Sabbath, as the inner hinge of Jewish existence, to the Lord's Day. For me, this revolution in our view of time is one of the surest proofs that on that "first day" something absolutely extraordinary occurred, that is, the real encounter with Him who is the Risen Lord.

Since then the structure of time has changed, and the first day is the day on which the community of believers meets with Jesus; time is structured around Sunday. This also changes the symbolism of our view of this day: while the Sabbath was the day of rest, shared between God and man, between man and all creation, the first day is the day of creation; for Christians it is the day of the new creation. We see that, with this day, creation begins anew and we enter into the dynamism of the new creation. But let us look more closely at how this happens.

Jesus enters through the locked doors. In this situation, we see the contradictory feelings of the disciples. Some of them remained in Jerusalem. Given the circumstances, it would have been normal to return to Galilee; instead, they are gathered, they are in an assembly, in other words, they are waiting for something. They are expectant, because they know that the tomb is empty; they themselves saw it; they heard the women tell about having seen the Lord; they heard Mary Magdalene, who saw and touched the Lord.

Therefore they are waiting so that they, too, will be able to have a sign, so that they, too, will be able to meet Him. But even with this expectation that follows the events of that morning, at the same time they are filled with fear and lock the doors. This way of looking at the situation is contradictory; it seems to me that it also tells us something about many situations in humanity, within the Church and outside the Church. The doors are locked out of fear. The doors are locked also for fear that God could perhaps be too demanding, that He could change my life, take away my security and my habits; then the door is locked against God, against Christ.

On the other hand, in our hearts there is still an expectation, the expectation that this God who showed Himself in history, who spoke to many men, who spoke to the Apostles, that this very same God would have to come to me, too, would have to touch me, too. In this contradictory view, which is the normal situation that runs through all of history, we pray that the Lord may come, that He may come through the locked doors of our heart, of many hearts: "Come, enter, show Yourself and show Your presence, give us the assurance that You are eternal love. Help us to see You, to touch You, to live together with You!"

The Lord enters and greets them: "Peace be with you!" Peace has an extraordinary newness in this moment, because He comes from the night of death, from the night of hell where He had descended to deliver Adam, humanity in jail. But at the same time, He comes from the power of God, from the light; God Himself brings the light and the peace of God. Thus Jesus changes the world, entering with His divine peace, entering as victor over death, over all these "jails" that keep humanity prisoner.

He says: "Peace be with you!" The reaction of the Apostles is beautiful: "Seeing the Lord, they rejoiced", the Gospel says. Anyone who sees the Lord rejoices. Once again, let us pray that the Lord may make us see a bit of His presence and touch our hearts with joy: "Yes, You are present; You are with us!"

Then we see the connection with the theme of the new creation, which is really the birthday of the new creation, the first day. The peace that He gives us has two dimensions. First of all, the dimension of peace-mission: "As the Father sent Me, so I send you." We are thus appointed messengers, bringers of His peace. Peace is not, therefore, a piece of property that the disciples carry like a treasure enclosed in their souls; peace—this new peace of God—is a gift that they must bring to the world, which lives amid many contradictions, conflicts, and acts of violence, which lives in opposition to peace.

Then Jesus "breathed" and said: "Receive the Holy Spirit." Here we really see the first day, the day of creation, in which Sacred Scripture with its beautiful imagery tells us that God forms man from the mud. The human body is made by God, but it is only a body; it is formed by God's hands, but at first it remains only a body. Then, God breathed, and man became "a living soul", Sacred Scripture says. Now, God breathes a second time, but human beings are already alive, they are "living souls", to use scriptural language.

The Lord breathed once again, giving the Holy Spirit. Saint Paul says: from being a living soul, man becomes "a life-giving spirit". A new dimension is added to the normal state of a human being: the Holy Spirit, the new breath of God. We can understand that the breath of Christ is the Holy Spirit and, so to speak, breathing with Christ means breathing the Holy Spirit, so that He might enter into us and transform us. Thus we are no longer only human beings, but we are penetrated by the divine reality, we are "a life-giving spirit", we become children of God in real communion with God.

This is the process instigated by the powerful fact of man's new creation: as on the first day of creation, the breathing, the breath of God enters into us and gives us a new dimension of belonging to God. The Church Fathers, in this context, had said that the phrase "created in the image of God" means: in anticipation of Christ. All human beings are made according to the model of Christ and thus are an image of God. This means that, insofar as we become similar to Christ, we are the image of God, and we become similar to Christ, the image of God, not through something external, but by means of the Holy Spirit who breathes in us, we breathe the breath of Christ. Interiorly we live as Christ, and thus we really become images of God, children of God, belonging to the family of God.

Along with this, the Risen Lord gives forgiveness. The Holy Spirit is forgiveness, transformation, renewal, purification of the human being, and only in this purification, in this overcoming of the mud of sin, are we really images of God. In recent decades, the words "sin", "chastity", and "purity" have been ridiculed, so much that it was almost impossible to pronounce these words.

Now the world itself speaks to us about sin as the root of all evil, speaks to us about the purity that we do not have. We see how true it is that sin is interior mud, the destruction of a human being, and we need the renewal, purity, and purification that can come only from this newness of God's breath; we need this purification that transforms us, renews us, and makes us really an image of God. Let us pray that the Lord may renew the world, that He may renew Christians, renew the priests, renew us all in the grace of His Spirit, in the beauty of His forgiveness, and in this way that He may make us an image of God, so that in us God appears in the world, because Christ lives in us.

Now let us look just briefly at the second apparition of Jesus. Thomas had doubted, and Jesus shows Himself to him in His bodily nature, so that Thomas can touch the wounds of Jesus. The Son of God is man eternally; human flesh has its place in the heart of God Himself and can be touched. This, too, appears to be contradictory: Thomas can touch the pierced heart of Jesus. In and of itself, a pierced heart is a dead heart, but Jesus lives, and His pierced heart is His heart open for us all. A heart in which we all can find divine love, which renews us and gives us the joy for which we thirst and which we need so much. The pierced heart of Jesus is a living, open heart: this is the newness of the Risen Lord, the source of our joy, of true life.

The Lord says: "Blessed are they who have not seen and have believed." Let us thank the Lord for this "beatitude", and let us pray that "although not seeing" in the sense in which Thomas did, we too might touch His heart—in our life, in our encounter with Christ, in the sacraments, in prayer, in many experiences of good in the world—and see that He lives. And let us pray with Saint Thomas: "My Lord and my God!" Amen!

John's Vision on the Lord's Day

April 7, 2013
Private Chapel, Castel Gandolfo

Second Sunday of Easter—Mercy Sunday (Year C)
Readings: Acts 5:12–16; Rev 1:9–11, 12–13, 17–19; Jn 20:19–31

Saint John the Apostle, on the Lord's day, was caught up in ecstasy to see Jesus. So the Book of Revelation tells us. John was in exile and could not participate in the life of the community, in the Eucharistic celebration of his Church, and the Church was deprived of the Eucharist because John was in exile. The Lord gave him His presence and, through his message, allowed the Church also to experience His presence.

Saint John was rapt in ecstasy on the Lord's day. "The Lord's day"—that is, the third day after His death, the first day of the week—was the day of the encounter with the Risen Lord, the day of the Church's liturgy, the day on which the Lord gave Himself to His followers.

We can see how Christianity revised the way in which time is calculated and structured. In the Old Testament, everything led up to the seventh day, the Sabbath, the Lord's day, the day of the pact between God and mankind. The moment the Lord shows Himself, though, the first day of the week becomes that day. The structure of the week changes: the first day becomes His day, the Lord's day, and the day of the Church's meeting. The day on which, again and again, she encounters the Risen Lord. From this fact we can guess that something resembling the force of lightning, some powerful reality burst in upon that day, so as truly to bring about a revolution in time. This first day, the Lord's day, the day of the meeting with the Risen Lord, is the permanent trace of an incredible event that changes everything, that changes the structure of time and renews the world.

Saint John could not preside at the Eucharist because he was in exile, and the community had no priest to preside over it. On this day, therefore, let us pray for all those who cannot go to Mass, for those who are in prison, for the persecuted, for the sick who do not have the opportunity to meet with the Risen Lord, so that the Lord might open the doors, help them, show Himself to them, and give Himself to them.

And let us pray not only for those who, because of sickness, civil unrest, and so many situations, cannot participate in the Eucharist; let us pray also for those who can but have forgotten the Lord's greatness. Let us pray for all Christians who no longer remember the great gift of the Lord's presence, of this possibility to meet with Life, with the force of renewed life, life that is victorious over death, with this explosion that opens the gates of the world and opens the doors of true life.

Let us pray that Christians will once again recognize the gift, that a new desire for the Eucharist may grow, a true desire for a meeting with the Risen Lord. Let us pray that we, too, may be able to understand, again and again and ever more deeply, what it means to say, "The Risen Lord is with us." The Risen Lord: the One who opened the gates of the world, who is the Life in which we already meet the new world.

Then, in his ecstasy, the Apostle hears a voice, as though of a trumpet. And he turns. The ecstasy starts, not with a vision, but rather with a locution. *Fides ex auditu*, tradition says: Faith comes from hearing, from the sense of hearing, from listening, not from reading, not from thinking. It is the product, not of our own invention or our ideas; it is the product, not of a process of reflections, but of a trumpet, of a voice, of a "you" who stands outside, who touches me and speaks to me, in the "you" of Christ, in the community of the Church.

And this trumpet of the word always demands that we turn around, that we change directions so as to see the risen Christ. Let us pray that this voice of the trumpet may touch hearts even today. Perhaps the Lord wants our voice, also, to be able to be that trumpet for someone else. So that our voice says: "The Lord exists." And we hope to be capable of converting again and again, of changing direction, so as to go toward Jesus, so as to meet Jesus, the true life.

Then John saw seven lampstands. And the lampstands are made of gold, and the Lord, too, has a golden sash across His chest. The seven lampstands remind us of those who stood in the temple in Jerusalem before the Lord's throne as a symbol of the people of Israel, of the believing people who surround the presence of the Lord, who is never alone. Thus the Risen Lord is not alone, either: He is surrounded by these golden lampstands, which are a symbol of the Church.

If the passage says that they are made of gold, we should recall that gold was a symbol for the early Church: it was the stuff of which heaven is made. If the seven lampstands are made of gold, this means that the Church is not made only out of the matter of this world, by our way of thinking; she is not just an association of human beings who want to do something, but she is made up of the stuff of heaven. In the Church, heaven is present among us in the communion of grace, in the communion of the sacraments, in the communion of the Word, in the communion of the Holy Eucharist. The golden stuff of the Church: a little bit of heaven is present on earth. We must love this Church, seek this gold of God's presence, and pray that it is not defiled by our sins.

But the lampstands give light. Thus the Church's mission appears, too. Her light is not for herself, but it is to give light to mankind. The Church must be a city on a hill, must be visible and a place from which one can see. She must be a light on the lampstand, and thus light must come from the Church into the world. The Church of the Gospel is not only for herself, for a little group, because the Gospel is light for the world. And the Church was created so that this light might touch the darkness of the absence of God.

Let us pray, therefore, that, even today, God's light may really touch the night of the absence of God.

The vision that John relates is similar to the one that the prophet Daniel had (see Dan 7:9–14). In Daniel's prophecy, not one but two figures appear. Besides the youth, there is an old man. An old man because he has white hair, a symbol of the God who transcends time, who has always existed. These white hairs therefore signify the "always" of God. In John's vision, the old man and the youth are one and the same: it is the Son of man Himself who has white hair. The God of history is the Son of man, because God was made flesh; He became man, and man became God.

It is obvious that, when he sees this, he cannot remain on his feet. John falls to the ground, as though dead. The whole tradition of the Old Testament says that, at the sight of God, no one can remain alive. The young man, however, approaches, places his hand on John's head, and says: "Do not fear." This is the moment in which John recognizes Him.

These are the same words that he heard when he was together with Jesus. The great God is also his friend, He is Jesus. Our judge at the end of time is the same friend with whom we were acquainted here on earth. He judges us, but we do not have to be afraid, because He puts His hand on our head and says: "Do not fear." This is why it is important to grow in friendship with Christ, so that we might recognize Him, some day, as our friend.

The hand on the head may also be a sign of the Eucharist. Thus symbolism once again makes its way into the liturgical context in which John finds himself. Jesus comes to us, gives Himself to us as our friend. In communion He places his hand on our head and says, "Do not be afraid, it is I!"

Let us pray to the Lord that His Word and His presence might always encourage us and lift us up in the midst of the trials of life: He is stronger than any fear and any evil in us and around us. Amen!

Emmaus: Always Good Friday and Always Easter

May 4, 2014
Private Chapel, Mater Ecclesiae Monastery

Third Sunday of Easter (Year A)
Readings: Acts 2:14, 22–23; Ps 16; 1 Pet 1:17–21; Lk 24:13–35

Two years ago, when I was making a pastoral visit to Cuba, one of the Cuban bishops said to me: "We Christians in this country, and many other Latin Americans, too, have not yet arrived at Easter; we stopped at Good Friday."

These words occurred to me yesterday, as I meditated on this Gospel, in which we find two men who are still at Good Friday, although it is a Sunday of Easter. They heard something about the empty tomb and angels, but remained at Good Friday: Christ is still dead; the world is empty; redemption has not yet come. They are not so unusual; they are almost permanent representatives of all humanity. We can say that these words of the Cuban bishop are true for most of the world: we have remained at Good Friday.

This is a real example, because even today Christ is thrashed, mocked, and tortured. Even today we hear *Ecce homo!* ["Behold the man!"] Even today Christ is in the world like a powerless man, and the faith seems to be in vain. There is no Easter; we are still at Good Friday. And if we think of all the dictatorships of past times, of those powers that were against God, while God appeared to be absent: they were Good Friday for all the martyrs, for all the believers.

Even today, although in a very different situation, we have these new forms of science that make it possible for us to make man and to destroy man, to treat man as our product. "Creatures" no longer exist; God is no longer visible, and it seems ridiculous to believe in the Resurrection, in the Son of God who became man, was crucified, and rose again.

In reality, the central image of the faith is the Crucified Lord. It is always Good Friday because we always live by the Lord's Cross, and the Crucified Lord with His open arms always stands before the Father, praying for us. Therefore, Saint Paul defines the Eucharistic celebration by saying: when you celebrate these mysteries, you proclaim the death of the Lord. Nevertheless, we do not adore a dead man, and we do not preach a dead man, but rather a Crucified Lord who is alive.

This means: yes, in the Church it is always Good Friday, but it is always Easter, too, because these two realities are always together! In human history, there is no Easter without the permanent presence of Good Friday; but it is not only Good Friday; it is always really Easter, too: the two realities stand together, and this is the essence of Christianity. We are always on a journey with the Lord, not having seen the Risen One, because we are not able to recognize Him, and nevertheless He journeys with us, opens our heart so that our eyes might be opened, too. Therefore, this journey to Emmaus interprets all of Church history: it is always Good Friday, and at the same time it is already Easter.

Just think, for example, of how the major forms of totalitarianism, which appeared to be invincible—whether

Nazism or Communism—have vanished now, while Christ continues to live. I think of the fact that from Vietnam, where Christ was totally excluded, the Head of State and the Head of the party visited me and told me that they have understood that the Church of Christ is an important factor in building their society.[1] Christ lives! Just think: the palace of the Emperor Diocletian, a great persecutor of the Christians, then became a cathedral of the Catholic Church.[2]

Christ conquers, but He always conquers on the Cross; even though all the negative major powers pass away, Good Friday always remains, and, only in this way, so does Easter remain. I think, for example, also about a little story related to me by Cardinal Van Thuan,[3] a great confessor, who was in a terrible prison and lived isolated in a cell no larger than a wardrobe, in total darkness, without contacts, completely isolated. In this great absence of God, in this great Good Friday, he managed—incredibly!—to have a few drops of wine, a few crumbs of bread, and thus, in the simplest but greatest way, he celebrated the Eucharist and touched the Risen Lord in the midst of that night; he experienced the fact that the Crucified Lord really has risen already.

This is what we should learn from today's Gospel. Our concept of God the redeemer might be a God who is a little like the Emperor Augustus, who exercises His authority over the world, who establishes justice and unites

[1] The president of Vietnam, Nguyen Minh Triet, visited Benedict XVI in Rome on December 12, 2009; the prime minister, Nguyen Tan Dung, on January 25, 2007.

[2] The Cathedral of Spalato is found in the ancient mausoleum of the Emperor Diocletian, in his palace in that Croatian city (Split).

[3] Cardinal François-Xavier Nguyen Van Thuan (1928–2002), archbishop of Saigon, was incarcerated for thirteen years. Ten years after being set free, John Paul II appointed him president of the Pontifical Council for Justice and Peace, in Rome. In 2017 he was declared venerable by Pope Francis.

everyone.... But this is not God's way of acting! God acts in His own way, and His way is not that of a worldly, military power, of armies, or of the economy, of economic power. His power is self-giving love, and this is the Cross. Christ, the witness of God, acts in a divine manner, and the divine power is not that of this world, but rather is self-giving love. And precisely in this radical donation, in this renunciation of all worldly power, God proves to be the true divinity: precisely in this way, by giving Himself, He lives and visits us.

This different way that God has of acting, living, and conquering is incomprehensible to us. We are always at the beginning, and we always say: "But what happened? We hoped that He would be the Savior of the world, and now we see how weak He is!" We think of all the scandals, of what is happening to belie Christ's victory.... Nevertheless, precisely in the humility of giving Himself, losing Himself, in the mystery of the grain of wheat that is given, dies, and thus bears fruit (see Jn 12:24), we see how God acts, we see the true way of divine action, which transforms and renews us in precisely this way. Jesus journeys with us as He journeyed with the disciples on the way to Emmaus. The Church's liturgy is this journeying with the Lord, who opens our heart for us and helps us to recognize Him; while we are not able to recognize Him, He opens our heart.

We know that, until Jesus, the interpretation of Sacred Scripture, of the Old Testament, saw only the triumphant Messiah, and Jesus was not that at all. He says: "How foolish and slow you are not to see how precisely the suffering Christ was foretold, the God who has no worldly power, but gives Himself in His love and thus is stronger than all the powers of this world!" It was a revolution in the interpretation of Scripture, because man started to see its true meaning: "Yes! Speak precisely about this, about Christ crucified and risen."

We must always rediscover this mystery in Scripture, in life, in history. The Lord waits for this attention from us as we journey, as we listen, as we do not let ourselves be captured by the appearances of things; he asks us to have the courage to go forward, not to abandon our search for Him.

The Gospel tells us that the two disciples on the road to Emmaus were searching; this is essential. Let us not simply allow life to fall into banality; we must walk with Jesus, listen to Him in the liturgy, in the dialogue of faith, and, finally, in the gesture of love. Jesus seems to go away. Only love holds Him back and finally opens the door to seeing Him. "Stay with us", they say; they take Him as their guest, and, after the dialogue of faith, the gesture of love makes possible the moment in which their eyes are opened and they recognize Him.

Let us say, too: "Stay with us, Lord!" May we not let Him go. Let us walk with the Lord, let us seek the dialogue of faith, of hope, the gesture of charity. By giving to others our love, our faith as we seek, our hearts are opened, our eyes are opened, and we can see: yes, it is He! He has conquered, precisely as the One who was crucified and arose, and He gives us life, and thus He teaches us, too, how to live really. It is not a triumph, but precisely in patiently bearing the sufferings of this world, we are blessed, because we are close to the Lord. "Stay with us, Lord, do not leave us!" Amen.

The Good Shepherd

May 11, 2014
Private Chapel, Mater Ecclesiae Monastery

Fourth Sunday of Easter (Year A)
Readings: Acts 2:14, 36–41; Ps 23; 1 Pet 2:20b–25; Jn 10:1–10

One of the most beautiful works of art of the early Church is no doubt the small, third-century statue of the Good Shepherd in the Lateran Museum. We all know it: a young shepherd carries a lamb, a little sheep, very tenderly and lovingly on his shoulders and brings it home. The poor sheep could no longer find its way, and it is no longer able to walk, and he carries it lovingly on his shoulders. The Christians of the early Church saw themselves in this sculpture; they understood the whole mystery of Christ, of our redemption, and of the Incarnation.

They knew that the Lord carries me, too, knows me by name, carries me very tenderly, because I am unable to find the way to go home, I do not have the strength to walk, but He carries me with His love. They understood: the Word of God, creative reason, the *Logos*, seeing mankind as a sheep that has gone astray, left His glory and took this straying sheep, mankind, upon His shoulders.

This is the Incarnation: the *Logos* takes human nature upon His shoulders; thus, this image is also a presentation of the Incarnation, of the mystery of Christ, who, being a man, took mankind upon His shoulders and carries us with great love; with this human nature of His, He carries each one of us. Christ, the eternal Reason, the Eternal Word who carries human nature with Him, is the true Shepherd.

In the Ancient Near East, the king, the great kings of the people were called shepherds, and in this way they expressed their authority, but also their responsibility. Isaiah was convinced that God alone can be the true Shepherd (see Is 40:11). In reality, God, in Jesus Christ, the Incarnate Word, is the Shepherd who carries us.

In the modern era, an objection has been made to this image, to this theology: "But we are not sheep! We do not need a shepherd! We have our reason and our own will. Man is not a sheep; he is autonomous and free and does not need these shepherds, any shepherd!" This statement of autonomy, this emancipation that is presented as though it were divinely willed, by Christ, is a lie, but it also conceals a truth. It is a lie, because we know that mankind is truly like a straying sheep, as we see even today.

The Lord speaks to us about these false shepherds, who manipulate mankind and its hopes, looking only at their own interests. Mankind needs help, while we see how even today many false shepherds create division, in small matters and in great; man needs light, a guide, but the true shepherd of man cannot be just anyone; he can be only creative reason itself, the divine light, and this is the mystery that appeared in Christ Jesus, the one true Shepherd. I think that this is the topic for a profound meditation: that Creative Reason, Truth itself, became involved with us, carries us, guides us, knows each one of us by name, and thus we are sure of really being brought to our homeland, to what is good, to life.

The Lord showed us where we must go, what job and what kind of task—we might say—the true shepherd has: to carry the sheep to the meadow where there really is fresh water and good grass. The Lord says in the Gospel: "I find pasture for you", and explains this by saying: "I came that they might have life and life abundantly." This is the meaning of being a shepherd: bringing us to life, giving us life, life in abundance.

But the question also arises: What is life? Everyone wants life, everyone promises life! There is a very beautiful remark by Saint Irenaeus, who writes: "The glory of God is man fully alive, and the life of man is to see God."[1] This is the life of a human being, this is true food, fresh water, good water: to see God. Only a human being who sees God is really alive; if man lives in the night of God's absence, he is not really alive. The shepherd, therefore, is the one who helps us, who brings us to see God, to know God, to be united to God, and to live truly. This, then, is His first task; Jesus showed us the face of God and grants us the grace to know God.

But not only this, because the knowledge of Christ is love. It is not only a matter of seeing; He gave us Himself on the Holy Cross, where His flesh becomes a sacrament, a presence for us. It is not only seeing: in the Eucharist, Jesus offers us this table that Psalm 23 speaks about today, where God Himself becomes our food, where the love of God makes itself food and gives itself.

Let us thank God for this, and let us pray that we may understand the mystery more and more, let us pray that our knowledge may become love: the Lord knows me by name and calls me; He gives Himself into my hands, into my heart, and thus becomes, from within, my shepherd.

We know that at this hour, nearby, in Saint Peter's, thirteen young men are being ordained priests, shepherds.[2]

[1] Irenaeus of Lyons, *Adversus Haereses*, 4.20.7.

[2] Traditionally, on the Fourth Sunday of Easter, Good Shepherd Sunday, the pope presides in Saint Peter's Basilica at the ordination of new priests.

Christ in the sacrament is the door through which to enter; He opens the door so that they may be true shepherds. With this image of the door, Jesus shows us that, ultimately, He is always the only Shepherd, but at the same time He also needs those who enter through the door, so that they may act as He does, in communion with Him.

Let us pray that these young men, who are entering through the door of the sacrament, may be more and more united to Christ, that they may know those who are "His" (see Jn 13:1), with Christ and through Christ; that they may love those who are "His", with Christ and through Christ, and thus may be able to guide them truly to the source of life, to the knowledge of God, to the love of Christ in the communion of the Holy Eucharist.

May the Lord help these young men, so that throughout their life they might always be true shepherds, that they may always enter by the door that He is. And let us all pray: "Lord, by ourselves we are always like straying sheep once again; be our Shepherd always and the guardian of our souls." Amen!

The Shepherd Who Guides and Defends against the Wolves

April 26, 2015
Private Chapel, Mater Ecclesiae Monastery

Fourth Sunday of Easter (Year B)
Readings: Acts 4:8–12; Ps 118; 1 Jn 3:1–2;
Jn 10:11–18

The image of the shepherd is in itself something majestic. The great oriental empires—the Sumerians, the Assyrians, the Babylonians—called their kings "shepherds" and the people their "flock", the "sheep" that they had to pasture; in this way, they expressed their authority, their greatness, but also their responsibility. The Lord, in calling Himself a shepherd, enters into this tradition, expresses the fact that He is the true king, the true king of the universe, the true shepherd; His kingdom is the eternal kingdom. In reality, only He who created us knows us and knows the truth of our being; He alone knows the pathways of life, and He alone can show us where to go in order to live.

Yet, at the same time, the image of the shepherd is also an affectionate one. Think of the beautiful little statue in the Lateran Museum, from the third century: the young shepherd Jesus very lovingly carries on His shoulders the lost sheep. We see that there is not just authority and greatness, but also love and closeness, a personal aspect that knows each one of us and carries us with great love.

In reality, Psalm 23 in particular tells us what a true shepherd does: "The Lord is my shepherd, He guides me to green pastures, He feeds me" (see v. 2). The shepherd, first of all, guides the sheep to green pastures, that is, he gives life, he gives food, he gives fresh water, he gives security, he gives beauty. The shepherd's first concern is to give life and to guide in the geography of being, in the mountains of Israel, the psalm says, where the sheep find this good grass and fresh water.

The mountains of Israel—on which we must journey in order to find the true food—are Sacred Scripture, the Word of God, in which the Lord guides us so as to find life, so as to find truth, love, and unity. This guidance of the Lord is the essential element, because it offers us truth, it offers us love, it offers us unity.

At the beginning of the modern era, there was a protest against this image of the shepherd who guides us. People said: "We are not sheep! We are free persons!", and they contrasted human autonomy with the idea of the "sheep-man". They said: "We do not need shepherds; we are autonomous, and we will find the pathway by ourselves." Yes! It is true that we are not sheep, that we are free persons with reason, free will, and love and have our freedom; but it is also true that this freedom of ours needs illumination: it is a participated freedom, it is a shared freedom; we do not know the path, we need the compass in order to find it.

Therefore this autonomy is a lie, because by himself man does not know where to go. If he takes only himself as his guide, he destroys himself and destroys others. Therefore our freedom and the guidance of the shepherd, with his love and his freedom, do not contradict each other: the guidance of Him who is love and truth is precisely what guarantees our freedom, too, guides us in the difficult mountains of the world, on which we can easily fall if we do not know the path, if we do not have the One who guides us and helps us.

In His parable, the Lord, knowing that these aspirations to autonomy put the human heart to the test, speaks also about "hirelings" and about "wolves", and He says that the wolves steal and scatter, that is, destroy also the unity that is essential for the human community. In our time, we have known these wolves that destroy. Think of the great dictators: Hitler, Stalin, Pol Pot, Mao Tse-tung; they all said: we are bringing mankind to its true happiness, to paradise. They were wolves, who destroyed the world in an unbelievable way, and behind them were the great philosophers, who created those tissues of errors on which the great dictators could then move.

Think of Nietzsche, who ridiculed Christians as weaklings and contrasted this weakness of the Christians with the strong man who destroys. Think of Marx with his promise: his paradise without God became a big concentration camp. Think of Freud and his destruction of the soul. Think, now, of the positivists who say that nothing is true unless it is material, and thus they say that even freedom is only an appearance, while in reality everything is a physical process that we can reconstruct: ultimately, the great work of freedom, autonomy, disappears amid the lies of positivism.

Think also of the violent men who kill in the name of God, who make a false God for themselves, destroy human lives, and behave like rulers over life and death. Think of the human traffickers, who treat human beings like beasts, like merchandise, and destroy them. They are true wolves! The world always ends up falling into the hands of the wolves, and in this situation we can only cry out to the Lord: Do not leave Your world, Your creation, to the wolves! Do not let them destroy the truth with their lies; love with their hatred; unity with their scattering! Lord, help us to defend man, Your creature. You are our shepherd; defend us!

In the history of the Church, the symbol of the shepherd is the staff. The staff that helps to find the path, to point out the path, to defend against the wolves, to guarantee safety. But the Lord's staff is the Cross. The Lord not only defends, but gives Himself and thus gives true life. We are no longer only a religion of the Word, but we are fed by the flesh, by the love of the Lord, who is the true Shepherd, who gives Himself and thus gives us life, opens for us the path of life.

If, at this moment, we pray to the Lord that He may defend His creation against the wolves, this prayer is always a word that also implies thanksgiving for the Lord, who gave Himself to us, who, in the midst of all the sadness and the tragedies of the world, created His Kingdom and defends it and builds it up. Gratitude, because we are called to be with Him in the Church. And gratitude also becomes a duty, to do all that we can to defend life, to defend the truth; to defend true freedom against autonomy, which is the lie of the wolves and destroys creation.

At this moment, in Saint Peter's Basilica, priests are being ordained: nineteen young men, ordained shepherds in the service of the Shepherd.[1] Let us thank the Lord, who called these young men, called young men from all parts of the world.

Let us pray to the Lord to help these men, His shepherds, to defend them, to help them to be true shepherds against the hirelings, against the wolves; that He may accompany them always and thus may help them to build up His Kingdom: the Kingdom of truth, love, peace, and unity. Amen!

[1] See note 2 on page 187.

The Multitude of Those Who Are Saved

April 21, 2013
Private Chapel, Castel Gandolfo

Fourth Sunday of Easter (Year C)
Readings: Acts 13:14, 43–52; Rev 7:9, 14–17; Jn 10:27–30

The Book of Revelation, from which the second reading is taken, often presents striking, unsettling images of the power of evil, horrible scenes in which the world of men is demolished. Today, on the other hand, it shows us the aspect that looks toward the definitive condition, an icon of hope. At the end, redeemed humanity is an immense multitude that no one can count. At the end, God wins.

Here, in this world, it always seems that the men of God are in the minority. Not only in the Book of Revelation do we see a situation in which few people believe, but also in our own experience, observant, staunch Catholics who live according to God's Law are in the minority. It seems that God is always in the minority. But at the end it is different: there is an immense multitude that no one can count. They are saved; they arrive in droves. And this is the joy that ought to touch our hearts. God wins, even though at first sight it seems to be a different story.

And they come from all the nations, from all the languages and peoples. This, too, is important: the fact that

God has His followers everywhere. God finds human beings in all parts of the world and of history. This also gives us a glimpse of the reality of the Church: on earth she always appears to be poor and simple; but if we look at the world as a whole, we see a family that surpasses all frontiers. God knows no frontiers between all the nations. Already today, in the Eucharist, this immense people exists. We are members of it and must thank God that this family of God exists beyond all frontiers.

In the second part of the reading, Saint John describes in a little more detail how these individuals will be saved. First of all, he says: they come from great tribulation. Tribulation, ultimately, is the way to make a human being mature. They come from tribulation, and thus they mature through their communion with God and with one another. At this moment, there are so many Christians who are in tribulation. So many—Pope Francis reminded us—are persecuted, are suffering for the faith. In these moments, let us pray for the Christians who live in great tribulation; and let us pray for all those who live in the tribulation of loneliness, poverty, misery, or the absence of God. Let us pray that the Lord will help them and encourage them, that He will give them His light so that in their tribulation they can mature for the joy and the beauty of the Kingdom of God. Let us pray to the Lord that He may guide us also in the tribulations of this world.

Then the Book of Revelation says that those who have been saved are clothed with light. They are men of light. This makes us think about two realities. First of all, according to tradition, Adam before the Fall was clothed with light, and only his fall into sin extinguishes that light, darkens that light and its ability to let God shine through. Men of light are men of heaven, because the material of heaven is light. Therefore, a second reminder: Jesus, on

Mount Tabor, is light, is clothed with pure light. Men of light are men of truth, without falsehood, without hypocrisy; and thus these men are close to God, they are in the image of God.

But how does this happen? Saint John takes up again the reality of tribulation with another surprising image. He says that those who have been saved have washed their garments in the blood of the Lamb, and thus they became white. It seems contradictory, because washing something in blood, as we know, does not make it white. Therefore, this is not about blood in the material sense: the blood of the Lamb is the love of the Lamb, the love of God who makes Himself a sacrificial lamb for us. It is the love of God who on the Cross gives Himself totally for us. This love is the washing that makes human beings pure; it purifies our hearts. And this washing is very effective.

In the sacrament of penance, which truly is communion with Christ's Passion, He washes us with His blood, makes us transparent once again, and purifies us from the stain of evil, of falsehood. In the Eucharist, we are united with Jesus Christ, with this blood of His, with this love of His that penetrates us, renews us, and makes us white, like the light. The sacraments involve our life; they make us enter into profound communion with this love of Christ. We must truly let ourselves be immersed in this love and thus become men of light, truly white, resplendent with the light of God.

Saint John tells us another thing, too. Namely, that these men live under a merciless sun. Think of the Middle Eastern world where Saint John wrote his works. But the Lord gives them a shelter, stretches out His tent over them, and thus gives them the shade that is necessary in order to live. What is this tent that the Lord gives us in this world against a relentless sun? According to the first chapter of the Gospel of Saint John, God's tent in the world is Christ's humanity (see Jn 1:14).

Christ, as man, is the tent that covers us. He covers against the merciless sun of rationalism, pure human thought that does not penetrate the mystery of God and ruins the shade under which to live. Thus we see how important it is to know and to love the man Jesus, to know the humanity of Jesus, which is like God's tent in this world, the tent that protects us against various forms of rationalism, against a relentless sun, and gives us a human standard, a place in which to live, where we can know God and really live.

This tent also has another meaning: it reminds us of the sacred tent of Israel during the forty years of the exodus (see Ex 33:7–12). The tent was the sacred temple, God's holy place, from which God guided His people. Therefore, the tent of Christ's humanity is also the tent of the Church, where Christ is with us, where we can live in communion with the other believers and thus be protected against the dangers of this world. Therefore, we have a second element, the tent, the humanity of Christ and the communion of the Church, which is the Body of Christ.

Finally a third element appears, that is, the fact that the Lamb guides us to the source of living water. Once again we see the aridity of the Middle East, where even a drop of flowing water is life. Jacob was the patriarch of water, because he had given the well, in which there was always pure water, ever-living water. Man lives on this water. Think of the gift of this water in the material sense, which is threatened: so many people do not have this clean water. Let us pray that clean water may always be protected against pollutants, so that all have access to clean water, which is living.

But Jesus sat with the Samaritan woman at Jacob's well (Jn 4:1–39). This makes it clear that man has an even deeper thirst, he thirsts for a deeper water, the water of truth, the water of love. But in this case, too, there is the threat of the pollutants that poison the waters of truth in this world.

Let us pray to the Lord to guard the world, the Church, and us personally against these pollutants; to help us to find the true water, the water that gives life, as He Himself said: "My words are life and truth" (see Jn 6:63; 14:6), and as Saint Peter said: "To whom shall we go? You alone have the words of everlasting life" (Jn 6:68), words of fresh, eternal water.

At this point, the reading is connected with the Gospel about the Good Shepherd, who guides the sheep to living water. Let us reflect that, in a few minutes, the new priests of the Diocese of Rome will be ordained in Saint Peter's; they are to be pastors, shepherds who guide the people to the living water, to the water of true life, and they must protect it against the things that pollute this water. At this hour, let us pray for these young men, that the Lord might make them truly pastors according to His heart and may help them to guide the people to the living water.

In this context, I am always struck by Jesus' words: "No one will snatch them from My hands." We know how the world seeks to tear priests away from the Lord's hands. Let us pray, then: "Lord, do not forget Your promise, fulfill Your promise: do not let anyone snatch them from Your hands. Give us good pastors, good priests who guide us to the living water of everlasting life." Amen!

Our Royal Priesthood

May 18, 2014
Private Chapel, Mater Ecclesiae Monastery

Fifth Sunday of Easter (Year A)
Readings: Acts 6:1–7; Ps 33; 1 Pet 2:4–9; Jn 14:1–12

The excerpt from the First Letter of Saint Peter, which we heard as the second reading, is probably part of a baptismal catechesis in which the Apostle explains to the candidates for Baptism, to those who are baptized, and also to us, what it is to be a Christian, what the essence of Christianity is.

He does this by citing the Old Testament, with these fine words: "You are a kingdom of priests, a holy nation, a people to offer spiritual sacrifices to God" (see Ex 19:6). This saying showed the dignity of Israel, a saying that God dictated to Moses on Sinai, to bring back to His people to explain what His intention was for Israel. If Saint Peter now takes these words addressed to Israel and applies them to the baptized, that is, to all Christians, it means that Christians have entered into the promise of Israel and are the true, definitive Israel, the kingdom of priests that God had spoken about.

Thus two very important things become clear. The first is that Baptism is not only an individual reality, in me, namely, involving the remission of original sin and the gift of sanctifying grace. This is naturally fundamental, but it is not only this. Baptism, so to speak, takes me away from myself and puts me into a new context, into a new totality; it creates a new relation, a new way of being in which there is in one respect myself, but there are also in another respect the others with me. I am no longer myself alone, because to be baptized means to enter into the great community of the people of God, into the "kingdom of priests", this community that transcends times and places and really is the family of God: it is entering into the communion of the children of God.

It is important to be aware that, as baptized persons, we are in this great communion that transcends the boundaries of the peoples: every one of the baptized is my brother; I am no longer only myself, I am in a great company on a journey and, thus, am in the true family of God. This implies my openness to the totality of the Church, an interior catholicity, and the fact that I do not live only for myself, but in this great community. I would say that the remission of original sin and sanctifying grace mean precisely this: that I am liberated from self-enclosure and that God introduces me into this great communion. We must seek to be ever more aware, to be ever more open to this great community, which is our true homeland.

There is a second element. If God calls Israel, and us too, "a kingdom of priests", a community of kings and priests, it means that a priest is not for himself but is always for others, in the service of others, and the king is not for himself alone; he is a king only if there are others over whom he rules. "He is a king!" means that a Christian is not for himself, but for others, as Israel was not for itself, but was like a beacon of light for the people, like the place of a divine presence in the world, from which it was possible to see and to begin to know that God exists.

Thus the Church, too, is not created only for herself, but as a presence of God that gives light to others; like a city on a hill—the Lord says—like light on a lampstand. And, as true as this is for the Church as such, it is true also for each one of us. I am not a Christian for myself alone, because to be a Christian means: "I am in service for others; from me a bit of light must come, so that God may be known in the world and present in the world."

In this way we have started to interpret what it means to say that we are priests and kings, that we are "a royal priesthood" (1 Pet 2:9). According to the classic definition, the purpose of the priesthood is for preaching, for proclamation, and for worship, for sacrifices. In reality, to be priests—and all of us, being baptized persons, are priests—means that we must first of all bring the awareness of God into the world. This is essential. Moreover, in order to bring this awareness of God, we ourselves must know God, the God who showed us His face in Christ. This is therefore a fundamental mandate of Christian existence: to know Jesus Christ more and more, to know God more and more, to know the Lord's voice today so as to be able to follow Him, so as to be able to make Him known to others.

Let us pray to the Lord to help us really to know Him and thus to make present in the world the light of His knowledge in the darkness of God's absence. Saint Augustine wrote a very beautiful parable on this task of Christians. He speaks about a father who suffered from sleeping sickness: the great danger is that, in falling into this sleep, he might not awaken again, and therefore it is necessary to bother him constantly, to awaken him, to call him back from this sickness against his will, so that he does not fall into death but returns to life. And so, Saint Augustine says, a good son must bother his father. The latter will say:

"Leave me in peace; I am so sleepy, I am so tired!" "No!" the son must say, "You must not abandon yourself to sleep!" He must bother him so that he comes back and returns to life.[1]

And the priest must do this, and therefore so must every Christian: not leave people in their sleeping sickness with respect to God. This is the great danger today, that the sleeping sickness with respect to God will cause people to forget God, and thus humanity will be lost. We Christians must be bothersome and not leave people in this peaceful sleep with respect to God, but rather bother them, resume the conversation about God, make God present with our words and above all with our lives.

The other task of Christians is worship, sacrifice. Humanity has always known that we are indebted to God, that we must seek to respond to God, to give a response of thanksgiving for His goodness, and so worship was born. Shepherds offered to God the little lambs as the most precious thing, while those who tilled the soil offered wheat and wine, and so on.

But the people of Israel understood increasingly well that this is not the response that God expects: God does not need lambs; He does not need wheat. In one psalm, God says: "Do you think, Israel, that I eat the flesh of bulls or drink the blood of lambs?" (see Ps 50:13). No! This is not the way to adore God or to respond to Him. In times past, there was also the immense horror of human sacrifices, but God is never glorified by the destruction of a human being.

This discussion took place already in very ancient times in Israel, with the initial prophetic responses, which show the path toward Christ. In the Book of Samuel, we hear:

[1] See Augustine of Hippo, *Sermons*, 400.10.12.

"I do not delight in sacrifices; I delight in obedience" (see 1 Sam 15:22); in the Book of Hosea: "I do not desire sacrifices, but the knowledge of God" (see Hos 6:6), and again: "I do not desire sacrifices; I will espouse you in faithfulness" (see Hos 2:19–20). And the Lord Jesus cites the Book of Samuel but transforms it: "I desire mercy, and not sacrifice" (Mt 9:13; 12:7). Thus four words appear as the true purification of divine worship: knowledge, obedience, faithfulness, mercy; these are the attitudes that transform a human being so that he himself becomes a sacrifice, the glorification of God.

Again, knowledge is like the foundation: if we do not know God, if we have the sleeping sickness with respect to God, nothing happens, and therefore the first point is: to be awake so as to stand before God, to see His presence, and to be attentive to it. And then from this, from our reason, so to speak, worship is transformed and goes to the heart, to the will, so as to be transformed into obedience. Obedience is not something external, but shows that we allow ourselves to be transformed according to God's will, which is our true vocation. And then fidelity, continuity: not only a moment of enthusiasm, but the humble continuity, day by day, of faithfulness in this transformation in God. And finally mercy, as love, which is an imitation of God's essence.

Thus it is clear that the true sacrifice is the living human person, a man who really lives and lets himself be transformed by God; we see that the fundamental element of the sacrifice is the transformation. One theory maintained that sacrifice is destruction, but what pleases God is not destruction; it is the transformation of our will, of our very being according to God's will, and by living in this way, we will be an image of God. Here we have arrived at the truly central point, which, however, we cannot develop right now: the true transformation of the world is accomplished in Christ's sacrifice, because He transformed death into an act of love and thus opened the path to God.

By entering into Christ's act of love, in the Eucharist, we ourselves participate in His transformation, in the transubstantiation of the world and of ourselves. Let us pray to the Lord, then, that we may become ever more really the people of God, that is, priests; that in us the world might be transformed and that we may accept this transformation of ours day by day, even though it may hurt our egotism. Saint Peter uses the image of stones that must be hewed in order to be fitted into the great house of God. Thus God works with us so that at last we may really be the adoration of God, that we may be transformed and renewed, part of His great house, in which we are all one body with Christ and thus become the true sacrifice, the glory of God.

Let us pray to the Lord to accomplish once again among us the mystery of transubstantiation and to transform us, too, so that we might truly be priests of the New Testament and a true glorification of God, as living men who are formed according to His will. Amen!

Remaining in the Love of the Lord, Who Knows Everything

May 3, 2015
Private Chapel, Mater Ecclesiae Monastery

Fifth Sunday of Easter (Year B)
Readings: Acts 9:26–31; Ps 22; 1 Jn 3:18–24; Jn 15:1–8

From each of the three readings for this Sunday I would like to take a little hint that, I hope, can help us on our journey of faith. Let us start with the first reading.

Saint Paul, on the road to Damascus, was struck down by the light of the Lord: the Risen Lord called him and gave him a universal mission: to bring His salvation to the world, even to the ends of the earth. Immediately after his Baptism, Paul had started to preach in Damascus, but very soon he had to flee, because of death threats. Thus he returned to Jerusalem, but not the Jerusalem from which he had come, that is, the city of the temple, of rabbinical theology, but to the new Jerusalem, the Jerusalem of the twelve Apostles, the Jerusalem of the Church of Christ. Here, too, Paul started to preach with zeal, entering into the heritage of Stephen, with the universal dynamism of his message. But he was suddenly threatened by death, and the Church of Jerusalem finally brought him to Tarshish.

We can understand this: not only to protect him against the threats, but also to protect the Church. At that moment, the Church needed peace and not the dynamism of Paul's great plan; she needed a silent maturation; therefore, there was no room for Paul, and they brought him to Tarshish. We can meditate a little on Paul's situation here: Jesus called him, but in the Church there was no room for him; not only was there no need for him, but he was a cause of irritation. In Tarshish, in that city which today is in Turkey, he was alone as a Christian: there was no church, no priest, nothing; he was alone, without a mission, without activities, and he did not know when his hour would come.

In the Acts of the Apostles, two chapters go by before the moment comes when Barnabas says: "Now I can go to Tarshish", and he looks for Paul and brings him back to the Church. But Paul does not know when that moment will be; he was left alone in Tarshish, and the Church has no room for him. He must wonder: Why did the Lord call me? What is to become of me? He has forgotten me!" He must have found himself in a difficult dark night. The Lord called him and at the same time forgot him; we can imagine how he suffered from this solitude, being left alone, not being useful, being forgotten by the Lord, and how he must have called on the Lord during that time.

But we can also understand that this was the moment, according to the words of the Gospel, in which the Lord pruned him so he would be able to bear fruit (see Jn 15:2). We understand that in these years of solitude, he suffered, but he always found the Lord interiorly, too; that his faith matured, that he entered into communion with the Passion and, in precisely this way, developed his view of the mystery of Christ. The Lord left him alone, but precisely in this sad solitude, in this dark room of his life, his intimate union with the Lord grew; otherwise, he could not have survived.

It seems to me that at this moment we should think of the many Christians scattered throughout the world who are left alone, suffer for Christianity, or are in danger. We can think of the many Christians who suffer because they do not find their mission. Let us pray for them all, that the Lord may always be near them, even in the dark nights of life. Let us pray to the Lord that we, too, in moments of darkness and in the dark nights of faith, will not be left alone, so that, precisely when the Lord prunes us, we can grow and sense His nearness, His presence, and not lose our hope for the day when He will return to call us, because when He needs me, the Lord comes and calls me.

In the Gospel, from this parable of the vine, which we can return to and meditate on more extensively next Sunday, I want to take just one word: "Remain!" says the Lord. This "remain" is a fundamental point, as we saw with Paul, who does not say: "Then I am useless" or "Seek me", but simply remains; he remains even in the dark night, remains faithfully, with perseverance. Saint Paul learned what later on Saint Augustine again learned, that is, that there are two elements in Christian life: conversion—the joy of the encounter, the newness of life, the knowledge of God in Christ—and perseverance—faithfulness and the patience to go forward even into the deserts, even in the night.[1]

At the moment of his conversion, Saint Augustine was full of joy, full of enthusiasm; he was sure that "now everything is new; the new life begins." Then, after years and years of the journey, he discovered that there is a second element: perseverance, walking, remaining even in the

[1] See Augustine of Hippo, *On the Gift of Perseverance* (PL 45 [NPNF-1, 5:521ff.]).

desert, and Christian life is made up precisely of these two elements together. On the one hand, in the time of perseverance, there must still be also the joy of conversion, the joy of having been encountered by Christ, of seeing Him and knowing Him; on the other hand, in the element of enthusiasm, there must also be perseverance, the patience to remain.

Precisely today, when some say that life is so long that people can no longer make decisions that last a lifetime, we reply: "No! It is possible!" Only in this way does a human being mature; only in continuity with the tree of life does the fruit grow also; life seems more interesting with continual change, but in reality it is ruined. True newness grows only in continuity; man is created to make definitive decisions; he is created to "remain", and, in precisely this way, he bears fruit.

Finally, in the second reading, there is a word that is one of the great words of Sacred Scripture, a word that is mysterious, too, which says: "If our heart accuses us, we are safe: God is greater than our heart and knows everything." In reading such a great verse as this: "God is greater than our heart; He knows everything", who would not think of the last encounter of Saint Peter with the Lord by the Sea of Tiberias after the Resurrection (see Jn 21:15–19), when the Lord asks him three times, "Simon, do you love Me?" The third time, Peter feels burdened by the weight of his sins, his infidelity, all his weakness, and he replies: "You know that I love You; You know everything." There it is, this exclamation: "You know everything; certainly you know my sin, my weaknesses, my failings, but You also know the desire for You, the desire for love, for faith, for truth that is in me!"

We know that the Lord is not our accuser, but our defender. "You know everything" is not a word of anguish but a word of confidence. Yes! God knows all our sins, better than we do, but He knows also the deep desire for love that is within us, and He is greater than our heart, and therefore He defends us. "You know it" is not a word of anguish, but a word of joy and confidence. For me it is interesting to recall that, before that encounter, Peter had said, "It is not a man, it is the Lord", adding then: "Depart from me, for I am a sinful man" (see Lk 5:8).

Man in the presence of God is afraid, he wants to go away from Him, wants to act as if God were distant; I think that this is a factor in many persons who do not believe: they want to distance God from themselves because they sense the weight of their sins. But in the second encounter, the last one, it is different: "Precisely because You know everything about me, I would like You to be with me"; because this omniscience of the Lord is not a condemnation but a grace; it sees our love in depth, and it is greater than our heart. The fact that God knows everything, that God's eye sees to the very bottom of us, is not a threat, but a great consolation, because "You know everything" means: You love me, You see me with the look of love.

Let us pray that the Lord will help us to come ever closer to this second encounter, and not to stop at the first, where we see only anguish because of God's greatness. In this second encounter, we see that God knows everything and, precisely because of that, He is kind to me and saves me. "Yes, Lord, I love You; You know everything. You are my salvation", and so from love comes the truth, from love comes unity, confidence, true redemption. Amen!

Giving Thanks, Asking, Journeying in Joy

April 28, 2013
Private Chapel, Castel Gandolfo

Fifth Sunday of Easter (Year C)
Readings: Acts 14:21–27; Rev 21:1–5; Jn 13:31–33, 34–35

With her liturgical prayers, the Church teaches us to pray. Thus she teaches us to live. She transforms the Word of God into a word of ours and creates a bond with God, the profound relation that makes us truly happy. Therefore, I thought: perhaps it would be helpful, once, to meditate on a liturgical prayer, on the Collect for this Sunday. Before interpreting it, I will read the text of it once again: "O Father, You have given us the Savior and the Holy Spirit; look kindly upon Your adopted children, so that true freedom and an eternal inheritance may be given to all who believe in Christ."

The prayer is made up of three elements: thanksgiving—immediately as the first thing—then a request and then a promise. It starts with thanksgiving and makes us understand that before we do anything, we are preceded by gifts. The principle is not our action, but God's gift, which precedes everything. And it is very important for us to realize deeply that before doing something, we have already received gifts. Because in this way we learn gratitude. A human being who is grateful becomes pure, also, becomes a joyous person.

The prayer mentions two gifts: the Savior and the Holy Spirit. But we must add that these two principal gifts are preceded by a fundamental gift: creation. God's first gift is life, is creation. We must take note of this reality, that the beauty of creation is a gift. The mountain, the sea, all the beauty of the world, and also whatever we may eat, everything is created, and we can live only by receiving from what is created. The gift of creation precedes us. Learn to love what God has created. Learn to be grateful for this gift of God.

And then the Savior, Jesus. God gave us not only something—certainly He gave us something, also: things to eat and to drink—everything—but above all He gave us Himself, the Savior, Jesus. We must think what life would be if we did not know Jesus. If there had been no Jesus, how empty the world would be! We must love Jesus as God's gift. And, in order to love Him, we must know Him more and more. Just think of what He gave us: the Gospels, the Beatitudes, the great parables, the good Samaritan, the prodigal son, the parable of a judgment where ultimately love matters and can justify everyone. The great, beautiful words of the Lord.

Then, all that He did for mankind: the whole history of the Cross, His suffering and Resurrection. It seems to me that every day we should think once more about these things so as to know Jesus, to understand Him, to understand the gift that He gave us, the gift that is Jesus Himself, the Savior.

And then the Holy Spirit. The Lord is Savior, not only in the past; He is present and works through the Holy Spirit. Think how poor the results of Church bureaucracy are, the attempts to reform the Church by our activities. God is the one who reforms; God is the one who renews with the Holy Spirit! Think of how God creates great figures: Chiara Lubich, Don Giussani, Padre Pio; in all times: Saint Francis, Saint Dominic, Saint Augustine, Saint Benedict. The whole company of the saints is a company of figures stirred up by the Holy Spirit. They are a gift of the Holy Spirit, and they renew the world and the Church. They inspire us; they truly are a great gift from God. From them come the movements: the Focolari, Communion and Liberation, the Neocatechumenal Way, which are true forces that renew the Church. The Holy Spirit is present and working, and He is the great gift of God for us.

The Letter to the Colossians says at one point: "*Eucháristoi gínesthe*," that is, "become thankful" (see Col 3:15; see Eph 5:20). This is a fundamental imperative. Truly, when we can understand what great gifts constantly precede us, what beautiful, great gifts precede us, we become thankful, and thus the whole tone of our being becomes different. Bitterness and the spirit of dissatisfaction cease; we are imbued with the joy of living, by the joy of receiving such great gifts from the Lord. God has bestowed the great gifts on us: Creation, the Savior, the Holy Spirit. Let us keep our eyes open to God's gifts, let us become responsive to God's gifts. In this way we are redeemed.

After this attitude of gratitude, which is the first act of the prayer—opening our eyes to the presence of God's great gifts and, thus, becoming joyful, because we are thankful—the prayer continues: "We pray that God may look kindly upon us and make us His adopted children." God's glance is not directed at a distant geometry of the cosmos, but it looks at me, it looks at me and you.

There is also a fear of this look: there is the flight started by Adam, who hides himself, because he does not want to be seen by God, because after his sin he sees God's presence as a threat (see Gen 3:8–10). In the modern era, people say more and more often that this God who sees us is a threat, a limit to our freedom, which does not allow us to be ourselves. Therefore, we hide from this look, we eliminate this look.

On the contrary, the look of God's love is the only thing that makes our life precious and beautiful. This look is necessary for our life, because the love of God—who sees us and renews us—is active and makes us alive. Think of Peter at the moment of his fall, when Jesus looks at him and this look touches his heart (see Lk 22:61–62). Yes, it causes great pain, but a good pain, a pain that renews, transforms, and purifies him and makes him good.

In this sense, like Peter, let us pray that the Lord may look upon us kindly and that His look will always renew our life once again. That our look may be touched by His, and thus we may truly become one reality with God. This look of God is not only a gesture; it is creative, it creates newness, it creates adoption. This look is also God's hand, which He places upon us, making us children of God. No longer are we merely creatures; we are members of God's family, we are children of God in God Himself. This, therefore, is the prayer: that God may accomplish this reality in us, that He may help us to be truly touched by His hand and to be truly members of His family, to live in His truth and reality.

Thus the request—the prayer that God may look upon us with love, with kindness, and transform us—becomes a promise: a promise of freedom and inheritance. The text says: "May true freedom and an eternal inheritance be given to us." Being children implies being free and being heirs. This is the essential quality of the son who belongs to the family: he is not a slave, nor a servant, nor a foreigner, but a member of the family, and therefore he is free. In the ancient world, only members of the family were free; the others were servants. And the son is an owner; therefore, he has a right to the inheritance.

Let us pray that the Lord may give us these two realities. First of all, true freedom. True freedom is not doing whatever comes to mind, but that I become conformed to the truth of myself. The truth of myself is my life, and thus truth and freedom are united in me and true freedom is realized. In this life, we are never completely free; we are on a journey toward freedom. Let us pray that the Lord will help us to be on a journey toward this true freedom, in which the truth of our being and our will coincide, and thus we can really, freely live what we are supposed to be.

And then the inheritance. What is this inheritance? In the Old Testament, the inheritance was essentially the Promised Land. The dream of the Israelites is their land, being free on their own land, which is to say, being free owners. But this is only a preliminary condition. The true freedom—which appears in the New Testament—and the true land of our being are God. God Himself is our inheritance: to be united with God thus means to find oneself in the fullness of being, of happiness.

Let us pray that the Lord will help us to walk toward this true inheritance, that He will be our lasting joy, our true life! Amen!

Faith in the Heart and Testimony on the Lips

May 25, 2014
Private Chapel, Mater Ecclesiae Monastery

Sixth Sunday of Easter (Year A)
Readings: Acts 8:5–8, 14–17; Ps 66; 1 Pet 3:15–18; Jn 14:15–21

As he did last Sunday, so today Saint Peter speaks with us, as he had spoken in the newborn Church, to build up the Church, to call us to Christ and to unite us in His body. Saint Peter speaks about faith with an approach similar to the one used by Saint Paul in the Letter to the Romans, which speaks about the psychological disposition of faith in a human being. Saint Paul says: "Believe in your heart that Jesus Christ is risen and confess with your lips that He is Lord" (see Rom 10:9–10): heart and lips. He distinguishes two aspects, so to speak, in faith. First of all man's interiority, where man truly touches God, because faith is an altogether personal thing, where we live with a name that no one knows except Him. Faith, however, while it is the intimacy of my being with God, creates a relation also: God introduces me to a new universal communion. Lips and heart express these two aspects of faith.

In today's reading, Saint Peter speaks first about the "heart" as the seat of faith. Citing Isaiah 8:12–13, he says,

"We must keep holy in our heart the presence of Christ." What does this mean? Recall that in the ancient philosophy of medicine there were two schools: one said that the seat of human life was the brain, the other said that it was the heart. The Fathers of the Church—naturally the Sacred Authors, too—did not enter into this controversy; nevertheless, in order to indicate what is ultimately the center of man they used the word "heart".

Clearly: faith is not only a matter of reason; it goes beyond reason. It is not only a sentimental, emotional matter; it is not only a matter of the will, and "heart" means the central unity of a human being, where reason, sentiment, and will are found, where flesh and spirit are joined and form a unity; this is the distinctive feature of man in the world, and, even more, it is what differentiates him from the pure spirits. The animals have no spirit; in man, the two worlds meet, and the distinctive feature of man is this "heart", that is, the interpenetration of matter and spirit, the interpenetration of the various forces of his being.

Faith is achieved only in man's unity between matter and spirit, between heart and sentiment and reason; only in this way do we encounter God. And we can say that faith creates this unity of man, this distinctive feature of the human creature, whereby spirit bears matter, flesh within itself, and thus is renewed and extended, and, on the other hand, matter becomes an instrument of the spirit, which is united to the body. We should add: Christ is man and God and, therefore, extends this unity of creation to the heart of God and, in precisely this way, as the One who unites all parts of creation with God Himself, enters into us to unite *us*, to create the unity of the human being, where matter and spirit, sentiment and reason, everything is united, is integrated into communion with Him who is the Lord of the world.

Let us pray to the Lord to grant that we may believe with our heart in this way, that is, that our faith may be the place of the unity of the human being and the place of the unity of being, of creation, with God. And finally it says: "You must keep Christ holy in your heart", that is, it is necessary to defend the desire in us and not let it be destroyed, "to keep it holy" as we keep a great treasure holy: Christ in us.

But then there is the second aspect: faith is communicative. The ancients used to say that "good tends to diffuse itself." In reality, if a person has found something of great beauty, a great love, a great truth, he cannot keep it to himself; he must communicate it; he feels the interior need to distribute the joy of the truth and to make the joy of the love present to others. Therefore, testimony is not something external to the faith, something added on in order to gain greater power for the Church, but rather it follows from the very essence of faith, which bears within it this necessity of diffusing itself, of communicating itself.

Thus we see two forms of testimony. First of all, testimony with our very life. Our life, our being must talk about our faith and must verify it, so to speak. Saint Peter in his Letter speaks about this a lot, about the suffering and the righteousness of Christians who suffer, but for the good and without doing evil. In reality, among the reasons why Christianity was victorious in the great encounter of the religions in antiquity, instead of being defeated, it seems to me that a very important one is precisely this: the testimony of their life.

In a world where corruption was normal, where violence was normal, where immorality was normal, in a world that no longer had a common commitment to the good, Christians lived without saying much, with righteousness, with integrity, with a good heart and with kindness; they suffered, but they did not do evil. A life like this was such a radical and obvious sign that it was convincing: a faith that creates this way of living must be true.

In reality, I would say, life lived in this way cannot be explained in terms of purely human forces but really proves that God is the One who gives this life. Thus, in my opinion, the testimony of Christian life is decisive for the victory of Christianity, in the future, too. All the other pastoral themes are necessary, but unless there is the testimony of life, this integrity, this righteousness, this goodness, we are not convincing, whereas if this testimony is present, then the Christian faith convinces and is victorious even today. Therefore, it is so important for us to let ourselves be guided by the Spirit of God and to seek to live what we believe, to live while "keeping Jesus holy" in our hearts.

This testimony of life is not only possible but necessary for everyone, yet we must add to it also the testimony on our lips. Saint Peter says: "You must always be ready to answer whoever asks you the reason for the hope that is in you" (1 Pet 3:15). In the Middle Ages, the great theologians considered this saying to be the very foundation of theology: not only the justification of it but the expression of the necessity of theology for faith: "You must be able to give the reason for your faith."

In reality, theology, that is, reflection in order to know the reason for the faith and thus to communicate it, is part of Christianity. If the faith is destined to belong to everyone, it must be comprehensible in its foundation; therefore, the essence of the faith must be communicable; thus it is evident that we must elaborate the reason for the faith so as to be able to communicate it to others. But this is not only the theologians' concern. Each one of us must have a faith that he lives out in a simple way, with feeling and practice, a faith that also is reasonable, that includes within it the integrity of the human being—reason, sentiment, and will—in communion with God. Therefore, catechesis is so important, even for simple persons, in order to understand better why we believe and to express it, not with major systems, but with simple reasoning, which justifies our belief and our Christian life. Let us pray to the Lord, therefore, that we may be able to integrate more and more all the dimensions of our faith, so as to be able to give an answer when asked why we believe and to give a reason for our faith.

I would like to touch on two more points from this very rich Letter.

Saint Peter says that we must do this with gentleness and respect. Gentleness, in other words, never being violent. The Christian view does not impose but proposes—Paul VI used to say. In other words, it invites but does not make use of publicity tricks, because we do not want to win persons over to some interest, but rather to open their hearts to Christ. Gentleness and kindness are essential for the Christian faith. And with "respect", the Italian text says; but the Greek text says *phobos*, with "fear". But this is not fear of men, which would be contrary to Christian testimony; it is fear of God, in the sense that we must really transmit what we have received from God; only this, but in its totality.

This means that we must be afraid of simplifying or scaling down the Gospel in order to be accepted. This is a great danger today: that we make a Christianity to please others, a Christianity that hurts no one, that causes no suffering. That is wrong! We must present the faith in its totality; only in this way is it true, only in this way does it give life. To me it seems important to avoid human respect, the fear of men that would cause us not to transmit the whole truth, faith in its totality and integrity.

The other point is that when Saint Peter speaks about giving a reason for the faith, he says: "the reason for your hope"; for him, faith is at the same time hope, essentially hope, and in precisely this way it is justified. While reflecting on this, I recalled a drug rehabilitation center that I visited in Brazil, and the testimonies that the young men gave after being cured and leaving the hell of drug abuse.[1] The essential thing that they said was always this: Now we can once again believe that it is good to be human beings; in the night of drug abuse, we had lost that confidence; we had lost the meaning of life, because we were in darkness.

Faith is hope in the sense that it gives us the certainty that it is good to live because there is a God, because we are loved, because the ultimate power is goodness, and we can have confidence in this ultimate power. We are sure that it is good to live even in difficult situations, because we know that God is good and stronger than all evils. This is the hope that justifies faith and is the foundation of our certainty.

Finally, Saint Peter says that we must be guided by the Lord. But—he says—the Lord suffered, set out on His path of suffering in order to lead us back to God—in Greek, *prosagōgein*, to guide us to God. We all know that our strength is not sufficient for this journey to God. Human strength is not sufficient for this height; we cannot arrive there alone, the path is too steep, too high: we need to be guided, if not hauled, by Him.

We see how there are different ways of being guided—an electric trolley, a walking stick, a hand—and thus, in different ways, we all need someone to give us a hand so as to be able to go where we should go and to arrive at God.

Let us pray to the Lord that He will guide us, each one in his way: that He will give us His hand to guide us

[1] Address at the Fazenda da Esperança, Guaratinguetá, Brazil, May 12, 2007.

along the path, to help us to go forward until we reach the height of God, the height of love and of happiness.

We know that in these days the pope is in the Holy Land in difficult situations; the successor of Peter is speaking to the world to bring the light of Christ. Let us pray, accompanying him with prayer, that the Lord may give strength and light to the pope so he can really give Christ once again in those lands. Amen!

Bearing Fruit: The Gift of Wine

May 10, 2015
Private Chapel, Mater Ecclesiae Monastery

Sixth Sunday of Easter (Year B)
Readings: Acts 10:25–27, 34–35, 44–48; Ps 98;
1 Jn 4:7–10; Jn 15:9–17

Today's Gospel is the continuation and application of the parable of the vine, which was read last Sunday. Last Sunday we already contemplated a key word of this parable: "remain". There is another dominant word in the Gospel for today: "fruit". Then there are others, too: love, friendship, joy; but in this meditation we intend to dwell on the word "fruit".

The vineyard, the vine is created to bear fruit, wine as a gift of festivity, joy, and love. Bread is the everyday reality on which man lives; wine, on the other hand, expresses festivity, joy. God, therefore, created the vine, also, to offer the sign of joy and festivity. Now, we must be branches on Christ's vine and bear fruit. The Gospel says: "Fruit that remains". The question is therefore: What is this fruit? What does it consist of?

To find the answer, we must, as always, go to the Old Testament, because the image starts already in it, the parable of the vine (see Is 5:1–2). There God says that He Himself planted a vine in the ground, so as to have wine from it, the gift of wine that is the wedding between God and man, and that this vine planted by the Lord in the ground was Israel, the people of God. He says also that He not only planted it but also protected, watched, and loved His vine, so that it might really produce this wine.

What is the wine supposed to be? The prophet Isaiah says: "Justice" (see Is 5:7), that is, life that is nourished by the Word of God, life that draws from the living waters of the Torah and, knowing God's will, becomes itself similar to God, becomes just. Think of Psalm 1; think of Joseph, the just man (see Mt 1:19), the man who really is rooted in the word of God, lives the Torah, and thus becomes the man that God designed him to be. The wine would then be justice.

But, look, God is betrayed, and the vine does not produce the wine of justice; instead, it bears bitter grapes, which in the end only become vinegar. We say that the culminating point in which this is manifested is Jesus on the Cross, where the gift that is given to Him is vinegar. Here we see that all the fruit borne by this vine was vinegar, unacceptable to God, an expression, not of festivity and joy, but of sadness and hatred. And we understand that this turn of events still continues; we are acquainted also with a bitter religiosity, a heart of vinegar; we also know Christians who go to church, but theirs is a sour Christianity; it is vinegar, and not the wine of joy.

God, though, does not give up; He finds a new way to arrive at the gift of wine. God personally—and this is the incredible thing—plants Himself in the ground, is made man. God Himself becomes man in Christ, plants Himself and becomes a vine, and we can be branches of this vine and, thus, with Him, bear fruit in Him. Here we see continuity and renewal: now, too, the fruit is supposed to be wine, but it is no longer called "justice"; it is called "love", love as the real nucleus, the essence of the Law. The whole Law, the Lord says, is summed up in this commandment: "Love God, love your neighbor."

The fruit that God expects is our love, and this comes from communion with Christ. Constant reading of the Law is no longer what makes man gradually understand the way. No: the Law is a person, Jesus, and He is the Word of God. Now to study and live the Law is to live with Christ, to know Christ, to be united with Him in a true friendship. This is the great simplification and, at the same time, the greater way. The Law is not made up of words; it is Christ. Christian life therefore consists of remaining in Christ, in the encounter with Christ, and, therefore, of being conformed and united with Christ. In this sense, we can bear fruit and be grapes that become true wine.

At this point an anecdote comes to mind; perhaps it is not altogether pertinent, but it will help you to understand what I mean to say. A professor friend of mine, at the end of his autobiography, speaking to his daughters, said that he wanted to point out to them one characteristic of their mom and one of their dad. He wrote that Mom had the intention of getting to heaven, to be with God, while Dad wanted to go down in history. He also gave an evaluation of this distinction between Mom and Dad—heaven for Mom, history for Dad. In order to go down in history, he had to make a monument of himself and write books that would still be read even after five hundred years; while Mom wanted to live for heaven, for God, for others. Thus he made something that remains for centuries, yes, but a dead thing; while she did God's will, lived for Christ, and thus bore the fruit of love.

But we must take a further step: the wine. In the Gospel of John, chapter 6, Jesus had spoken at length about bread: the true bread, the true manna that gives life to mankind, that nourishes man is Christ Himself, God who became man. But in chapter 2, He had already spoken about wine: at the wedding feast in Cana he had spoken about "His hour"; He had anticipated His hour and had spoken about the best wine, the abundant wine. Now here, in today's Gospel, which is in many ways connected with the one about Cana, Jesus returns to this: the wine is His blood. The true wine, the fruit of the vine is the blood of Christ, the Eucharistic gift. Here we really have the wedding between man and God: He gives Himself; the wine is the gift of Himself, total love, which thus creates unity, creates the wedding, creates the joy of life.

In this sense, the parable of the vineyard is also a Eucharistic parable, and it tells us that the great fruit matures in communion with Christ, on the Cross, in the act of self-giving: a gift that finally creates joy, because love is joy, and he who lives in love lives in joy. But the great joy springs from the Cross, and Jesus gives it in the Eucharistic wine, giving Himself, so that we might enter into His movement leading to the Cross and the Resurrection.

Let us thank the Lord, because He became a vine, He became wine in the gift of Himself, and thus we are not only His creatures, but His friends, united to Him in love, in friendship, in the Cross.

Let us pray to the Lord: "Help us to enter into this communion." Let us give thanks for the great gift of the Eucharist, for the gift of His wine, and let us pray that our lives may bear fruit, so that they produce the true and good wine, the wine of God's love and joy. Amen!

The City of God with Mankind

May 5, 2013
Private Chapel, Mater Ecclesiae Monastery

Sixth Sunday of Easter (Year C)
Readings: Acts 15:1–2, 22–29; Rev 21:10–14, 22–23; Jn 14:23–9

The passage from the Book of Revelation, the second reading for this Sunday, shows us the destination of history, the end for which it was created and which it awaits: God becomes our fellow citizen, and we become fellow citizens of God. It is the city of God, and, precisely thereby, it is also the truly human city: only where man has arrived in communion with God does he become completely himself.

The Letter to the Hebrews tells us that believers have journeyed from the start, until the present day, and that all times are on a journey toward this city: to live is to journey, and faith is journeying toward this city (see Heb 11:14–16). It says that the saints and believers have understood that no city in this world is the destination and the true homeland. The true homeland is beyond. If that were not so, if the cities in this world were the destination, the whole journey would be merely a journey toward death.

But human life, according to God's plan, is not a journey to death, but rather a journey to life. Therefore it transcends all these earthly cities; it goes beyond these cities and becomes a journey toward the true city. The light of God in our temporary cities transcends them, yet it intends to illuminate the city of man also. All our cities are temporary, and therefore we must go to the true city, but allow our cities also to be formed by this city. Even the Church, the city of God, is not yet the definitive city. Certainly, God dwells with us, but still under the veil of the sacraments, and therefore we see that the Church still has a temporary tent, even though she already bears within her the dimensions of the new city, and these indicate also the criteria for the life of the Church.

What does the Book of Revelation tell us, today, about these dimensions of the city? I would say three elements.

The first element is this: it is a city that has walls and gates. It has a wall; in other words, it is connected together like a house; it protects us and gathers us together in communion. This city is not an indefinite reality; the Lord says that it has a definite identity, and ultimately I would say that this identity is the truth. The truth is at the same time a wall and a gate; it defines and separates between truth and falsehood, between love and hatred; thus it is a wall, which defends the citizens against falsehood, against hatred, but it also defines, in the sense of the whole richness of the truth. I thought also that this truth—which ultimately is our city—is the Incarnate Word, with the flesh that is the living Body of Christ, and this Body is a wall and a gate at the same time. Hence the city has walls, but it also has twelve gates: it is a city that gathers together, but it is an open city. In reality, the truth is precisely the thing that is open and opens. In history we see these gates: many cultures of the world have entered into the Church, many worldly realities form the Body of Christ. Many realities enter, but many also go out: how much wealth has gone out of the Church into the world and has transformed the world! It is an open city and at the same time a city that protects and gathers together.

The second element: this city has foundations, and the foundations are the Apostles. The Apostles are not something from the past, two thousand years ago, but are present; they are the perennial foundation that supports the city. But how are they present? After the end of the apostolic era, the Church had to ask herself this question: How do the Apostles remain present? How can this definition, this reality of the Church be preserved, that she is alive and open and nevertheless also firm in her continuity, in the unity of the truth?

In those days there was a great temptation, the so-called "gnosis", whereby everything was dissolved into thoughts, to ideas in a certain philosophy relative to the cultures. The Church wanted to look for a way to find walls and gates, to preserve the presence of the Apostles as a living presence. She found three criteria that define the structure of the Church, that are, so to speak, the presence of the foundation that lasts in the structure of the Church.

The first criterion is the "canon" of Scripture, the Word of God: it defined which writings belong to the Word of God and which are only human. Thus it created this canon, in which we encounter the living Word of God. A twofold relation appears here. On the one hand, it is the Church that forms Scripture: without the Church there is no Scripture, but only an ancient literature, like other literatures. Only the Church finds the culture of God, encounters it as a Word of God; hence Scripture, as Scripture, lives and is Scripture only in the living Church. On the other hand, this Scripture, acknowledged as the Word of God, is the standard that the Church obeys. Both elements are important: the Word of God is our standard, the criterion of the Church, the criterion of Christian existence; but at the same time, Scripture lives only in the communion of the Church, of the Body of Christ; otherwise it perishes amid world literatures.

The second criterion for defining this mutual relation is that the Church draws life from the witnesses, from the successors of the Apostles. The Apostles remain present in their successors in the episcopate. The bishop is a witness: on the one hand, he is a guarantor of the objective Sacred Scripture, so that it really remains a living voice; on the other hand, he is subject to this Word. This is the importance of the episcopal office: to preserve this relation with Scripture, so that it remains Scripture, our standard, and it does this only in the living communion of the Church. This seems to me a good opportunity to pray for the bishops, that they may really be guardians, a presence of the Apostles, their successors, and thus be their true presence. An opportunity to pray that the Lord might help us to find at all times which are the true pastors, the true witnesses, the successors of the Apostles.

And finally a third criterion: the Creed. In the Creed, the Church found the summary of Scripture and tells us the essential content of Scripture. This is therefore also the gate through which to enter into Scripture, if I seek—as Scripture itself says—to find this gate. Thus, the eyes of faith are the eyes that make us see the Word of God. Only the eyes of God, the eyes of faith, can truly see the presence of the Word of God. Let us pray to the Lord that the Creed might form us, transform us, and help us to enter ever more deeply into the Word of God.

Finally, this city is the city of God; here we are certain that God dwells with men. To dwell with the divinity has always been the desire of mankind. All cities were built so that man could cohabit with God, be in communion with God, a fellow citizen of God. But we cannot draw

God in; God is the one who must come to meet us, and He achieves this in the new city that comes down from on high. Thus we become fellow inhabitants with God in His own city.

I said that the Church is an initial anticipation of this city in which God really dwells with us, although under the veil of the sacrament. Nevertheless, God is with us in this way, and we walk toward the city where God is openly sun and light and the center of our life. Let us learn to love this presence of His and to find cohabitation with God; to see in the Church, in the bodily presence of Christ, the presence of God Himself: in this way, let us be on a journey toward the true city, and let us prepare the true city that comes from on high.

A city built by us alone becomes a city without true humanity: only if God builds the house do the builders not labor in vain (compare Ps 127:1). Let us give thanks to God because He gave us His veiled presence; let us love this presence of His, and thus let us be on a journey toward the definitive city, in the joy of being fellow citizens of God. Amen!

The Church Awaiting the Spirit

May 17, 2015
Private Chapel, Mater Ecclesiae Monastery

Seventh Sunday of Easter (Year B)
Readings: Acts 1:15–17, 20–26; Ps 103;
1 Jn 4:11–16; Jn 17:11b–19

The nine days between the Ascension of the Lord into heaven and Pentecost were, and in a certain sense still are, days of waiting for the gift of the Holy Spirit, for the birth of His Church. The Apostles, returning from the Mount of Olives, knew very well that the hour of their mission had come, but they knew also that by themselves they could not make the Church. The Church, the community of the Gospel, is not a thing that can be made; she is a living thing, and living things are born, they are not made. Moreover not only is the Church a living thing, but she is vital through the Holy Spirit: in other words, in the Church, ultimately, the subject is God Himself, and therefore only He can create her.

Then what must the Apostles do? They know that now they cannot sit down and make a constituent assembly to develop a system by which they could create the Church; they know that they cannot develop a strategy for proclaiming the Kingdom to the world, because this goes beyond human capabilities. But they know also that they cannot simply wait, that their expectation must be an active waiting. Therefore what do they do? Several things.

The first, Saint Luke says, is to go to the upper room, to the room where the Lord celebrated the Last Supper with them. They go to the upper room: there is also symbolism here, because it reminds us that Jesus prayed on the mountain and that praying is always an ascent on the mountain, a departure from everyday routine, a departure from common things, an elevation of bodies and hearts. The Apostles know it, and thus they ascend to the upper room, they leave everyday things behind, and go out before the face of God, to accept and to receive spirit and life from Him.

This ascent to the upper room is important in order to lift up one's heart, but it is also important because it is precisely where the Lord celebrated the Last Supper with them: it is going into communion with the Lord, going to the place where He is and gives Himself to us. If we want the Church to be born, we must also do this once again, take the first step and go toward the Lord on high, go in the context of His love, which is given in the Eucharistic assembly.

As a second step, the Apostles seek those who want to be with the Lord, and finally they find 120 of them: not only the Twelve are gathered, but also Mary, the brothers of the Lord, and other believers. This already outlines somewhat the multiplicity of the Church, with her wealth of gifts, of spiritual and human resources, in which is reflected the richness of the unity of the new humanity.

Then, finally, the third step. Peter knows that he is responsible, because the Lord charged him to be the shepherd of His flock, and he takes the initiative to complete the college of the Apostles, which is no longer complete after Judas left it: there must be twelve of them. This is not simply a matter of having a sufficient number; but rather, twelve is a symbolic number: if the Lord created the group of the Twelve, it means that Israel is born once again.

Israel was born from the twelve sons of Jacob, and now Jesus, the new Jacob, creates the new Israel, no longer with a carnal origin, but with His word as its source. Twelve who represent the new people: a symbolic gesture in which the Lord expresses that from it comes the true Israel, the universal people of God that is born of the Holy Spirit, born of His word, born of obedience to His word, of the joy of knowing the Risen Lord. This, therefore, is the act that needs to be performed: so that this symbolic reality, which already expresses the whole future, may be restored, so as to give a fresh start to the journey toward universal communion.

But how should this be done? How can the work be completed? It is interesting to note the cooperation between Peter, who takes the initiative, the whole assembly, which is also involved, and finally God Himself, who must decide. And He decides through a lottery! We see that in this election our discernment is surely important, that is, that we do all that we can to seek, to awaken vocations, to help, accompany, and discern. Our initiative, our cooperation, our discernment is fundamental. Nevertheless, ultimately, the decision is the Lord's. In this cooperation, between our attentiveness and the gesture made by the Lord, the vocation is born. We must always pray to the Lord once again to show, both to the persons concerned and to us, what His will is, and in this way is born, again and again, the mission of the Apostle, the witness to Jesus.

Another important thing is the requirement for an Apostle, for one of the Twelve. It is expected that he knew Jesus from John's Baptism until the Resurrection, hence he knows the person, the teaching, the words, the life of Jesus and, above all, is a witness to the Resurrection. This always remains decisive for witnesses to Jesus: knowing

Jesus and how Jesus lived on this earth, but above all the risen Jesus who speaks today.

This is the same criterion that Jesus Himself had expressed when, as Saint Mark relates, "He appointed twelve to be with Him, and to be sent out" (see Mk 3:14–15). Those who are with Him, and thus grow in the divine life, at the same time are sent; being with Him and being sent go together. Let us pray to the Lord today also, in our time: "Lord, help us, awaken men, accompany persons; show Yourself, help us to be with You and thus to be on a journey with the people to show Your presence." In summary we can say that Saint Peter does two things: on the one hand, he takes the initiative, he is active, he decides, and, on the other hand, he is obedient, because God acts. This is always the model for the Church's action: our initiative and activity, but above all openness to God's will, to the Word of God, so that ultimately God creates, and we do not.

It is interesting to reflect that at this moment Saint Peter, with the already existing Universal Church, completed the college of the Twelve. But, not long afterward, the Lord Himself would complete the Apostles again in an unexpected, totally new way with the mission of Saint Paul (see Acts 9). Then the important thing will no longer be the symbolic number twelve, but rather the charism of the vocation, of the mission to the whole world.

And, almost at the same time, there will be another event: the imprisonment of Saint Peter, his death sentence, and his flight, which compel him to leave the Holy Land (see Acts 12) and to go to pagan countries. Thus he must take responsibility for Churches that come from paganism, for Christians who come from the Jews, and to be truly the universal pastor for the whole Church. Then we can go even farther, when the charism of John comes to light as a third element, and thus we see the rich and profound panorama of the Church developing through the Lord's activity.

But now, I would like to take a look also at the Letter of Saint John. Last Sunday we read a very beautiful verse: "If our hearts condemn us, God is greater than our hearts" (see 1 Jn 3:20). Today, too, we find in this Letter a grand verse, one of the most beautiful verses in Scripture, I would say of world literature. It says: "We have known and believed in love, God is love." Here the essence of Christianity truly appears. We know that the essence of Christianity is not a philosophical system, a system of thought, it is not a program about how to do something, it is not a moral system, but it is a person, Jesus, and the encounter with this person. Here, the same thing is expressed in an even more profound way: this person is love, and we have known love and believed in love.

We have known: because in the Incarnation, in the Cross, we see what love is. Love is this radical gift in which God alone can give Himself to the point of being lost in the night of death, in the night of hell. God really gives Himself and thus exercises His power and thus can transform the world. We have known love!

Second act: we have believed in love. In other words, we have not only known but also believed; we are convinced that this love is the heavenly power, that it is stronger than all other powers, capable of redeeming the world with all its sorrows and its dark nights.

And, third point, God is love. Thus, we see all Christianity from the perspective of this beauty of having known love. Seeing how God acts and believing, we entrust ourselves to this love, and in this way we can live; in this way we are redeemed.

"Lord, thank You for having shown Yourself in Your love. We pray You, help us to believe, to live by Your love, to be witnesses to Your love, which gives us true gladness, the gladness of true love." Amen!

"Come, Lord!"

May 12, 2013
Private Chapel, Mater Ecclesiae Monastery

Seventh Sunday of Easter (Year C)
Readings: Acts 7:55–60; Rev 22:12–14, 16–17, 20; Jn 17:20–26

In the second reading, we heard the conclusion of the Book of Revelation, in which John summarizes once again the essential theme of his message and, at the end, concentrates it into a single word: "Come!" But, even before that, he shows us, once again, the figure of Christ and the figure of redeemed man. Let us try to understand a little of what he says. Christ is characterized with three predicates: Alpha and Omega (first and last); root of David; bright morning star.

Alpha and Omega: Christ is the beginning of God's whole creative Word (see Jn 1:1–3; Col 1:15–17). He is the concept of the world that is reflected in God and that created the world. He is the beginning of everything, He is hidden in all realities, which come from Him: He is the creative word. But Christ is not only the beginning and the first, He is also the last. Today many people say: "Christianity is a thing of the past, and Christ is a figure from the past." In reality, the figure of the historical Christ, which some reconstruct, actually encloses Him in the past: He is not a living, present man, but someone from the past. They say: "The time of Christianity passes; others are decisive now."

But He is the Living Lord, the Risen One; He is not only the first; He is always present and will also be the last. All other things pass. If we look at the history of the last two thousand years, we see how many things pass away, and many things have passed away, but Christ always appears anew and at the same time as the Last, as the One who is always decisive. Standing with Christ, we are on the right side, because we know that not only are the first and the beginning in Him, but at the end He is the one who decides and concludes. To be with Christ: only in this way are we at the root and at the destination.

A second characteristic of Christ: root of David. Here we marvel, because one could say: not the root, but the fruit; not the root, but the son of David. But I think that Saint John deliberately wrote "root", because he meant that in Christ appears the original concept of David, which is realized only imperfectly in the figure of David. The true origin, the idea that God had of David, is realized in Him. He is the true David: He is the "root of David".

It seems to me, however, that we should see in what respect David announces Christ. It is not easy to make it out, because David, as we see in the Books of Kings, is not altogether attractive. Nevertheless, we must seek the decisive factor in this man, where the One who is the root and the end appears.

We see an initial aspect, it seems to me, when Samuel anoints David king: he is still a boy, the youngest of the family, who is pasturing his father's sheep (see 1 Sam 16:1–13). No one ever thought that he could become king of Israel, much less become the bearer of God's promises. David comes from a simple life; now simplicity, the simple life, a simple heart are fundamental for faith in Christ, for the figure of Christ Himself, who was born in a stable in

Bethlehem, was born of a simple Virgin, had a carpenter as His protector, and was Himself born as a carpenter.

Simplicity: Jesus Christ Himself called the simple blessed; only the simple of heart can understand revelation. In all the circumstances of life, we must preserve a simple heart and also a simple life. This seems to me to be a point that Pope Francis quite correctly emphasizes: not losing simplicity and thus being open to those who are simple and to the great truth of God.

A second aspect of David: for a long time in his life he was exiled, excluded from the land of the promises, excluded from the promises of Israel; he was persecuted, and thus he announced the mystery of the Cross (see 1 Sam 20–30). This problem of persecution and exclusion is always part of Christianity, because it must always be in communion with Christ crucified.

It seems to me that we must pray a lot for the persecuted Church, for the persons who suffer under the pressure of intolerance, pray that the Lord may protect them, in their faith and in their life. We must be spiritually close to the persecuted Church of today. And here is also a subtler persecution, namely, the cultural and intellectual marginalization of Christianity, the creation of an anti-Christian culture, which oppresses Christianity spiritually. It seems absurd today, still to be a Christian. In the name of freedom, the freedom to believe is oppressed; homosexual marriage is proclaimed in the name of freedom, abortion as a libertarian right, based on a false freedom that is opposed to the freedom of our faith; so much so that it appears almost absurd to be a Christian still in this world. It is a spiritual persecution: we must be open to the Lord so that He may guide and keep us, and we must also help the little ones, so that in this context they can remain faithful.

There is also a third aspect. David created the city of God: he conquered Jerusalem and transformed it into the seat of Israel's worship, into a city of God (see 2 Sam 5–7). In reading the Books of Kings,[1] we ask ourselves: "Why is David the chosen one of God? How can he be the exemplary king? He was an adulterer, a bloody man, who also killed persons and committed many other crimes...." What remains in him, nevertheless, as a positive element, which makes him the bearer of the promises? I think that it is precisely this: that for him God was always the central reality. Even though he did not succeed in living according to God's will, he always maintained a great reverence for God or submitted to God. Even though he did not always live accordingly, he understood the centrality of God and expressed it in the construction of the sacred tent in the city of Jerusalem. He was not the builder of the temple, but of the tent of the Ark, and thus of Jerusalem as God's seat, where above all God lives, and we with Him.

It seems to me that these two things are still important for us: the centrality of God—acknowledging God as the point of reference of our life, not losing sight of God as Creator, as Redeemer, as Judge—and creating space for God. David created this space for God in the city of Jerusalem, in such a way that Jerusalem became the image of the future. Creating space for God in our time, having a space for God on our earth, having a space for God. Let us pray to the Lord that this centrality of God may be ever stronger in us and may be ever more realistic; so that adoration of God becomes more and more the center of our life; so that God may have space in our time, where He is obscured and seems to disappear. Jesus Christ is precisely that God-with-us, totally in unity with the Father and, in precisely this way, the seat of the Father's presence.

[1] The stories about David are related in the Books of Samuel (1 and 2), which in the Vulgate Latin edition are called the Books of Kings (1 and 2).

Finally, the third characteristic of Christ: the morning star, the bright star of morning. This means that Christ announces the day; the night is not permanent. The day comes and orients us, shows us where to go. Therefore, He is the star of hope, He announces to us the day, announces to us that there is hope, that there is a God, that God is hope.

Again, briefly, a word about the figure of redeemed man. He washes himself; the redeemed wash their garments with Christ, they have access to the tree of life, they have access to the Holy City. Washing their garments with Christ means accepting the purifications of the Lord, purifications through the truth, through charity, the purifications in the sacraments. Having access to, having a share in the tree of life, the tree of the Cross: having a share in the tree of life means that life is something to be given, not to have for oneself alone. We need to observe the great freedom of Christ: he who wants to have life loses it; only he who gives life finds it. And finally, access to the Holy City: let us give thanks to God that we have access to the communion of saints in His Holy Church, and let us truly live this communion of the Holy Church with gratitude and joy.

At the end, there is the word: "Come!", which sums up the whole essence of Christianity, the whole message of the Book. In reality, the whole liturgy of the Church is walking toward Christ; it is a single cry: "Come!" And the whole Christian life is walking toward Christ, and crying "Come!"

We do not pray that the end of the world will come, but we pray that Christ may come into the world; that He may come into me, into the situations in which I am needy: "Come, Lord! Many times we truly and personally need You to make us feel Your presence. And come in this period of world history, as You will: may Your presence be strong, stronger than the negative things! Come, Lord!" Amen!

The Mystery of the Holy Spirit

June 8, 2014
Private Chapel, Mater Ecclesiae Monastery

Pentecost Sunday (Year A)
Readings: Acts 2:1–11; Ps 104; 1 Cor 12:3–7, 12–13; Jn 20:19–23

Each of the three readings of this Pentecost liturgy brings to light an essential aspect of the mystery of the Holy Spirit. I would like to point out briefly these three elements, which appear in today's liturgy.

In the Acts of the Apostles, there is this wonderful narration of how the Church is born. She is born in the sense that they all speak in all languages and everyone hears the Apostles speaking in his own language. The Church is born Catholic; from the first moment, she is a universal Church. It is not that first a local Church is born and then the others, and then a confederation is made. No, first there is the universal Church, which speaks in all languages; she is immediately catholic, and then she is communicated to others and creates particular Churches, and all of them are expressions of the one Church.

The Holy Spirit creates understanding, opens up boundaries, gives peace, unity, and charity and thus unites. Behind this event, we hear the echo of another story, that of the Tower of Babel (see Gen 11:1–9), which recounts that mankind had been united at the center of the world, had acquired incredible power, and felt that it was capable of building a tower to reach heaven. They no longer needed a divinity, because they themselves, mankind, could create access to heaven for themselves; they were capable of making their own god, of doing everything; they could do it all. But precisely in that moment of extreme power, they became disunited, one man no longer understood the other, one was against the other, and thus the tower was not built, it was not completed.

This seems to me an image of our situation. Man has really acquired impressive power: we can make a human being, we can destroy mankind, we can build the world, we can do everything, we do not need God, we ourselves can create our heaven. And, precisely at this moment of extreme human power, the more superfluous God appears, the more conflicts arise among all human beings: violence, war, destruction. Where there is the spirit of pride, so the Gospel tells us, true humanity does not grow. Apparently man can do everything, but he cannot do the essential thing: love, know the truth, live in unity with others, and thus live in a world of love and truth.

Pride, human power, and science do not build the gate to heaven, but God Himself does; in His humility, He gives Himself to us. Even today the unity of mankind grows precisely through the humility of faith, which creates islands of peace, islands of charity in an ocean of violence, of human and spiritual poverty. Thus the Gospel invites us truly to put aside pride, to become open to the gift of the Holy Spirit, to live by faith in Christ, to live our catholicity and thus to live by the unity of God, who creates the unity of mankind. As a Catholic, each one of us speaks in all languages, because we belong to the Church that speaks in all languages and is a force of love and of reconciliation beyond all boundaries.

We come to the second reading. In the story from the Acts of the Apostles, we heard also that the Holy Spirit comes under these two aspects: wind and fire. The fire, a force of the transformation and renewal of the world, appears in a very particular way, under the form of tongues, and everyone receives one of them; that is, this fire of the Holy Spirit is not a shapeless force that becomes destructive, but rather a personal force, in which each person receives a tongue of fire.

In his Letter to the Corinthians, Saint Paul tells us what this tongue of fire consists of. The answer is very surprising, perhaps very disappointing, because it does not appear to be a great reality. No, this tongue of fire given to each one of the believers is a word, a word with the force of the true Word, a simple and profound word: "Jesus is Lord." This is the tongue of fire, the tongue of the Holy Spirit, which God gives us at the moment of Pentecost. "Jesus is Lord": this is the fundamental confession of the Church, which builds the Church, by which the Church lives. This simple word is truly a word of fire, because it creates the communion of the Church, places us within the communion of the Church, and thus creates the unity that alone can be born from the lordship of Jesus: that catholic unity that we spoke about is born precisely from the lordship of Jesus.

By believing in and confessing Jesus, we enter into the universal communion of the Church, and this profound unity is created. We must also keep in mind that the word "Lord", in the Old Testament, was an expression signifying God: no one dared to pronounce the mysterious name of God, Yahweh, and instead of God, they simply said "Lord", *Kyrios*. Thus we see the communion between the Old and New Testaments: Jesus is the Lord God, He is this hidden God, Jesus, the Lord, is God! And this very reality, the fact that God is not a "spiritual thing" but is our Lord, changes everything; it gives us the standard of our life, it gives us the strength to live according to this standard, and it really renews us.

And now the third reading. The Gospel tells us how Jesus, on the evening of the day of the Resurrection, with the doors closed, comes among His Apostles. The Holy Spirit knows no doors; He enters even through locked doors. We saw, in this past century, how He entered and was present even in the prisons and entered and was present even in the palaces of ideology. The Holy Spirit enters even through locked doors; this is the good and beautiful news of today's Gospel.

Then Jesus, after greeting His followers, "breathed", the text says, on His Apostles. Here we see a repetition of the morning of the creation of man: Genesis relates that God had formed the shape of man from the dust, but that this figure became a living being thanks to the breath, the breath of God; in this way, dust became a living being. Jesus repeats this gesture of creation at a higher level. Yes! The human lung functions only if there is air to breathe, but man needs more than physical air in order to breathe: the air that man, as man, must breathe is love and truth. And Jesus, who breathes on man, recreates man; it is once again the day of creation, and if only man can breathe the air of the love that comes from God, then his physical life is good, too; only this new creation completes and justifies the first creation.

Jesus creates by breathing the Spirit, and here we see also that the breath of Jesus is the Holy Spirit, and we are close to the Holy Spirit if we are close to the breath of Jesus. This is the important message of this day: we are always close to the breath of Jesus, to Jesus Himself, and only in this way are we precisely in the breeze of the Holy Spirit.

Then the Gospel adds that this breath of Jesus, this new life, is a spirit of forgiveness. Only forgiveness makes us live, only if there is forgiveness can we accept the truth of God's norm, can we accept the truth about sin; if there is no forgiveness, we must deny our guilt, we must deny the norm. Forgiveness gives us life; we exist in the strength of Jesus' forgiveness; this is the breath of Jesus, it is the Holy Spirit. And finally Jesus gives the Apostles and their successors the power to forgive: the sacrament. Through the sacrament, He Himself holds the Church in His hand: we are not the ones to decide "so and so", because in the sacrament He Himself remains the Lord of the Church, He remains present and acts in the midst of humanity. Let us thank the Lord for this gift of His permanent presence, which grants also a permanent Pentecost.

In this Gospel, I particularly like one sentence: "The disciples rejoiced to see the Lord." We can understand that after the scandal of the Cross, the night, the doubts, they see Him and rejoice because of it: to see Him is to rejoice. The true gift of the Lord, the gift of the Holy Spirit is the joy that Jesus exists, that there is a God who knows us and is present with us. The true gift of the Spirit is the joy of the Holy Spirit, it is the joy of being loved and known, that Jesus is not distant, but is close to us. Let us pray to the Lord: "Come, Holy Spirit, give us this joy of seeing Jesus, the joy of being loved and of loving with You." Amen!

Pentecost: Universal Communion, Transforming Love, Purifying Wind

May 27, 2007
Private Chapel, Apostolic Palace

Pentecost Sunday (Year C)
Readings: Acts 2:1–11; Ps 104; Rom 8:8–17;
Jn 14:15–16, 23b–26

In the account from the Acts of the Apostles, the Holy Spirit appears in three forms: one image is taken from salvation history and two are cosmic images.

The image taken from salvation history is represented by the tongues, which are a symbol of the human ability to speak; they are a symbol of speech. By means of speech, man can open his mind; he can create understanding with another, and understanding also means communion. Thus the Holy Spirit appears as this force that opens us and creates communion.

Behind this image there is a reference to the story about the Tower of Babel, in which pride scatters mankind, creates incomprehension, separation, and opposition (Gen 11:1–9); that story shows that man had arrived at the point where he thought that it was possible for him, with his own forces, with the technology of that time, to build a tower that would reach heaven, to create "heaven" by himself, access to heaven.

But precisely this pride of man, who thinks that he no longer needs God and makes a "God" of himself, who raises himself up to be God, this very pride that creates "greatness" at the same time destroys man, creates incomprehension, opposition, destroys mankind and scatters it, as we ourselves see.

This image—in which speaking all languages creates incomprehension because of the diversity, but then also creates unity and communion in the diversity of the languages—reveals that pride in our power or the progress of science cannot do everything; they cannot create a man-God, they cannot give man redemption. Rather, the humility of faith, which opens itself to God, and the gift of love, which is always given, are the real force capable of creating that understanding that becomes communion.

At the same time, in this Pentecost event there is also an anticipation of the Catholic Church. This first apostolic community speaks at that moment ideally all the languages of the earth. It thus expresses the universality created by the Spirit of God, by communion with the divine Spirit, who is the only One capable of creating universal communion. And it tells us: the Spirit is the One who creates communion, who creates universality, who is capable of creating this universal family of God that speaks all languages and nevertheless speaks one language.

This tells us also that not only are love and faith essential, but this love and this faith are forces of unity that create the Universal Church, the Catholic Church; being in the communion of the Church, in the humility of this communion, in the language of the common faith, is a sign of the Holy Spirit. The Holy Spirit creates this community, the Catholic community.

Thus Saint Augustine could correctly say: "One loves the Church to the extent that one has the Holy Spirit."[1] Love for the Church is a fruit and sign of the Holy Spirit. The Holy Spirit does not move generically, but rather has His proper place; He creates the Catholic communion, and therefore Pentecost is always a new invitation to catholicity, to the great communion, to communion with the Church of all peoples and of all times.

Let us turn to the two cosmic images: the fire and the wind or breeze. In the ancient tradition that spoke about the four elements that make up the world—namely, fire, air, earth, and water—fire and air were considered the celestial elements that make up the heavens. Therefore, if fire and wind arrive, it means that heaven has opened, that heaven enters into earth, that the arrival of the Holy Spirit, the Spirit of the Son who comes from the Father, is the entrance of heaven on earth and the embrace of the earth by the heavens.

But let us look more closely at these two elements. First of all, the fire. In the history of civilization, it was always thought that the discovery of fire was the beginning of civilization and culture, because fire is the element capable of transforming reality. Fire makes it possible to transform things and, in precisely this way, to create new realities. With the power of fire, with its transforming power, man could finally change the world, could create his own new world.

Fire is a force for transformation, renewal, and creativity. But fire is also heat and light, and thus it reminds us of the truth, which is light, and of love, which is heat, and makes us understand that the real transforming power—that transforms the world and creates culture in the deepest

[1] Augustine of Hippo, *Commentary on the Gospel of John*, 32.8.8.

sense of the word—is made up of truth and love. But immediately it appears evident also that, while fire transforms, it also burns, that the transition from one state to the other is a painful passage like all renewal, a passage that burns and, only in this way, renews.

Recall that Jesus promises His disciples, after the Baptism of John, the baptism of fire as the real renewing baptism. And, with this promise of the baptism of fire for the disciples of every era, we must connect the fact that the Lord considers His own Passion as a "baptism". His Passion is a baptism; it is the baptism of fire. The fire that transforms man and the world, that creates the Resurrection and the newness of the new life, is His Passion! Jesus was baptized in His Passion, the center of which was not His bodily pains: the nucleus of the Passion is the love that transforms, it is the love that moves Him to give Himself even unto death.

The love of the Son, accomplished in His Passion unto death, is the power of God Himself and of the Holy Spirit, which transforms Christ in the Resurrection and thus opens up for us all the definitive transformation in the newness of life, in the new risen Body of Christ. Because the fire of the Holy Spirit speaks to us about communion with the Passion of Christ. Here the love of God is present; it transforms us and renews us, and precisely in the pain of this transformation, in the pain of the passage with Christ to the new life, heaven really arrives in us, it arrives on earth.

Finally a few words about air: this is the element for breathing, and therefore it is fundamental for our life. Today we speak, rightly, about air pollution, which makes our respiration increasingly unsafe; we have to inhale so many poisons that they endanger our physical life. Everyone speaks anxiously and rightly about this material pollution, but that is not all there is.

There is also, above all, the pollution of our spiritual air. We inhale spiritually so many poisons that destroy our true life, destroy the capacity for truth and love in us. The Holy Spirit is the One who purifies, who cleans the air and makes us breathe the fresh air of divine life. Therefore, we have great need of this purification of the spiritual air, of the miracle of Pentecost; we need the Spirit to come as a strong, purifying wind and to make us once again breathe the true divine air and thus live!

Let us pray that the Lord will purify us, transform us with the fire of His love, that He will purify the air of this world, of our times, and that He will unite us all in His Holy Church. Amen!

Pentecost: The Feast of Catholicity

May 19, 2013
Private Chapel, Mater Ecclesiae Monastery

Pentecost Sunday (Year C)
Readings: Acts 2:1–11; Ps 104; Rom 8:8–17;
Jn 14:15–16, 23b–26

In announcing the Second Vatican Council, Pope John, and with him all of Christendom, hoped for a new Pentecost, in a new strength of the Holy Spirit, a strong presence that would break the barriers of hearts, of structures, and would open them once again to the presence of God, thus creating a new springtime in the Church's faith.

At the latest in the year 1968, we saw that this was not the reality, and that even a council cannot "organize" a Pentecost; we can create the conditions for the coming of the Holy Spirit, but He is the one who gives Himself. Nevertheless, every year, in the ten days between the Ascension and Pentecost, the Church prays that there may be a new Pentecost, that the Spirit may come again to enliven His Church, to transform the Christian community. If we pray this way, if we still await this event, we must also ask ourselves what Pentecost is, what we are really waiting for, and what it consists of.

The reading from the Acts of the Apostles gives us three signs of God, three elements that define somewhat the reality of Pentecost. The first is this strong, driving wind; the second is the flame, the fire, in the form of tongues; the third is languages, the comprehension that opens one person to another in a new unity, a unity in diversity, in fullness. Let us look a little more closely at these three elements.

The first is the strong wind that transforms, renews, changes. It is true that God had manifested Himself in times past in an earthquake, in fire, in a wind that was so tremendous that the people said: "We do not have the strength to bear it" (Ex 20:18–19). It is true that sometimes God visibly shows His power, but God's language is normally different. After hundreds of years, the covenant with Israel that had been created on Sinai seems almost dead, ruined.

In the time of Elijah, he alone had remained as God's servant, against hundreds of priests of Baal. The covenant was destroyed, and so Elijah was called once again to Horeb, to Sinai, for a new beginning of the covenant. God promised him a new beginning, as a return to the beginning, a theophany: a visible, perceptible encounter with God, and he awaited this encounter (see 1 Kings 19:4–15). A driving wind came, but God was not in it; that is not God's language. A devouring fire came, but God was not in it; that is not God's language. Finally, a very gentle, almost silent breeze came, and this is the expression of God's language; here God shows Himself.

Thus we see that God's language is not that of the powers of this world; it is not the language that destroys or builds en masse; God's language is a gentle breeze. The power of God is different from the powers of the world, and thus the true and continual Pentecost is revealed, not in driving winds, but in a very gentle and silent breeze.

If we open our eyes, we see that this Pentecost is present even today. Think of the many Sisters who in Africa, in the midst of the violence, continue to do good, to perform works of charity, to teach, to help life continue; think of the priests, the missionaries, the simple people who continue to do good: in them we see this gentle breeze. Yesterday, these two testimonies[1] showed us the same thing in a different way: a man who truly, like the prodigal son, had utterly fallen, but the Lord found him and lifted him from the dust, renewed him to experience a new joy in the faith, a new strength of witness; and then this minister who knows that he risks martyrdom and deliberately continues to do good, to help the Christians in their faith, in their charity, and in precisely this way he shows the presence of the Holy Spirit.

The gentle breeze, God's true language is present; Pentecost is present; every day there is a new Pentecost, and this feast invites us to be attentive to this language of God, to His presence. It invites us so that we ourselves might become servants of this presence, that we might participate humbly, each according to his mission, in this silent but at the same time strong presence of God, which is the presence that saves.

God's victories are different from the victories of the world. If we expected mass conversions, with violent transformations of the world, these are not God's victories. God's victories are this man who is ready for martyrdom, the humble souls who day by day offer their service to the truth, to charity: this is the presence of God, this is the true, renewed wind of God.

The second sign of Pentecost is fire. But not a devouring, destructive fire; it is a fire in the form of tongues, a reasonable fire, so to speak, a warm fire, a fire that is warmth and

[1] Benedict XVI is referring to the testimonies at the Vigil of Pentecost, celebrated in Saint Peter's Square with Pope Francis.

light. The Acts of the Apostles tell us a second thing, too, besides the form of tongues, and this is that the fire comes down on each one of them, in other words, that this fire is personal; the fire of the Spirit is not a collective thing that creates destruction or something else, but rather is personal; God is personal and speaks to persons. Fire in the form of tongues means at the same time charity, in other words, love and truth.

At the same time, this is what characterizes the *Logos*. Saint John tells us that the word "reason" is creative, but this creative reason, this *Logos* is at the same time charity, love. We could also say that in the beginning is love, because in theory the two realities—creative reason and creative love—are only one thing. These flames in the form of tongues are precisely the expression of this reality, which signals the beginning of the world: this unity, and identity, of creative reason and charity is the life of the world. Let us, too, think about this reality; let us pray to God that this fire may revive in us, too, day by day.

And finally the languages. This is the sign contrary to Babel (see Gen 11:1–9). In Babel the arrogance of power, the arrogance of creating a tower to reach heaven so that man could make himself God, disrupts unity; everyone is alone by himself; no one understands the other anymore. The confusion of tongues in Babel is an expression of the arrogance in which egotism rules, in which each person becomes divided from the others, in which men are separated, do not understand each other, do not stand together, but are one against the other.

Pentecost is the comprehension of everything; it overcomes this separation. It tells us: the new Jerusalem is against Babel; it is born from God's love; it is born from the faith that offers and opens itself to God's love; thus, one understands the other, thus in diversity unity is created, true catholicity, into which all cultures enter, all temperaments, all charisms, yet all in their diversity form the unity of Christ's love, the unity of the Body of Christ.

In other words, from her first moment, the Church, although she was made up of only these twelve Apostles and a few others, was already catholic, and this fact is expressed in the miracle of the tongues of fire, of love, of reason. The Church was able to be and to become externally catholic only because internally she was already catholic, because internally she already bore within her all the breadth and openness of the Holy Spirit for all, the reconciling force of diversity. Only this interior catholicity, which is the first thing to keep in mind, creates then the possibility of concrete external catholicity. Thus Pentecost is also a feast of catholicity, of the joy of being Catholics, of the joy of belonging to this universal community, in which we all understand one another in the diversity of languages and cultures.

Let us pray that the Lord may help us to be ever more catholic, to be able to say with ever greater conviction: "*Credo Unam Sanctam, Catholicam et Apostolicam Ecclesiam.*" [I believe in One, Holy, Catholic and Apostolic Church.] Let us thank God for the Holy Spirit, for the Pentecost that He gives us today, and let us pray that we ourselves may be instruments of this catholicity, of this Pentecost, and that we may thus be full of His joy and may give joy to others. Amen!

SOLEMNITY
OF THE MOST HOLY TRINITY

Trinity: Joy Because God Is Near

June 15, 2014
Private Chapel, Mater Ecclesiae Monastery

Most Holy Trinity (Year A)
Readings: Ex 34:4b–6, 8–9; Dan 3:52–56;
2 Cor 13:11–13; Jn 3:16–18

The feast of the Most Holy Trinity is different from all the other feast days of the liturgical year. In the other feasts, we commemorate events in the history of God with us; we repeat, as it were, the course of that history. We start with the millennia of waiting for the Lord, the Savior, then we arrive at Christmas, the Nativity of the Lord, until the Paschal Mystery and Pentecost, the gift of the Holy Spirit, at the beginning of the Church. Today, on the feast of the Most Holy Trinity, we do not celebrate an event, something that God did for us, but simply the source of all, God Himself: it is the feast of God's joy.

The content of the feast is expressed well in the line from the Gloria: *Gratias agimus tibi propter magnam gloriam tuam.* [We give You thanks for Your great glory.] We give thanks for Your beauty, for You. The joy that God exists, that He knows us, that we know God. Just as the beauty of the mountains, the majesty of the sea, the beauty of a tree in bloom give us joy, without our wanting something in exchange for it, because in the experience of beauty there is always a joy per se; so, too, God is joy, and it is a joy to see that He exists, and we want nothing else but to give thanks for His Beauty, His Goodness, His Love.

Research into the history of religions has produced one result that, I think, is unexpected: the novel feature of biblical religion is not monotheism as such. The research showed that all religions—at least the archaic religions that have to do with many demons, deities, etc.—know that all these deities are not God, but that there is only one God; they know that there is the God who is the one God, and all the others are not God; they are deities, they are powers with which man must reckon.

This God is known and, nevertheless, unknown also: this superior divine Being, who is greater than what can be known, is not adored; there is no worship for Him. The reason is simple: this God—so they thought—is not interested in us. He is too great. He is God but does not rule us. He is too great to be interested in us, and we cannot speak to Him; and, above all, this God is good, and therefore there is no reason to fear; it is not necessary to reconcile Him with us and to have His favor. Therefore, this God remains without worship, and, although He is known, He remains an unknown God who is too distant, too great for us. Real life, on the other hand, has to do with the present powers, with the forces of this and that other demon, and thus systems of worship arise, and also of sorcery and so forth, in the search to defend oneself against those powers. Life is full of these beings, who also threaten human life.

The new feature of biblical revelation is that God, the God who is so distant, so silent, knows us, and that the distant God makes Himself a God who is near: the true God is not an absent God, a being who is too great and superior, but rather He has a face, a voice, and He speaks, He becomes the God who is near (see Deut 4:7). Thus everything is different; there is no longer any need to struggle with these powers of the world or to adore them, because He is the power and has the power, He who is the true God.

Think of Abraham: when Scripture speaks about him, we find no great philosophy about monotheism or about polytheism, but there is one very important thing: this God who is so near, who speaks with Abraham and guides him, is his friend (see Is 41:8), and at the same time the God who can speak in Mesopotamia, and call him to go to the Holy Land, can protect him in Egypt. In other words, He is a God who does not depend on one place or another, but rather is a God who is a person, who works with persons, who becomes the friend of persons and thus enters into history and nevertheless remains God, who is God everywhere and not only in a certain place. God is near: the true God creates friends for Himself, creates a people for Himself so as to enter really into the life of the world, into our life.

In the New Testament, we see a new step: this great, distant God, this God who has become near, makes Himself so near that He becomes a man! He becomes one of us: it is not possible to be nearer than that; He is one of us, with us, and thus the face of God is, so to speak, visible, and He gives Himself into our hands in the Holy Eucharist. He is still the great God, the Creator, who has power over all, but at the same time this great God is the God who is near, who is one of us, who lives with us, for us, and in us.

Here we are at the point where we can also understand something of the mystery of the Trinity. God did not speak to us about the Trinity in order to tell us: "I am a mystery"; He truly wanted to show Himself. The great Greek philosophers, for example Aristotle, knew, as the religions do, that there is one God, but just with his philosophy, his rationality, he was convinced that this one God cannot have relations with us, because we change, while He is eternal and therefore cannot enter into relation with the things that change; otherwise, He Himself would no longer be eternal, because He, too, would be subject to changes. Therefore, this one God exists in Himself, He is "thought about thought" and the geometry of the cosmos, so to speak.

Jesus Christ makes us see another reality: this God not only has relations, but *is* relation; He is not only the geometry of the world, but He is love, and love always indicates relation, and the greatest reality is not the geometry but the love. God is love, and therefore He is relation, and since He is relation, He can also have relations, involve us in His relationality, in the mystery of His love. This is the Trinity, and this means that God not only loves, but is relation, is love! God is Father, Son, and Holy Spirit, and precisely in this way He is one. The Trinity does not destroy monotheism; it tells us that the unity created by love is deeper and more unified than the unity of an atom.

So we return to the beginning: it is beautiful to know that God, the God, the one God, is so great that He has time for us. Precisely because He is great, because He is immense, He has knowledge, He has time for each one of us, knows each one of us, and we can know Him in our manner. The new feature for the Christian is that God is not distant, but near, and that God is so great that He loves us and becomes one of us. It really seems to me that this is a reason for joy: God, the true power, the ultimate, good power, knows me, loves me, and therefore we know that it is good to be alive, because we are in the hands of this God. Let us thank God for His goodness, let us thank God for having revealed Himself, and let us pray that He will help us to be ever nearer to His goodness. Amen!

A God So Near!

June 7, 2009
Private Chapel, Apostolic Palace

Most Holy Trinity (Year B)
Readings: Deut 4:32–34, 39–40; Ps 33;
Rom 8:14–17; Mt 28:16–20

If we listen attentively to the first reading, taken from the Book of Deuteronomy, we can discover something surprising. God says to His people: "Consider heaven and earth, consider especially all of history and all the religions that surround us, and you will see that your faith is incomparable, that it is unique and different from all these religions."

Today we normally think the contrary: that the history of religions demonstrates that they are all similar, that "religion" is a genus and that all the individual religions are species of this same "reality religion". The Lord tells us instead: "Look attentively, and you will find that this revelation of yours, this faith and religion of yours is unique, incomparable, different from all the rest. You will see that in these religions," says the Lord, "there is always a god to whom belongs a definite part of the land, a people, or a majority of this people, but is not the God of everything." It is always a question of "this" god, of "this" people, of "this" land. This people needs its god and his power, but the god also needs this land, his people; otherwise he will no longer be present as God. In contrast, *you* do not have "your" God who is yours alone. The God who spoke with you is not "a" god, but "the" God, the God of everything and of everyone, the God who created heaven and earth: everything is His, and He rules over all. For He is not the God of a definite land, but, among all the peoples that are His, He chose you, in order to enter with you into the history of them all. He found you in Egypt, He guided you into Palestine, He gave you this land, but He could give You all the other lands; it was His free choice to give you this one; He can also expel you from it and scatter you throughout the earth. He always remains the God of all, who has spoken to you; with an ineffable love He made Himself your God. This fact—that not just "a" god, but "the" God spoke to Israel, that He chose it among all the peoples and all of them are His—is to this day the great joy of Israel, its pride. In another passage of Deuteronomy, it says: "Is there a God who is so near to His people as our God is, who speaks with us in His word?" (see Deut 4:7).

Now, as Christians, we must keep in mind that history does not end with Israel, with the Old Testament. On the contrary, history arrives at its summit, at its intrinsic finality, only with Jesus Christ, with a new uniqueness, which ought to be our joy, the joy that brings our life to its fulfillment and shows us the path of life. We ought to ask ourselves: Where is a God, who is the God of all and created heaven and earth, so great and so near as to speak with us? Moreover, we can say: Where, in the whole world, is there a God who became man, really man, one with us, our brother, who lives eternally as man and remains God? Where is there a God who suffered as we do, who shares our passion and suffering? Where is there a God who descends with us into the abyss of suffering and death?

Where is the God who brought the human being, with his body and soul, into God's interior life, so that now God is man's space and we find our eternal dwelling in God's interior life? Where is there a God who forgives us with a valid word of absolution? How many times we ask for His forgiveness! And where is there a God so near to us that He gives Himself under the form of a bit of bread into our hands, into our hearts, really gives Himself to us, really with the body and the soul of His human-divine being? And where is there a God who granted to the world, to the people, a glimpse into His interior life and allowed us to discover that God is an eternal circle of love between Father, Son, and Holy Spirit?

We must also truly consider the world as Christians and discover the beauty of knowing God and of being known by God. And where is there a God who, through His people, created such a light of charity as God created over the centuries in Christ through the Church, in the world, and for the world? The verse of the psalm that we recited as the antiphon: "Blessed is the people chosen by God", is true all the more for the Church, for us, and it should be a reason for interior joy.

The solemnity of the Most Holy Trinity is a feast of God, and, considering God and entering into relation with Him, we discover that God is joy, that joy is not only knowing God, but also being known by Him, being loved by God, loved until the end.

Let us pray to the Lord that this joy of God may penetrate our hearts, so that we may know God better and better and thus the beauty of being known by Him. Let us pray that this joy of God may become the ruling force of our life. Amen!

On the Mountain: Promise and Commission

May 31, 2015
Private Chapel, Mater Ecclesiae Monastery

Most Holy Trinity (Year B)
Readings: Deut 4:32–34, 39–40; Ps 32;
Rom 8:14–17; Mt 28:16–20

The last meeting of the Lord with His disciples took place on the mountain. It simply says "mountain", without specifying. The mountain must be the mountain of Jesus' prayer, the mountain to which He withdrew, to the height above the evil of the world, on which He meets with the Father. Thus, in this word "mountain", the Trinitarian mystery appears: the Lord, the Son, who speaks with the Father, meets with Him in the Holy Spirit.

At the same time, another story appears, another mountain, the mountain of the temptation, about which Matthew speaks in his account of the temptations (see Mt 4:8–11). The devil had guided the Lord to a very high mountain, from which all the kingdoms of the earth could be seen, the glory of these kingdoms, and he had said: "All this is Yours, if You adore me." It was the offer of worldly power, and this same thing seems to be the content of the "redemption" offered by Satan: having power in the world.

But Jesus had not said "yes", because He does not adore Satan; in other words, He does not adore military or economic might or the power of public opinion as the ultimate power; He does not acknowledge this as the true power; He is not available to adore worldly power, material things. The devil's reply was the condemnation of Jesus to death, and so the matter would be ended. But Jesus rose and now can say: "To Me is given all power in heaven and on earth." What is the difference between the power offered by the devil and this "all power" of the Lord?

An initial difference appears immediately: the Lord's power is "power in heaven and on earth". While the devil offered all the glory of economic might, etc., but nothing of heaven, Jesus now has at His disposal all power in heaven and on earth. Now, only a power over heaven, too, is a real power: a power that is totally closed off from heaven is a destructive power; only a power united to heaven, open to heaven, is a true power for man's true happiness.

Certainly, today, a secular State cannot be a religious State; nevertheless, even if it remains neutral, it cannot close itself off from the great fundamental values, from the great descriptions of heaven, of human nature; in this sense, it must always be open to this other power.

The second concrete difference is that the Lord's power is the power of the Crucified, a power that is given through the Cross. His mountain is the mountain of the Cross; His height is the height of the Cross, that is, the height of the love that is given, the love that is the true power, even if it must let itself be killed. Furthermore, it is the power of truth, which is not imposed on the heart with instruments of domination, but is imposed only by free conviction. This is the power of Jesus, the power of the Crucified; this is the true power that conquers, that really redeems, even if it is not convenient for us.

Because of this power—since He has all power in heaven and on earth—Jesus now can commission His eleven Apostles to all parts of the world, to all the nations, so as to make all the nations His disciples: only this power makes this possible. Externally it appears ridiculous that these eleven persons should go into the world and try to make all the peoples of the earth disciples of Christ.

They speak only one language, they are persons without higher education, they really are commissioned by the Lord as sheep in the midst of wolves, so that they might appear "as sheep" in the eyes of the academics, who know all the philosophy, all the culture in the world, whereas they know only Jesus. They appear to be "sheep" also in the sense that they are then victims of violence. And, nevertheless, the incredible, incomprehensible thing is that these eleven actually succeed in making disciples of Christ in the world, in spreading the truth of Christ, the truth of the Crucified, of the God who shows Himself in the Son and in the Holy Spirit.

It is the same situation even today. We Christians, in comparison with today's "enlightened" culture, seem like sheep confined to our corner on the height of the temple, sheep who are killed in the name of the powers that be; but, even and precisely today, we remain certain that the true power is the power of truth and not of falsehood, the power of love and not that of hatred. Externally, the power of hatred and of falsehood seem much stronger, and nevertheless in the end the sheep are victorious and not the wolves.

Saint John Chrysostom, in the light of his experience of the Christian Byzantine Empire, once said that we Christians are always tempted to turn into wolves, in order to be sure of our victory; but the moment we appear as wolves, we have already lost, because we no longer bear invincible love, we no longer bear the truth, which has no need of violence and does not accept it. Thus, even today, the Lord commissions us and tells us to be assured that at the end the wolves are not victorious, but the sheep, that at the end the Crucified is victorious and not the one who says: "All this is mine...."[1]

At the end of the Gospel, at the end of the earthly life of Jesus, stand the promise and a commission.

The promise: "I will be with you all days until the end of the world." This is the great certainty: the Lord is present even today. Sometimes we do not see Him, but He is really and truly present, His promise is true, and this is the great joy of Christians: He is with us until the end.

The commission: "Baptize all the nations in the name of the Father, of the Son and of the Holy Spirit." "To baptize" means to immerse, to immerse man in the ocean of God. This is the true reality: that Christianity finally immerses us in the ocean of love and truth, and precisely by facing it, and in a certain way by dying to ourselves, we truly live.

"In the name of the Father, of the Son and of the Holy Spirit": Jesus reveals to us God the Trinity: the Son meets us, guides us, and unites us to the Father in the Holy Spirit. The beauty that God pours out is ultimately not a monad, but rather it is love, and, if love is the ultimate reality, this essentially implies relation; therefore, it involves the Trinitarian mystery; and, since God is relation, He can also enter into relation with us; or rather, He needs, so to speak, to give His beauty to others.

This is the beauty of this day. Here the words come to mind that Nehemiah said to the Israelites, who were sad

[1]John Chrysostom, *Homilies on the Gospel of Matthew*, 33 (PG 57:389–90; NPNF-1, 10:219–220a).

upon their return from exile to their country, which was now poor, without resources, and without protection: "The joy of God is our strength!" (Neh 8:10). Yes, the joy of God is our strength! In this sense, we celebrate the feast of the Most Holy Trinity: with the joy of God. Despite all contrary appearances, He possesses the true power and gives us true joy, because true joy is love and truth. Let us thank the Lord for this revolution of His; let us thank God and really pray with the Lord: "May Your joy always be in us, and may it be our strength." Amen!

We Give You Thanks for Your Great Glory!

May 26, 2013
Private Chapel, Mater Ecclesiae Monastery

Most Holy Trinity (Year C)
Readings: Prov 8:22–31; Ps 8; Rom 5:1–5;
Jn 16:12–15

The feast of the Most Holy Trinity is different from all the other feasts of the liturgical year. All the other feasts are a commemoration of an event in the history of God with mankind. We have two liturgical cycles: that of the Incarnation—of Christmas—and that of Easter. In the cycle of the Incarnation, we repeat the journey of mankind toward Christ, because we all must walk toward Christ once again, as in Old Testament times, as in the times of all centuries. And there is the memory of the events: Nativity, Epiphany, down to the Cross and Resurrection, to the Ascension and the Holy Spirit.

But I would say that in reality there are three cycles, because the Sundays of Ordinary Time are not an empty space, but rather are a time of the Holy Spirit, a time in which the Holy Spirit, as the Lord proclaimed in the Gospels, introduces us into the memory, makes us enter into the depth of the memory, and thus we can understand more and more, and in a way that is ever new, the memory of the Incarnation, the Resurrection, and the Ascension, as a time of the Holy Spirit.

The feast of the Most Holy Trinity is not the commemoration of an event; it is a commemoration of God: simply put, we do not celebrate an event, we celebrate God, the joy that God exists. The content of the feast of the Most Holy Trinity is stated very well in a beautiful phrase from the Gloria: "We give You thanks for Your glory, for Your great glory." We give You thanks for Your great glory: this is the content of this feast.

What is the meaning of this? I would say: we celebrate the mountain in its beauty, we are happy, we are grateful for this beauty; we celebrate the beauty of the sea, the beauty of a tree in bloom, the beauty of a human being; we listen to the beauty of a piece of music, we are always grateful for the gift of beauty in which the light of creation appears, the beauty of Being. And all these beauties, for which we are grateful, are only a ray of the beauty of God. Thus, ultimately, we rejoice in everything and are grateful, because You, O God, are so beautiful, so good. This is the content of the feast of the Most Holy Trinity: thanks, thanksgiving, joy because of God's great glory.

But do we know God? The specialists who do research in the field of religion, or the history of religions, tell us that all religions know the one God, even the so-called polytheistic religions. They know that these deities, which are the content of their religion and their worship, are not "the" God, that God Himself is unique, and that the deities are not God.

But a religion deals only with deities and not with God, who remains outside [its scope]. But why? Because this God, of whom everyone has a certain knowledge, is inactive—they say—that is, too great to deal with us, too far away, too distant from the little creatures that we are, with our little problems, which do not interest this God. This God is self-contained. Aristotle, a great Greek philosopher in antiquity, says the same thing in a philosophical way. He discovered the unity of God, but says: God is concerned only with Himself; He does not take up relations *ad extra* [i.e., external relations]; thus his philosophical monotheism coexists with a religious polytheism. This is the situation in the history of religions.

During *ad limina* visits, I always asked the African and Asian bishops about these ancient, pagan religions, and they assured me: they know that God exists, that He is one, but He is not interested in religion, because this God is too great and does no evil; on the other hand, the deities—the forces of the earth, of the sea, of the mountain—these deities are dangerous, and therefore it is necessary to placate these deities, to practice worship, to give something to these deities so as to live in peace with them. The religions know that God exists, but God does not know us, does not love us, has nothing to do with us; therefore, religion deals with the dangerous lower spirits, and by worship man defends himself against the danger of these deities.

The new feature of the Old Testament is therefore not monotheism; the new feature is that this one God is also God-with-us. This one God is not an inactive God, who lives only in Himself, in His eternal beatitude, but is a great God, so great that He knows us, too, that He is concerned about us. The new feature is that this one, true God is also God for us and with us.

Thus religion is changed, because we no longer need to be afraid of demons. The pagan religions for the most part are fear and defense against fears. And the revelation that God has power on earth, too, that He is God-with-us, is above all a liberation from fear. So it was in antiquity, and so it is today also: in the countries where there is paganism, conversion to the one God is automatically liberation from fear. Except that the faith of these persons is not full, and thus these fears continue, because they do not believe deeply in the one God. Perhaps this is true of us, too, because we do not believe sufficiently that He is with us and that no other power has power against Him. God, the true God, is also God-with-us; this is the fundamentally new feature of the Old Testament, and this becomes even more radical in the New Testament.

God is radically God-with-us, down to our flesh: Jesus Christ. God is with us so profoundly that He is one of us; not only with us, but one of us, and we can enter into the interior life of this God; we are really capable of touching God, of entering into communion with God, even to the sacrament of the Eucharist, in which He enters into us, and we enter into this God.

Let us understand this new feature: God went out of Himself, and, precisely because He went out of Himself, we can enter into God, and this fact allows us a glimpse of the intimate mystery of His being. This mystery is Father, Son, and Holy Spirit, but is it compatible with God's unity? Not only is it compatible, but this mystery is the true unity. Thus we see that God is love, and love always implies an I, a Thou, and a We, and in precisely this way it is the perfect unity, the deepest and most real, the unique and most radical unity.

God's unity is not that of an atom, of a tiny invisible quantity, but rather is the greatest unity: it is the unity created by love. This is really the perfect unity, and thus the Trinitarian God is the one God. But His unity is the unity of love, and thus it applies also to us: because God is love, He can love us little creatures, too, and we can love God.

Therefore let us give thanks to God for His immense, glorious beauty, for His being-with-us, for His being-love.

In this sense, the feast of the Most Holy Trinity is a feast of joy, and the joy is redemption. Saint John identifies joy with the Holy Spirit. We are redeemed to the extent to which we enter into this joy of God who is Love. Redemption is wrought by Jesus Christ, but we are on a journey of redemption; we journey toward redemption, and faith is this journey toward redemption.

We will be totally redeemed when faith becomes vision, when we are really immersed in the today of God's goodness and love. Now we are on a journey, and we pray to the good Lord that we may be filled more and more with His glory and thus may live well, live in love, and may transform the world and ourselves: "We give thanks to God, to You, O Lord, for Your great glory." Amen!

FEASTS THROUGH THE YEAR

Commending Oneself to God to Enlighten the World

February 2, 2014
Private Chapel, Mater Ecclesiae Monastery

Feast of the Presentation of the Lord
Readings: Mal 3:1–4; Ps 23; Heb 2:14–18; Lk 2:22–40

Forty days after the birth of Jesus is the day of the purification of Mary, His Mother, of her readmission to public worship, and thus also the legal, formal conclusion of the birth of the Child. Therefore Mary, Joseph, and the Child go to the temple and in that way fulfill all justice.

Just as Jesus let Himself be baptized without having sins, so too Mary lets herself be purified although she has no need of it, because this birth is the true purification of the world, and from this birth comes the purification of the world, of us all; precisely because Mary is the Mother of God, the light of this birth is the pure light from the beginning and, thus, shows us where the true purity of the world comes from: it comes from this birth that renews us all.

Part of this ritual is the sacrifice of a few doves; this is the sacrifice of the poor, of simple people; so we see that Mary and Joseph, the family of Jesus, belong to the poor of Israel, to those simple of heart, the poor in spirit, who can truly be the place in which the Lord enters into the world. A pure heart, which is not covered with arrogance, shut by ideologies, prejudices, impurity, corruption, and arrogance; a simple heart that is open, a pure heart that sees God and thus welcomes Him, lets Him enter.

The pure heart. Let us pray to the Lord that we, too, may always have once again a simple heart, a heart that can see what is essential. Only a simple heart is capable of seeing what is essential, of seeing God. Mary, the poor woman of Israel, invites us to be among these simple people whom the Lord praised because they see the mystery, see the grace of the Son.

But Mary, Joseph, and the Child come to the temple with another purpose, also. The Book of Exodus (see Ex 13:2, 11–16) and the Book of Leviticus (see Lev 5:7; 12:8) prescribe that, since every first-born son is God's property and belongs to God, in order to be able to live legitimately with his parents, in order to return to the normal world, he must be ransomed from God's ownership, so that he becomes a free man like us. So they come to the temple for this purpose, too.

According to the tradition of Israel, though, it was not necessary to go to the temple for this purpose; it was enough to bring a small sum of money to a priest in one's own region without entering the temple. But Mary and Joseph come to the temple, not to ransom Jesus; on the contrary, they come to give Jesus to God, to give Jesus back to the Father definitively. Indeed, the Greek verb *parastēsai* means that they not only give Him back, but they offer Him, so to speak, sacrifice Him to God. Jesus is not their property; truly He is only the property of God; they acknowledge this: the Son who was presented to them is given back to the Father, and, precisely in this way, being the Father's alone, He is with us and for us all.

Here the mystery of the Cross already appears: Jesus is presented, given back to God, He is sacrificed, and thus He opens the gates of heaven for us; by entering into the mystery, He opens the gates of heaven. In the background of this episode we recognize Psalm 40, which says: "Holocausts and sacrifices You do not desire, but You prepared a body for me. Behold I come to do Your will" (see Ps 40:6–8; the psalm is cited as it appears in Heb 10:5–7, according to the Greek version). The temple is the place of holocausts and offerings, but God is not interested in bulls or sheep. God needs something else. God's concern is one reality only: that man should come to Him alive. "A body You have prepared for me": the Son is incarnate in a body and thus becomes a body prepared for You; now this body is handed over to God and, in Him, mankind itself is handed over, is given back to God.

Think also about the broadening of the word "first-born" in the New Testament. In the Resurrection, Jesus becomes "the first-born of many brethren" (Rom 8:29) and, indeed, Saint Paul tells us that "He is the first-born of every creature" (Col 1:15); with Him creation begins, and we are once again made free.

Let us pray that the Lord will help us to be handed over to God with Jesus, that He will help us to say: "A body You have prepared for me; I go to do Your will; I do not give You some thing, I give You myself." And that He will help us to understand every day what it means that we ourselves are in communion with Christ. Christ offered the true sacrifice; He opened heaven and draws us to Himself as brothers and sisters, so that we, too, with Him, can hand mankind over to God, starting with ourselves.

And then the great words of Simeon! I would like to cite or interpret only two of them. Simeon says—and we just chanted it—*lumen ad revelationem gentium*, this Child is "the light of the Gentiles", or nations, and thus "the glory of Israel". Simeon quotes here the song of the Servant of God, which says about Him that He will be not only a light per se, but a light of the Gentiles (see Is 42:6; 49:6). In quoting this Servant song, he tells us that this Servant is the king. The true king enters in order to serve, and only in this way does he truly reign.

The king, who is the light of the nations, illuminates everyone. In antiquity there is this desire for light, and not only in antiquity, but in the hearts of us all there is the desire to know, to see what there is, what stands behind this greatness of the world, whether God exists and who God is. He is that light which, according to the prologue to the Gospel of John, enlightens all those who enter into this world (see Jn 1:9); He Himself, this Child, is the true light, shows us the face of God, shows us who and what stands behind the world, who we are, who God is, and thus He enlightens the world. He comes to enlighten. Let us pray that this light may really shine on the world! We see what a great absence of God there is today, how much darkness concerning God, concerning man. The Light has come, but the world did not accept it, as Saint John also says (see Jn 1:11).

Let us pray that the light may be stronger than the darkness. Let us give thanks, because in His life, Jesus revealed Himself to us as Light, and let us, too, seek to show this true Light that enlightens and, thus, to help the world to be in the light.

This word about light also gave the external characterization to this day, with the procession of the "lights" or candles. It is a day of light; with the light of the candles it professes Christ, who has arrived in the world as the One who is the true light, light who is God Himself. In the Roman liturgy, the phrase "light of the nations" also has a particular emphasis.

In ancient pagan Rome, in these first days of February, they used to hold a procession of "lustration", the meaning of which was the expiation, the purification of the city. The Romans were aware of how much corruption existed, how much fraud, how many injustices, how many lies, that the city was in danger of being only a muddy swamp, of sinking into these lies, and therefore they held this procession in order to expiate, to renew, to start over. Their sentiment was this: "We cannot keep going on like this; we must free ourselves from this mud, we must start over from zero and be renewed!", and that was the meaning of this procession with animals as sacrificial victims. They circled around the city to free it from these malignant powers; it was a loud cry of renewal, of liberation from the weight of the mud, from the evil that moves about in the city.

When Christianity was professed, they could not simply abolish this procession, because the awareness of the mass of corruption, and of the necessity of renewal, was so strong that the procession could not disappear, and thus it was transformed into a procession with Christ, the true Light. And because of this day, the verb *lustrare* meant two things: to purify and to illuminate—the light is what gives purity, and the purity is light.

Thus the coincidence of this fortieth day after the birth of Christ with this event is obvious: the Light has come, the Light that really transforms the world, the Light that made itself a victim on the Cross to renew the world and that frees the world from the burdens of evil, from its filthiness. Therefore, the procession was initially held with black vestments, and people walked barefoot as far as the Basilica of Santa Maria Maggiore; later on purple vestments were adopted, until the liturgical reform, yet the deep meaning is always the same: that the light goes against the darkness; it purifies and frees the world.

Today we see how our world, both in Italy and elsewhere, needs renewal, a light that not only enlightens but transforms, renews interiorly. We know that our prayer is no longer only a cry, as in the pagan procession, but that we really bring God's force for renewal, because Jesus on the Cross took upon Himself all this mud and thus renews the world and is the place of the renewal of the world. From this place we draw light; therefore we light our little candles by drawing from His great light; thus we are with Christ who conquers, and we are renewed and can help in the renewal of the world.

Let us pray, precisely in this hour of our history, that the Lord may be light and strength, a flame of renewal that transforms the world, that He may help us, too, to be bearers of His light, to be renewed and instruments of renewal.

One final word. Saint Simeon says to Mary: "A sword shall pierce you." Saint Luke wrote these words decades after that event, surely after the death of Mary, and knew—the readers knew—that Mary bore that cross, that sword: he knew that Mary beneath the Cross had suffered interiorly with Jesus, had borne with Jesus this purifying, transforming light, which becomes a sword and renews precisely in this way.

The Fathers of the Church said: "The real sin of paganism is its insensitivity, its lack of compassion." God Himself, in contrast, is compassion in Christ Jesus, and Christians must be compassion with Christ and in Christ. With Mary, the image of the Church, of the true Church, we are thus invited to enter on this day into the mystery of the Cross, of the sword that pierces, to let ourselves be transformed, renewed and, by carrying with Jesus the weight of the world, to see the light, to be light.

Let us thank the Lord for the gift of His light, for the gift of Himself! Let us ask Jesus to renew the world and to renew us. Amen!

"Listen, My Son": Saint Benedict, Teacher of Wisdom

March 21, 2006
Immaculate Conception Monastery, Albano Laziale

Memorial of Saint Benedict
Readings: Gen 12:1–3; Ps 45; Jn 17:20–26

The first reading spoke to us about Abraham; in this figure, we can see features of our saint: Saint Benedict. Like Abraham, Benedict [*Benedetto*] is a "blessed man" [*un benedetto*], he is a source of blessing for many others, and, like Abraham, he is the father of many peoples. But wherein lies the mystery of this father Benedict, this Abrahamic mystery from which new fruitfulness still emanates, from which a new blessing continually comes?

The essence of the message, of the figure of Saint Benedict, appears immediately in the first words of his Rule: "Listen, son", words taken from the wisdom literature of the Old Testament (see Prov 1:8). Taking these first words from the wisdom of the Old Testament, Saint Benedict indicates that with his Rule he introduces us into a school of wisdom, into a school of the art of living, the art of being human beings, the art of finding the right path. And the key of the wisdom of this art of living, of the spiritual art—as he says—is precisely in the word "listen".

Saint Benedict makes his full humanity evident in this word. Adam was unwilling to listen; he only wanted to follow his own will, his own idea, and precisely thereby, by not listening and not obeying, he destroyed the path of humanity. And Benedict says immediately, in the first phrase of his Rule, that we must turn back from the mistaken path of Adam and start over from the beginning, by listening.

Abraham was someone who listened. This is the mystery of Abraham: listening, attention to the mysterious Word of God that spoke in him and with him. And, of course, this listening was not only perceiving some information, something that is known or not known; listening was "formation", not "in-formation"; it was letting himself be formed by the Word, letting himself be assimilated to the Word, entering into the Word, becoming conformed to the Word. Listening was obedience and, thus, a journey.

Saint Benedict invites us to this kind of listening, to this sensitivity of the heart to the presence of God, who speaks in us, who speaks in our conscience, of the God who speaks in creation and of the God who speaks out loud in Sacred Scripture, speaks in Jesus Christ and in the Church. A sensitivity of the heart, an openness of the heart that becomes attentive and capable of listening and, precisely in this listening, allows itself to be "formed" and [thus] goes to the "school of life", of prudence.

In reality, Saint Benedict says in his Rule that the monastic community is a "workshop" in which one prepares to live a righteous life and in which one finds the tools "of the spiritual art". The art to be learned is being human; the art to be learned is living well; the art to be learned is listening to and following God. And all the parts of the Rule are parts of this instruction, of this "school"—as Saint Benedict says (see *Prologue*)—of spiritual discipline, of this "workshop" in which one prepares for true wisdom and learns to live, learns about the true path of life.

"Listen, son." In these fundamental words, in which we already find the summary of his insight and personal experience, Saint Benedict also echoes another word, namely, the wedding Psalm 45[44], where we read: "Listen, O daughter, look, and incline your ear; . . . and the King will desire your beauty" (verses 10–11). Here the mystery of wisdom appears in depth; it appears in its more profound center; the mystery of God's love appears, which prepares the wedding of His Son and thus His wedding with humanity. Wisdom appears as a mystery of love revealed in Christ, who, for love of us, descends from heaven to be united with us in the flesh, even unto death.

Thus the second dimension of this word "listen" appears. Yes, "listen" first means being open to God's "speaking"; it is learning the contents thereof and the way of life that results from the contents. But finally the ultimate nucleus of this message appears: it is the person of Jesus and His love that searches for the lost sheep, which we are. Learning wisdom becomes learning to know Jesus and to love Jesus and, thus, to be united with Jesus.

"Listen, daughter, and the King will desire your beauty": behind this word stands the mystery of the Church, of the Bride, of humanity that has become the "bride" whose beauty pleases the King: it is the mystery of the love between God and the new humanity that is presented in the Church. But it also appears that this daughter-Church, who is sought and loved by Jesus, lives in every soul and, thus, this word speaks, not just to nuns and monks, but to all Christians as well.

To be "an ecclesiastical soul", as the Fathers of the Church say, to be Church in person and, in this way, to realize in one's own life this spousal mystery, to go to the center of wisdom, of the art of true living, by knowing Jesus more and more, by loving Jesus and by being united with Jesus. This is thus the ultimate and most profound invitation in the word "listen": that we ourselves should become *Ecclesia*, "Church", and really become a soul that is a bride of Christ, that lives in His love and thus really finds life.

"Listen, son." Along with these fundamental words, another text comes to mind from the New Testament, from the first chapter of the Book of Revelation. Here there is a great Christophany [manifestation of Christ]: John sees the Pantocrator [Ruler of the Universe] in all His immense greatness and newness, the Risen Lord with all His power, and describes the details of this figure of Christ that appears to him, and says: "His voice was like the sound of many waters" (Rev 1:15). The Fathers of the Church interpret this comparison, "voice like the sound of many waters", by saying: in reality "many waters" are "His voice", that is, all the rivers of Sacred Scripture, the many waters that make up Sacred Scripture are "His voice" and speak about Him; with this voice Christ speaks. In reality, the waters of Sacred Scripture, which are so different, a thousand years of writings, are rivers that all flow toward Jesus and are His voice, if we listen to it correctly. The many waters of Scripture are the voice of Christ.

Saint Benedict, in composing his Rule, did not claim to write an original book that was his alone, with his private voice, which has been the claim of the great thinkers of the modern era, who wanted to show their own genius, with thoughts that were theirs alone, and to create, with their books, a monument to themselves, so that, in reality, the history of modern philosophy is a cemetery, with many monuments of dead philosophies.

Benedict did not do that; he did not want to highlight only his personal voice; on the contrary, he wanted to let

Christ speak and to make the voice of the "many waters" heard. And this is the greatness of the Rule: that here we find the confluence of all the many waters of Sacred Scripture and of the experience of the Church, of monasticism, of the spiritual life of the Church. With all the voice of the Head and of the Body, with the voices of Scripture and of the living Church, with the "many waters" of this tradition, Christ really speaks with us, and we really hear in the "many waters", in their sound, the multiplicity, the richness, the beauty of the voice of Christ, the voice of the Truth.

And thus, it seems to me, we can, on the one hand, learn the humility of someone who does not highlight himself, but seeks to become part of the greatness of the Truth itself, and, on the other hand, we can hear this polyphonic concert and thus enjoy the richness, the beauty of the truth, really hear Christ the Pantocrator who speaks with us, with all the voices of creation and of history, and thus we can meditate on the Rule word by word, so as to hear more and more the richness of the Truth in its great voice.

In all this richness, my favorite chapter is the fourth, "The tools of the art of living", where there are incredibly magnificent words, with a beauty that is ever new: "Prefer nothing to the love of Christ", "Confess the truth with your heart and with your voice", "Desire eternal life with a true spiritual yearning", and so on.

But behind all these numerous voices that resonate in the "sound" of the Rule, so to speak, once again we must finally seek the one, central point. We have already said it: it is the point of being open, having a heart open to the voice of the Lord, listening in silence, letting oneself be formed, finally the point of knowing and loving Jesus as the nucleus of truth.

And this last point helps us to listen to the Gospel. In his high-priestly prayer to the Father, the Lord says at the end:

"I made known to them Your name, and I will make it known" (Jn 17:26). What does the "name" of God consist of, which Jesus makes known to us? In the Old Testament, Moses appears as the great mediator of revelation, because to him was revealed the "name" of God, and thus he could make the "name" of God known to the people. But very soon, and more and more over the course of the centuries, Israel understood that the "name" of God does not consist of a word, the "name" of God is something much greater, and therefore that word was no longer pronounced. Because there is something much greater: "Name" of God means that God starts a relation with us. If I know a person's name, I can call him: the relation with him has started.

If God is the unknown one, infinitely distant from us and inaccessible to our thought; if God gives Himself a "name", meaning that He makes Himself accessible, allows others to call Him; it means that the Infinite makes Himself finite so as to be able to speak with us, that He who dwells in inaccessible light goes forth from this inaccessible light and makes Himself accessible. The "name" of God is the accessibility of God, the "name" of God is God who made Himself one of us, so that we can have a relation with God, so that He is a God who listens, to whom we can speak, and a God who responds.

This is the mystery of God's "name": He made Himself finite with us, someone who dwells with us, in whose presence we can express ourselves, with whom we can speak. This mystery of God who, beyond His infinite greatness, makes Himself finite so as to become the "God-with-us", is only at the beginning on Mount Sinai and is completed in Jesus Christ, because Jesus Christ really is the "God-with-us", the Infinite who has made Himself finite, man, touchable, one of us. Christ really is this being-with-us, this divine making-Himself-accessible, and in this sense Christ is the "name" of God, is this cohabitation of God with us. The name of God is not a word; it is a person: it is Jesus Christ, the God-with-us.

Thus, this mysterious saying of the Lord, in His high-priestly prayer, says that He makes God known, by making Himself present as God's "name", the accessible God. In saying this, He invites us to seek to know more and more in Jesus the accessible, touchable God, the God-with-us, with whom we can speak and who speaks with us, and to make known to others, as Saint Benedict did, this "name" of God, this God-with-us.

This twofold content ultimately is the true "art of living"; it is the content of the listening: to know more and more in Jesus the "name" of God, that is, the living God who made Himself finite for us and with us, and thus to enter more and more into a living relation with this God who embraces us, and to help others so that they may know Him and can love Him.

We come once more to Psalm 45[44]: "Listen, incline your ear, the King will desire your beauty" (v. 10). Let us offer our life to this communion with Christ; so we become "blessed" and so we also become sources of blessing.

Today let us thank the Lord because He gave us this great father, and let us pray to Saint Benedict that he will help us to listen, to know, and to love. Amen!

The Mission of Peter and the Offering of Paul

June 29, 2014
Private Chapel, Mater Ecclesiae Monastery

Solemnity of Saints Peter and Paul
Readings: Acts 12:1–11; Ps 34; 2 Tim 4:6–8, 17–18; Mt 16:13–19

I did not prepare a real homily, but I would like to say only a brief word about each of the three readings for today, because each one of them reflects, in a different and particular way, the mystery of the mission of Peter and Paul and, thus, the mission of the Church and our vocation as Christians.

First reading. The event is impressively dramatic: Peter is in prison, in chains, in utter darkness, flanked by two guards; it is impossible for him to get out; then again at the door there are two more guards, then another iron door. All the worldly power is present, and nevertheless God can open the doors and make the chains fall. This drama foretells the mystery of the Church of all times, in which the Church ultimately seems already conquered. Diocletian thought that after his persecution no Christians would be left. Today his empire has disappeared, and so on.... But this drama shows us the power of God, the power of the Crucified, because the Crucified Lord is alive and victorious.

We must keep in mind also a word that is central to this passage, when it says that the Church was united in prayer. While Peter is in prison, the Church prays, and this prayer calls on the power of God; this prayer is a power in the world. It reminds us of another passage from the Acts of the Apostles, at the beginning of the persecutions, where it also says that the Church was at prayer and that finally the earth shook (see Acts 4:31). In reality, prayer caused the earth to quake because it transforms the earth, because it makes God's power enter in. This is an important part of the first reading: God's power, the helplessness of our reality in the world, and the power of prayer.

But there is also another important part: this incarceration of Peter nevertheless has, in God's plan, the outcome of a mission. Until then, Peter had been only in Jerusalem and in the neighboring regions in order to form the Judeo-Christian Church, whereas now he must flee from Palestine and go out into the world of the pagans; in this passage it says only "to another place" (Acts 12:17); it does not say where, but it makes clear that ultimately the other place would be Rome.

Saint Peter, who formed the first Church in the Holy Land, now must go out into the world of the pagans; he must inform the whole world about the Church and thus take his universal responsibility for the Church. This violent act of persecution nevertheless enters into God's plans and causes a second phase of Peter's journey to start, that of his universal responsibility, the final expression of which will be his martyrdom in Rome. Jerusalem cannot be the place of his martyrdom; he must also go to Rome, and that is where he ascends to the primacy, and that is where he causes the universality of the Church of Christ to appear. We see how, even in wicked action, God creates new salvation for the whole human race.

Second reading. These are the last words of Saint Paul: he knows that he is condemned, that his martyrdom is imminent, and nevertheless he is not disheartened; on the contrary, he offers us a marvelous interpretation of his martyrdom, saying: "It is the moment in which I am sacrificed, as though poured out as a libation for God." He interprets his mission in the sense of a libation, a sacrifice to God. Here we must keep in mind that in antiquity, whether among the Jews or among the pagans, it was customary first to take the wine, to offer the gift to the deity of wine, that is, a part of it was poured out for the deity: it started with a sacrifice to God, so as to receive properly the one who is the gift of God.

Saint Paul says: "Now I am poured out, I am now the moment of this libation, of this sacrifice." What is true of his martyrdom is true also of what his whole life has been: his whole life as an Apostle was an act of pouring himself out for God. Worship, liturgy, and life are no longer separate; all of life is a libation, an act of worship, a sacrifice to God; martyrdom only concludes what his whole life was and makes Saint Paul enter deeply into the mystery of God. Christ, who is the Holy Eucharist, poured Himself out in the gift of the wine, which is His blood, still pours Himself out, through all the centuries, in the Eucharistic meal, and the life of Saint Paul, too, becomes Eucharistic, as he enters into this act of allowing himself to be poured out. Let us pray that the Lord may help us to understand this mystery and that we, too, with our whole life, might become Eucharist, a gift for the Lord.

Then at the end, Saint Paul says: "The Lord saved me from the lion's mouth." This is a reference to the first trial, where he was acquitted at the end, but it is also true now, because—although sentenced and killed—the Lord saved him from the lion's mouth: he did not fall into hell, he did not fall into wickedness, he did not lose the faith, and thus, by dying as a martyr of Christ, he is saved. Even though externally he is killed, nevertheless he is saved, because he is in the Lord's hands as a martyr; he lives in a new way; martyrdom is life even in death.

Finally the great Gospel of Matthew. How many times we have heard it and meditated on it! Saint Peter, in the power of the Holy Spirit and for the first time, pronounces the confession of the Church for all times: "You are the Christ, the Son of the living God." Living with Jesus, he received knowledge about Jesus. Many people are more or less acquainted with Him, know something about Him, but have not entered into the intimacy of His mystery, into the intimacy that consists in the fact that He speaks with God as His Son: Jesus is not only a prophet who sees something, but He sees the face of the Father, He is the Son of the Father. And at this moment the knowledge becomes confession, a confession that is still the Creed of the Church.

It is important to see that here Saint Peter received a gift from God; he himself is not the one who invented this word. Now his duty is to live and to die for this confession of Christ and to be the guardian of this truth. Thus an important reality appears: the faith is not our invention, but a gift from God. Therefore it is not at our disposal; we cannot change it as we like; it is a gift from God to be kept and lived, and thus it grows in its depth.

The second aspect that appears is that the pope is not an absolute monarch, who can do whatever he wants. On the contrary, the pope cannot do whatever he wants; he is the guarantor of obedience; he is the one who guarantees obedience to God's gift, which is the world's real treasure: to know the truth, to know love, to be loved, and thus we, too, learn love and the gift of God. The pope is the guarantor of obedience to what we did not invent; rather, it was given to us and is the real treasure of this world.

As we know, today the pope confers the pallium as the sign of pastoral responsibility on twenty-seven bishops of the world, in whom the catholicity of the Church appears.[1]

Let us pray for these pastors, that the Lord may help them, that the Lord may grant them the grace to be true apostles, that He may accompany them so they can make present in the world the Gospel of Christ and gather the Church in a mighty prayer that changes the world. Let us pray also for the pope himself, that the Lord may guard him and always accompany him in his responsibility of being the first confessor of the faith: "You are the Christ, the Son of the living God." Amen!

[1] Traditionally, on the Solemnity of Saints Peter and Paul, the pope confers the pallium on the new metropolitan archbishops who were appointed over the course of the past year.

The Faith of Thomas: Only a Believer Touches Jesus with His Heart

July 3, 2009
Private Chapel, Apostolic Palace

Feast of Saint Thomas the Apostle
Readings: Eph 2:19–22; Ps 117; Jn 20:24–29

The Gospel of Saint John records for us four episodes from the life of the Apostle Thomas and thus offers us a sort of essential portrait of this disciple and Apostle of the Lord.

First little story. Jesus, knowing that death awaited Him in Jerusalem, is on the other side of the Jordan River, in present-day Jordan, together with the Apostles, until He is informed about the illness of Lazarus. After the death of Lazarus, He decides to go to Jerusalem, passing through Bethany. The disciples know that He is going toward His death, apparently delaying a bit, and Thomas speaks up and says: "Let us go with Him, and let us die with Him!" (see Jn 11:1–16). A great and beautiful saying of this Apostle, in which we see, on the one hand, his realism: he assesses the situation correctly, knows precisely what is going to happen; but we see, together with this realism, also his profound fidelity to the Lord, his faith in Christ Jesus. We see that he is willing even to die with and for Jesus: this means that Jesus is for him more important than life; He has become his life, he has really found his life in Jesus, and he follows Him even to death.

Second story. In the Cenacle, Jesus speaks to the disciples and speaks about His Father's house with its many mansions, and adds: "I go to prepare a place for you, and you know the way." And Thomas, with his realism, his candor and sincerity, says: "But, Lord, we do not know where You are going; how can we know the way, the path?" And he receives this grand reply from Jesus, one of the key sayings of the Christian faith: "I am the way, the truth, and the life" (see Jn 14:1–7).

Thus Thomas must learn a new and deeper way of journeying with Jesus: not only journeying with Him on the roads of the Holy Land, from Bethany to Jerusalem and so forth, but journeying spiritually with Jesus, with his heart, journeying on the true path that is the Lord, the path of truth, the path of always being on a journey toward the Father, and from the Father to the people; he must learn this art of following Jesus with his interior life, with his whole existence, and thus must also learn another way of dying with and for Jesus, that is, leaving himself aside, going out of himself, allowing himself to be transformed by the truth and the true life, and thus being reborn in Jesus. He must learn the imitation [*la sequela*] of Jesus, which is more than obedience for someone who follows Him on the paths of the world: it is an interior communication with Jesus; it is an identification of my heart with the Heart of Jesus, and in this sense it is an infinite journey, it is a glorious journey.

Third story. We heard in today's Gospel that Jesus is risen, but Thomas did not see Him. And again Thomas' realism appears: for him it is not enough for the others to tell him: "He is risen and we have seen Him"; he does not want to follow impressions, hearsay; he does not want to follow a mere idea. For him it is not enough for the

Resurrection to be perhaps a spiritual vision, an idea about what ought to happen; he wants to touch, he wants a strong, indeed, a materialized realism.

We may be surprised, but this realism belongs to the very structure of the Christian faith. In his Second Letter, Saint Peter says: "We did not follow fables, but have seen with our own eyes" (see 2 Pet 1:16). And Saint John, in his First Letter, says: "We have touched the Word of truth" (see 1 Jn 1:1). "Touched" is what Thomas wants: to touch the Word of truth, to see.

In reality, God made Himself touchable, because the Christian God is not a mythological god whose stories may have happened always and never, but rather He is a God who lived a real, historical life in the material state of this earth and left His mark on this earth. There is an imprint of God on the earth; we can see the roads where Jesus really walked; we can see the place where He was born; we can see the sepulcher; we can also see Golgotha, the place of His crucifixion.

He left His imprint on this earth; He wanted to be touchable: in this sense, it is right that Thomas wants, not to follow rumors alone, but also "to touch", that is, to have a real certainty that this Resurrection is true, that this Jesus really is risen and lives. And so it happens: Jesus comes while the doors are closed and stands in their midst, and Thomas puts his hand into His open Heart. And here, he touches and learns a new dimension, a second dimension of touching and seeing: he touches the mortal wound, and this person, who ought to be dead because of the mortal wound, is alive.

Thomas touches the death of Jesus and thus sees the life of Jesus and also sees that Jesus entered the Cenacle through closed doors, that He is a man and nevertheless is touchable in the truth of His Resurrection. He touches Jesus, touches His Heart of flesh, and touches even more:

with his heart he touches the Heart of Jesus and sees Jesus, and sees more than the man: at that moment, by seeing and touching the man, he sees God with the eyes of his open heart. On his knees, he adores and gives us one of the most beautiful prayers of Christianity, an essential confession of our faith: "My Lord and my God!" Therefore, there are two dimensions of touching here: Thomas touches the material imprint and with his heart touches the true Heart of Jesus, and thus he sees more than what his bodily eyes see.

This second form of touching is the essence of the faith. In the light of the Gospel that we heard a little while ago in the liturgy, we can understand better also the Gospel about the woman who for twelve years had suffered constantly from a loss of blood, had given her whole fortune to the doctors without any improvement, and, when she heard about Jesus, put all her hope in Him (see Mk 5:25–34). Jesus was traveling toward the house of Jairus and had contact with the crowd; they were touching Him on all sides, but the woman approached and touched Jesus, touched Him not only with her hand, like all the others, but touched Him spiritually with the faith of her heart.

And Jesus says, to the great surprise of the Apostles: "Who touched Me?" They reply: "Lord, You see that everyone is touching You!" "No", Jesus says. Then, He sees this woman and says: "Your faith has saved you." She touched Him with her hands, yes, but more than that, she touched Him with her heart and thus was cured. This touching with the heart is faith. And this touching, which is faith, heals: it is salvation. We can observe the same thing even today: many people touch Jesus, like those in the crowd, because they know the Scriptures; they know so much about Jesus, they can say this and that about Him, they have gone to the Holy Land, they know everything; but they touch Him as the crowd did and do not truly touch Him. Only someone who believes touches with his heart and thus is cured.

Let us ask the Lord to grant that we may touch Him externally like Thomas, like the many people who can touch Jesus in the Gospel, but especially that we may learn to touch Him with our heart, so that in this way He may cure us and give us salvation.

Fourth story. We find it in the last chapter of the Gospel of John: it is the miraculous catch of fish (see Jn 21:1–13). Saint John tells us that there were seven disciples who participated in this fishing expedition: Peter, Thomas, Nathaniel, the two brothers John and James, and two others who are not named. These seven took part in the miraculous catch of fish and hauled in 153 large fish.

No doubt, we can and should see this catch of fish granted by the Risen Lord as a metaphor for the Church's mission, for the work of the fishers of men, who draw out of the salty waters of this world the fish of the Lord and guide them in the light of the Gospel, in the light of the truth. It is a parable about what starts after the Resurrection: the great, miraculous catch of fish is the construction and the growth of the Church.

Thomas, after Peter, is mentioned as one of these seven, and this means that he was one of those who really brought the Gospel to the ends of the earth, that he is one of the great fishers of men who built the Universal Church. A very ancient tradition says that Saint Thomas brought the Gospel to India, to the great Indian subcontinent, where he is venerated as the Apostle who set up the Cross there, the sign of the Redeemer. Let us pray that India in particular, the continent of Saint Thomas, may find more and more the light of Christ, may ever more really and profoundly touch Jesus and thus say: "My Lord and my God!" Amen!

Being Conformed to the Cross of Christ

September 14, 2014
Private Chapel, Mater Ecclesiae Monastery

Feast of the Exaltation of the Holy Cross
Readings: Num 21:4b–9; Ps 77; Phil 2:6–11; Jn 3:13–17

The feast of the Exaltation of the Holy Cross, which is celebrated today, had its origin in a historical memory.

As we know, Saint Helena, the mother of the Emperor Constantine, in the early fourth century had found the Cross of Christ and had solemnly built a church on Mount Calvary. From that moment on, the Cross became the most precious relic in the empire, an expression of the whole Christian mystery, and when it was set up on Mount Calvary, it said: "Christ has conquered" and was the expression of Christ's victory. All the adversaries had disappeared; Christ conquered; His reign had been established.

Yet at the same time, this relic also had a spiritual significance, because the Cross is a very particular victory; it is not a victory with power and wealth; on the contrary, the Cross is the most profound shame possible, the most terrible defeat. Therefore, this victory of Christ is always connected with a love that descends into the depths of the human being, to the ultimate humiliation of the servant, about which the Letter to the Philippians speaks today. Thus this Cross was also a decisive measure, a criterion for the kingdom, for the empire as such. What is decisive, then? That one cannot live by earthly glory, by wealth, by military power, and that the ultimate standard of everything always remained this Cross as the source of true victory: the love of Christ who gives Himself.

In the fifth century, wars began against Persia, which increasingly threatened the Byzantine Empire; in 614, on account of a major defeat of Byzantium, the Cross fell into the hands of the Persians. Its external loss was clearly also a spiritual loss for the Byzantine Empire. The emperor therefore had to ask himself: What happened? The answer is obvious: we lost, spiritually also, the Cross of Christ, the victory of Christ, the standard of our being. The emperor then ordered a time of major repentance, and finally, in 628, the Byzantines won against the Persians, regaining the Cross of Christ. A fundamental victory for them, an expression of the fact that Christ was still their true emperor.

Then it was decided to carry the Cross in a solemn procession with the emperor, with the whole court, with all the bishops, to Calvary, and the emperor himself, adorned and clothed in all his solemnity, with gold and jewels, carried the Cross. Legend has it, strangely, when they arrived at the gate of Jerusalem, the emperor could no longer move, could not enter by that gate, because, inexplicably, he was incapable of any movement. Then the Patriarch Zachary, Bishop of Jerusalem, having received an enlightenment, allegedly told him: "Do you not understand that the Cross of Christ, with which He made Himself our servant, on which Jesus with His love descended to the depth of a slave, cannot be carried with gold and precious stones? Therefore, you must become like Christ, who descended into humility for us." The emperor put off his regal garments, the purple and the beauty of the jewels, and went on clothed like one of the poor people on the street, and only in that way could he carry the Cross to the height of Calvary.

We do not know whether there is a historical basis to this legend. In any case, it expressed a profound spiritual truth: the Cross of Christ can be effectively present, as a means of salvation and joy, only if we are conformed to it. The Cross of Christ demands conformity with what it shows. Only if there is humility in us—this descending of Christ by which a Christian takes up his cross every day—are we in conformity with Christ Himself, with His humility, with His love; only in this way can we carry the Cross and with the Cross have victory, God's great promise.

We know that this way of the Cross, the *Via Crucis*, is not a thing of the past; it is a permanent presence. Especially the Letter to the Hebrews, but also the Letter to the Philippians and Saint John explained for us that the way of Christ's Cross was not limited to a certain historical moment and a certain historical place. The Letter to the Hebrews tells us that Christ's *Via Crucis* passes through all the degrees of the cosmos and finally arrives at the face of the Father (see Heb 4:14; 10:11–14; 12:2–3). This unity of divine love and human love, in Christ, throws open the gates between God and man, between Creator and creature [*tra creatura e creatura, sic* = between one creature and another], opens the heavens and Christ brings His love and us, His beloved children, with Him before the face of the Father. And in the love of Christ, which reconciles God and the world, is contained every flame of love kindled by Christ in history, and finally all human beings are one flame of love in Christ.

This fact is once again present, in particular, in the sacrament of the Eucharist, in the Holy Mass. The Holy Mass is the movement of Christ, in which we are all involved in the passage from earth to God, on the journey by which Christ presents us to God and reconciles us, gives us His love; the journey on which the words are fulfilled: "God so loved the world that He gave Himself, His Son for us." The Eucharist is the reality of the Cross and the Now of the Cross: in the movement of the Eucharist, we are involved in the movement of Christ, which invites us to be conformed to His love, to His humility, and, in this way, we can really find the joy of the redeemed.

Let us pray to the Lord to help us to accept, to understand spiritually the message of the Cross and to be conformed to it, and to celebrate really with all our heart, with all our being, the Holy Eucharist in such a way that it becomes the strength of our life, redemption, and joy. Amen!

God's Love Leads Us on High

November 1, 2015
Private Chapel, Mater Ecclesiae Monastery

Solemnity of All Saints
Readings: Rev 7:2–4, 9–14; Ps 23; 1 Jn 3:1–3; Mt 5:1–12

The Church presents to us today, on All Saints Day, the Sermon on the Mount, the core of Jesus' preaching, so that we might be convinced that the saints are the true interpretation of the Sermon on the Mount, an interpretation made, not with words, but with their life: This is how you live, this is how you become blessed, this is the path of the blessed, happy life!

Cardinal Wojtyła, before becoming Pope Saint John Paul II, in 1975 preached the spiritual exercises for the Roman Curia[1] and related how the Russians from the beginning imposed Marxism on Poland as the State philosophy and also as the required conduct in everyone's life. For the Church, it was obvious that she had to show that that was not the true philosophy, but rather Christian life, the word of Jesus, shows us the path of true life. In this foreseeable debate, the Marxists thought that the discussion would essentially concern natural science, and therefore they sought

[1] The meditations of then Cardinal Karol Wojtyła are collected in the volume *A Sign of Contradiction*, revised and updated translation (Cluny Media, 2021).

to demonstrate that modern natural science excludes God, rules out the Christian hypothesis: Christianity today is not scientifically acceptable; it is a religion of yesterday, and only Marxism is scientific in the life of today. But that was not the case, because the real problem was not modern science; the real problem was the model of human life, in other words, who could show the better model for how to live. The Marxists said: "Your Christianity is unacceptable; we show true modern life." But Christianity was not overcome, because this Marxist faith is not a model of how to live, while the Christian faith is a model even today.

Parenthetically, I would like to note here that in the famous dialogue, too, between the Emperor Michael Palaiologos and the Muslim, about which I spoke in Regensburg,[2] after the first few rounds the emperor had reached the point of saying: "The essential question between us is who shows the better model of life." His interlocutor declared: "But your life, your model is too lofty; it is idealism, no one can achieve it; it is not a truly possible way of life, whereas we with our realism show the path." And the Christian replied: "Yes, our ideal is very lofty, but you with your realism degrade man; you drag him down; with the greatness of our faith, we draw man upward, toward his true greatness." But let this be said only parenthetically.

Even today the question is this: Who shows how one can live a better life? Many are convinced that Christianity is not acceptable: it has too many commandments, too many difficulties, and freely we can live even better. The exodus from Christianity at the beginning of the modern era was based precisely on this statement: Christianity is unacceptable; it makes man a slave; we show how to live.

[2] The reference is to the famous speech by Benedict XVI at the University of Regensburg on September 12, 2006, about which a heated debate developed.

The modern critique, I find, is summed up especially in Nietzsche, who said: "But what do you offer?" The critique of Christianity is not so much a critique of the dogmas, but of Christian morality, of Christian life, which is not acceptable: you are bent over, like that publican who does not dare to raise his head; you are bloodless weaklings; the religion of the Christians is a religion of those who have had no success, who were incapable of living and then justified themselves by saying that their life of humiliation and lack of success was the better way. No! We do not want these plaster saints; we want vital persons who live life in all its beauty; we want to live, to have it all. As Albert Camus also said: "The kingdom of Christ is not of this world, but I say: our kingdom is of this world!"

What is the response to that? We can say that all these critics were wrong and that we wish to show instead that the Christian life, Jesus' model of life, is really the true one. I cannot go into the details now; I will take just one of these beatitudes: "Blessed are the pure of heart, for they shall see God." Purity of heart springs from the truth; it springs from the courage and the humility of the truth, which dares to remain faithful to reality even against the ruling powers. If we think about the times of dictatorships, the great were not the ones who trampled on the others and had power; the great were the ones who dared to stay on the side of truth even if they were destroyed, trampled on, despised: they were the real witnesses of the truth, the apologists for man; they had true life despite their external defeat; they opened the door to the future. Humility and the courage of truth are truer and greater than the force of the violent.

And thus we can continue: not the violent, but the peaceful, the peacemakers; not those who resort to violence, but the meek are the true life of man. It is true that Christians are not plaster saints, because precisely with the vitality of the faith they live the true life, which can be hard, but ultimately is true life. In other words, Yes! Our journey is a noble journey, but we can say that it is noble because the love of God precedes us.

This is the essential point: the love of God precedes us and inflames us, carries us with it, and thus we can endure hardships, too. By traveling through the dark nights of life, too, we arrive at the true light, because we are carried by the love of God, which precedes us, accompanies us, and lifts us up again and again, even if we have fallen; because we know that this love is indestructible, it is the true light, the true vitality of the world.

On this day, let us pray to the Lord, then, to help us always to be on His path and thus to find true life. Amen!

Living Stones in the Body of Christ

November 9, 2014
Private Chapel, Mater Ecclesiae Monastery

Feast of the Dedication of the Basilica of Saint John Lateran
Readings: Ezek 47:1–2, 8–9, 12; Ps 46; 1 Cor 3:9c–11, 16–17; Jn 2:13–22

The Church, in the liturgy of the Roman Rite, celebrates today the feast of the Dedication of the Lateran Basilica, which is the first church built after peace with the Roman State was declared by the Emperor Constantine. It is therefore a feast of joy and gratitude: God is with us; God visited us not only for a moment, but remains with us, dwells with us, is, so to speak, a citizen of our cities; and we can visit Him, hear Him, because He gives Himself into our hands.

For more than a thousand years, this feast was only a feast of the city of Rome; then in 1565, it was extended to the whole Church. It was the time of the rise of Protestantism and division in the Church, and this feast said, yesterday and still today: "Even now there is only one Church in all the Churches of the world, and Peter, the Apostle, the Bishop of Rome, is the guarantor of this unity." It is the feast of the Church, the feast of Christ, a feast of God, but also the feast of our unity.

The readings of today's liturgy present the essence of the Church, especially in the Gospel, in the comparison with the temple in Jerusalem. Therefore, in order to understand correctly the statement: "This is the Church", we must first understand what the temple is. The temple was unique, an expression of God's oneness, and it was essential that there could be only one temple, one place where God dwells with us, where the worship prescribed in the books of Moses is carried out. The synagogues are not the house of God, but are the house of the community, where the community gathers to celebrate, to listen to the Word of God, and they are not houses of worship; in contrast, the temple is the living expression of God's oneness, of Israel's oneness. Three times a year, the Israelites, therefore, were obliged to make a pilgrimage to Jerusalem, and thus Israel remained, as it were, in a perpetual procession toward the temple, and it declared its willingness by this repeated pilgrimage.

But now, what is the Church? It seems to me that the Word of the Lord that we heard in the Gospel is especially important, where He says: "Destroy this temple, and in three days I will rebuild it." "Destroy this temple": the temple was destroyed! And the Lord rebuilt it in three days. The new temple is not an edifice made of stones, but the temple is the Risen Lord; He is the Living One who is the true house of God in the world, with which He draws us into His Body, and thus we ourselves become God's temple, the place where God dwells. There is a correspondence with the temple of Israel, but our churches made of stone are not the equivalents; the correspondence is: we are the living Church! We are the living temple; the Church herself is the Body of the Risen One, in which He who is the Lord dwells, God with us.

From this several consequences follow, also: we are stones—Saint Peter says, for example—of the one living Church, of the living temple of the Lord: we are stones and must be incorporated into this temple (see 1 Pet 2:4–5).

Therefore "to become Church" means that we must allow ourselves to be incorporated into her and also let ourselves be "remade", so to speak, so as to be really incorporated into His temple. In order to become a temple, for our part, we must let ourselves be formed by the Lord, let ourselves be grafted onto the unity of His temple.

Yes, we are the Church; it is true. We are not only a specific group that calls itself by that name, but we are Church inasmuch as we enter into the great community of the Body of Christ, a body that is vertical and horizontal, synchronic and diachronic, in other words, that lives between heaven and earth and at all times. Precisely by being grafted onto this great "we", and emerging from the limits of our own body, we are in the community of the Body of Christ.

This is therefore the first essential point for meditation on this day: what corresponds to the destroyed temple is the risen Body of Christ, and all of us baptized persons are grafted onto this Body. In reality, the temple was made for divine worship, but this Old Testament worship had value only inasmuch as it signified the true future worship. And the true worship of God is this great act of adoration, of love, which is the Cross, and thus, on the Cross—which is the true worship of God, as an act of the utmost love of God for us and of man for God—what was provisional and only symbolic is destroyed, and the new fact is that on the Cross of Christ the true worship of God is accomplished.

Now the question remains: What then do the buildings mean, starting with the Lateran Basilica, which is the mother of all the churches in the world? Are they like the synagogues, only places of the community, of the assembly, and not houses of God? Yes, in a certain sense they are above all meeting places, but the [Latin] word *ecclesiae* (the churches) means "those who are called together" and the moments of this convocation, and already as such they are more than a place for listening; they are an expression of this permanent convocation in which the great God gathers us in the Body of Christ.

In the second millennium, another understanding developed: it was understood that God, that Christ, the Lord who fundamentally transformed bread into His Body, remains present and is always present. And thus, when we enter a church, the crucified and Risen Lord, the Eucharist is present; therefore by entering into the church, we enter into this permanent Eucharist of the world, into this act in which heaven is opened and heaven and earth meet. This entering into a church, where there is a tabernacle, is entering into the permanent Eucharist and, thus, celebrating with the Lord the act of love and allowing oneself to be formed, renewed by this act.

In his Gospel, Saint John also makes another important statement about this set of problems. To the Samaritan woman who had asked, "Is the true worship found on Mount Gerizim or on Mount Zion?", the Lord replies: "True adoration is not on one mountain or another; true worship is in spirit and truth" (see Jn 4:9–24). This is the great renewal accomplished at the moment of the Cross: mountains no longer matter, this place or that; what counts is the new place of adoration, which is the living Christ.

In this sense, Christianity is a fundamental transformation of the history of religion, and the moment of Christ's crucifixion, in which the old temple falls, is the moment of this transformation of all religion. Not this or that mountain, but "in spirit and truth": this is the true religion, that we adore God in spirit and truth. The moment of the Cross is the renewal of the Old Testament in love and really is the decisive moment in the history of religions. But "spirit and truth" does not mean an abstraction; it is not saying that everyone has his own spirit, his own truth. Certainly Christianity is a spiritualization, inasmuch as we transcend all externals, but it is also a new incarnation, a new corporeality.

Jesus says: "I am . . . the truth" (Jn 14:6), and the Spirit is not just any spirit, but is the Spirit of Christ, about whom Paul says: "We are one spirit with Him" (see 2 Cor 3:17–18). Adoring in spirit and truth does not have an "illuministic" meaning—we might say—namely, that everyone follows his own spirit. No, it means that the Spirit and the Truth are a Person and that by entering into the liturgy with this Person, we are in the true temple, we are in the true adoration. Spirit and truth are above all interior realities, and nevertheless they are not abstract realities, but concrete realities: the Spirit gives Himself in the Body of the risen Christ, and the Truth—the truth of the One who comes from the Father—is Truth in Person!

Finally, let us thank the Lord for this gift, through which He Himself became the true temple. Let us pray to Him that He may help us to be ever more truly Church, to be united with Him. Let us pray that, in this moment in which He gives Himself into our hands, He may renew in us faith, charity, and hope, make the Church grow, and be more and more God in all. Amen!

Mary Is Close to Us Because She Is Immaculate

December 8, 2013
Private Chapel, Mater Ecclesiae Monastery

Solemnity of the Immaculate Conception of the Blessed Virgin Mary[1]
Readings: Gen 3:9–15, 20; Ps 98; Eph 1:3–6, 11–12; Lk 1:26–38

The teaching of the Church that Mary was preserved from all stain of original sin appears to us generally today as remote from our life. It seems that it has little to do with us, and some think that a life without sin is a rather tedious life, like the life of an anxious person who has not dared to put out into the deep on the ship of his life.

Some think that the greatness of the human drama, of human life, appears only in the experience of guilt, because where there is no experience of the grace of forgiveness, an essential dimension is missing; true human greatness does not appear if the human being has not even fallen into sin and risen from sin. Only in this way does a human being seem really to mature in himself, to arrive at the fullness of his life.

[1] In 2013 the Immaculate Conception fell on a Sunday and therefore took the place of the Second Sunday of Advent.

In reality, behind this idea—that only with the experience of sins do we arrive at the full greatness of the human adventure—stands another very important position, a position that Goethe formulated and put in the mouth of his devil Mephistopheles, who introduces himself with these words: "[I am] part of a power that would alone work evil, but engenders good."[2] This means that there is always a dialectic between good and evil and that in the final analysis even evil is necessary and serves the good; evil would therefore not be an absolute evil, but only relative, inasmuch as it appears evil in itself, but in the totality of the dialectic of being it has an irreplaceable function, because only in this dialectic does the greatness of human history arise.

This position has some truth to it: that is, it means that there are very different words, different charisms, which are also in tension with one another, that there is diversity and difference, and the fullness of being grows only in the tension of these values, in the richness of the differences and diversities, also. But difference or diversity is one thing, and opposition [*contrarietà*] is another. True evil is not a difference or diversity, but is opposition; it is a "no!" to good, and therefore it does not build but destroys.

Hatred is never right, and falsehood is never right; true evil does exist. To deny this and to make everything relative is to destroy the truth of being, our truth. An evil exists that is not difference but opposition, and it destroys and does not create; and the adventure of good does not need this evil. Certainly, in the dialectic of values, the richness of the drama increases, but it is destroyed, seriously damaged by the opposition of true evil.

Presently I am reading the life of Don Bosco, and I see the greatness of the adventure of a life of sanctity; this life

[2] Johann Wolfgang von Goethe, *Faust*, pt. 1, trans. Philip Wayne (Penguin, 1949), 75.

of his with a major dimension of social concern and love: an adventure that demonstrates that the world of love and truth is much richer than the world of hatred, evil, and falsehood; and that really the adventure of good is greater, more beautiful than the adventure of evil, that we do not need true evil to arrive at the greatness of our human existence.

Mary is like that! We see what a life she led! What an adventure! To be invited to be Mother of the Son of God: what a challenge! And then the stable, the birth of Jesus in Bethlehem, the flight into Egypt, then the everyday life led in simplicity and in depth; and then the public life of Jesus, and Mary apart from it, then the Cross, the Resurrection, being together with the disciples in the Cenacle and the beginning of the Church.... What a magnificent life! Because the adventure with God is the true adventure that opens up for us true life in all its greatness.

Another objection, very similar to the first one, is: Mary has no sin and therefore does not really know us. As though solidarity in sin were necessary. If she does not share in sin, she is another type of person and does not help us. Only someone who knows sin understands us sinners, too. But this is not true, either!

Sin does not know; sin does not make a person know; the more someone sins, the less he knows that he is a sinner. Sinning is precisely what makes the sinner blind; it does not give us knowledge but excludes us from knowledge; sin does not recognize itself, but hides itself and hides our life from us. And, as for solidarity, sin is essentially and precisely de-solidarization; we see this today in the first reading. When God speaks with Adam, the latter immediately says, "It was her fault!" and the woman says: "It was the serpent's fault." The essence of sin is non-solidarity, because only love creates solidarity.

Therefore, we must say that the closer a human being is to God, the closer he is to other human beings. Mary can be close to us all only because she is with God and shares in God's openness. Only God is close to us, closer than we are to ourselves; only someone who is with God is truly close to another person. Already in the third century, they prayed in Egypt: *Sub tuum praesidium confugimus, Sancta Dei Genitrix.* "We fly to thy patronage [protection], O Holy Mother of God." Precisely this being-with-God brings Mary quite close to us: everyone can have immediate access to her; everyone is sure of the solidarity of the mother with her suffering children, suffering because of sin. Only because we know that she has no suspicions, she has no shadow of egotism, can we go to Mary with such great confidence, knowing that, precisely because she is with God and in God, she understands us; precisely because she is full of love she loves us; because she is full of truth, she helps us to be true, also.

Thus we see that precisely this "immaculate conception" makes Mary close to each one of us and helps us to understand life, to find the courage to lead a true life. If we think that a life without sin is not possible, Mary tells us: "Courage, choose life!" So God spoke to Israel, and so Mary repeats: "Choose life and choose yourself, choose love, choose truth, choose God" (cf. Deut 30:15–20).

Let us thank God for the gift of Our Lady, which He has given to us; this great Lady who went ever deeper into humanity, from the little house in Nazareth to the Cenacle, to the Gothic cathedrals, to Guadalupe, to Lourdes, to Fatima, to us all.

Let us pray: "Holy Mary, help us in the adventure of life; give us the courage to lead a life of love and truth and so really to find life, the human adventure in all its greatness." Amen!

SUBJECT INDEX

LITURGICAL CALENDAR INDEX

Easter Season (*continued*)

Ordinary Time

CHRONOLOGICAL INDEX OF HOMILIES

December 21, 2014 (Fourth Sunday of Advent, Year B)
"Mary's 'Yes' and the Fulfillment of the Promise," 60–63

March 8, 2015 (Third Sunday of Lent, Year B)
"The Decalogue and the Fulfillment of the Law," 112–17

April 26, 2015 (Fourth Sunday of Easter, Year B)
"The Shepherd Who Guides and Defends against the Wolves," 189–92

May 3, 2015 (Fifth Sunday of Easter, Year B)
"Remaining in the Love of the Lord, Who Knows Everything," 204–8

May 10, 2015 (Sixth Sunday of Easter, Year B)
"Bearing Fruit: The Gift of Wine," 221–24

May 17, 2015 (Seventh Sunday of Easter, Year B)
"The Church Awaiting the Spirit," 230–34

May 31, 2015 (Most Holy Trinity, Year B)
"On the Mountain: Promise and Commission," 264–68

November 1, 2015 (Solemnity of All Saints)
"God's Love Leads Us on High," 304–7

February 21, 2016 (Second Sunday of Lent, Year C)
"Entering into the Light, Becoming Light," 101–5

February 28, 2016 (Third Sunday of Lent, Year C)
"'I Am': God Watches Us, and We Can Call on Him," 118–22

March 6, 2016 (Fourth Sunday of Lent, Year C)
"The Joy of Being at Home with the Father," 142–45

March 12, 2017 (Second Sunday of Lent, Year A)
"Listening in Order to Go Out and Be a Blessing," 92–95

March 26, 2017 (Fourth Sunday of Lent, Year A)
"Man Lives When He Sees God," 135–38

April 2, 2017 (Fifth Sunday of Lent, Year A)
"Eternal Life: Held in the Lord's Hand," 146–48

SCRIPTURE INDEX

Bold page numbers indicate the primary readings for the day.

Old Testament

New Testament